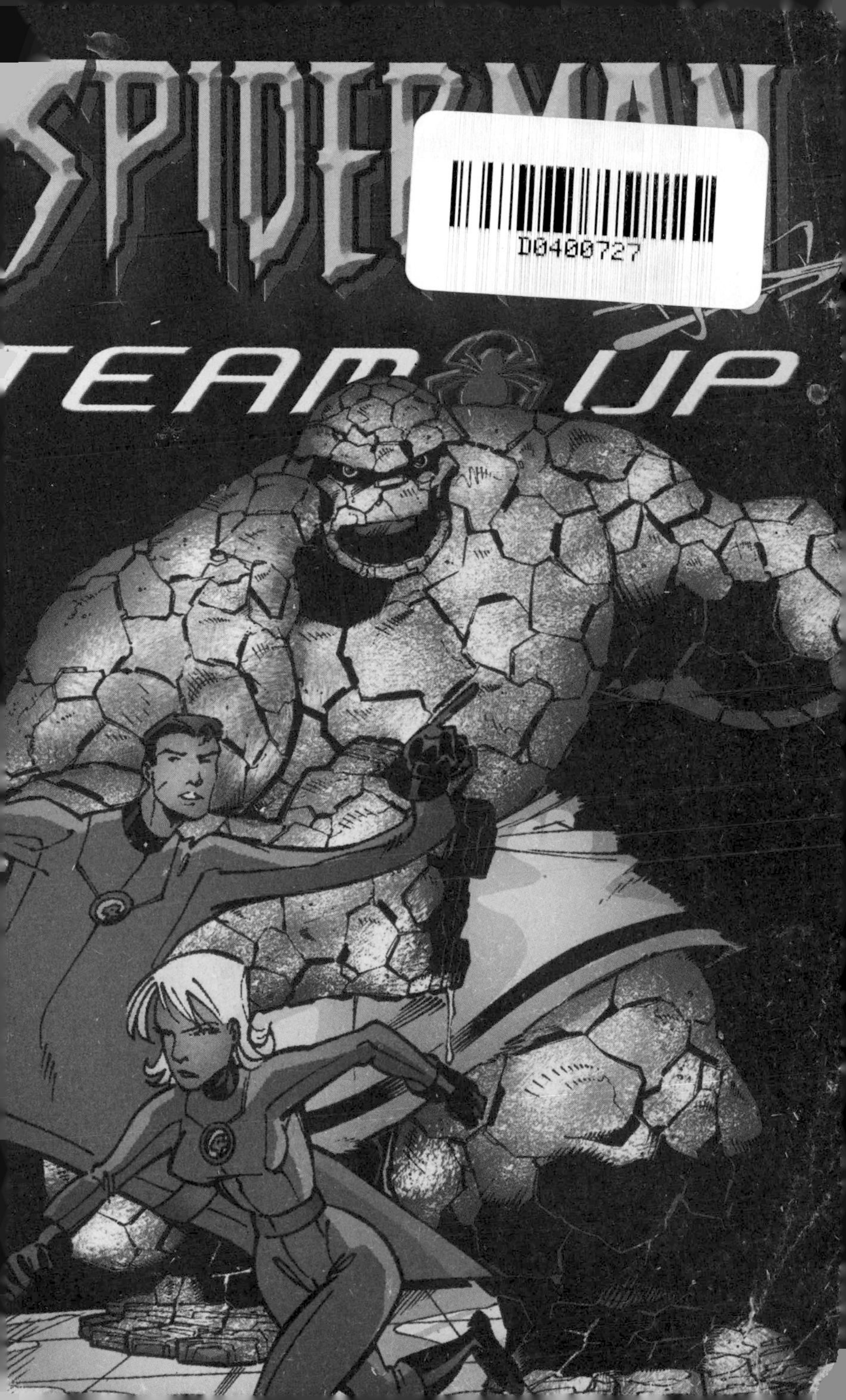
SPIDER-MAN
TEAM UP

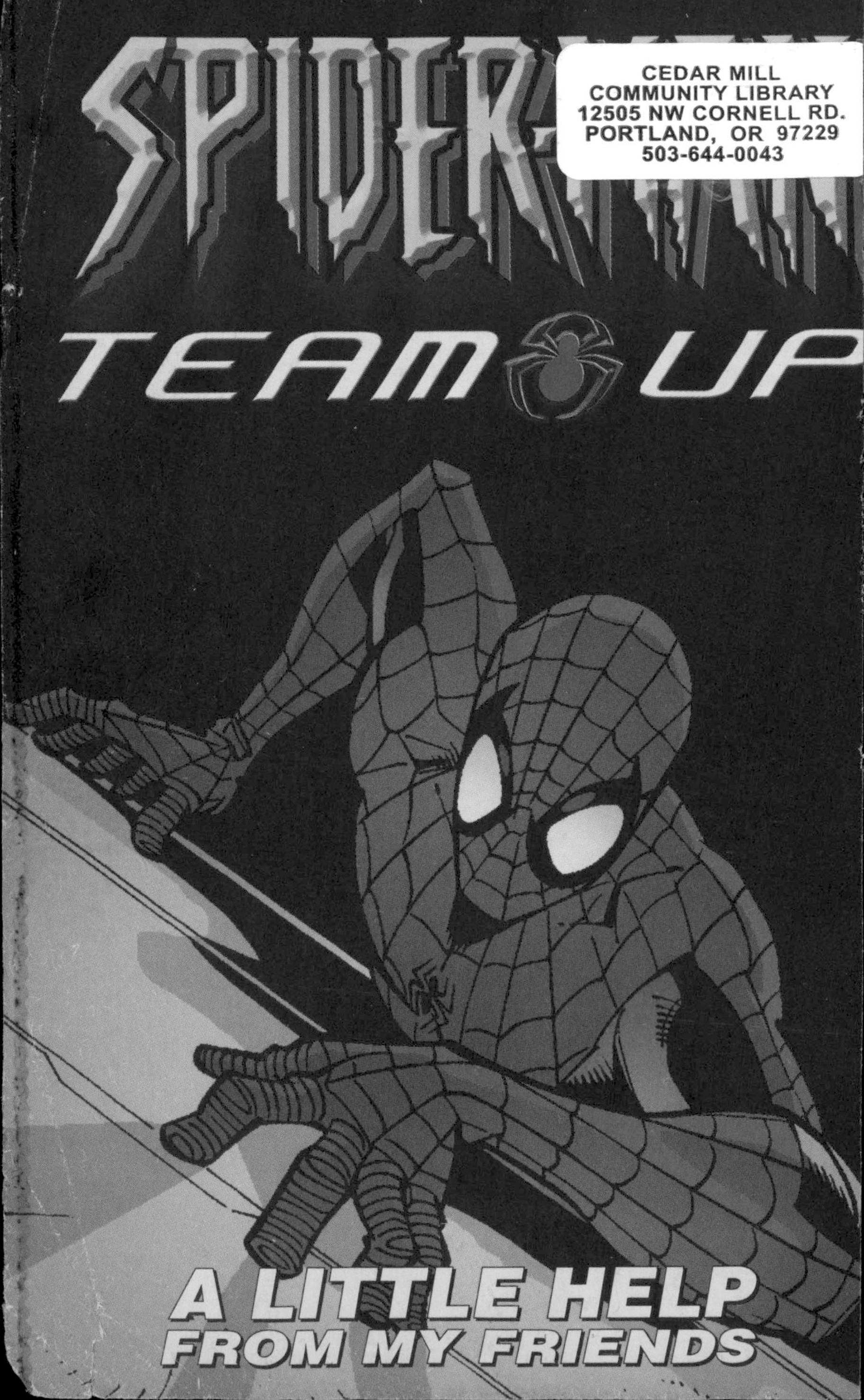
SPIDER-MAN
TEAM UP
A LITTLE HELP
FROM MY FRIENDS

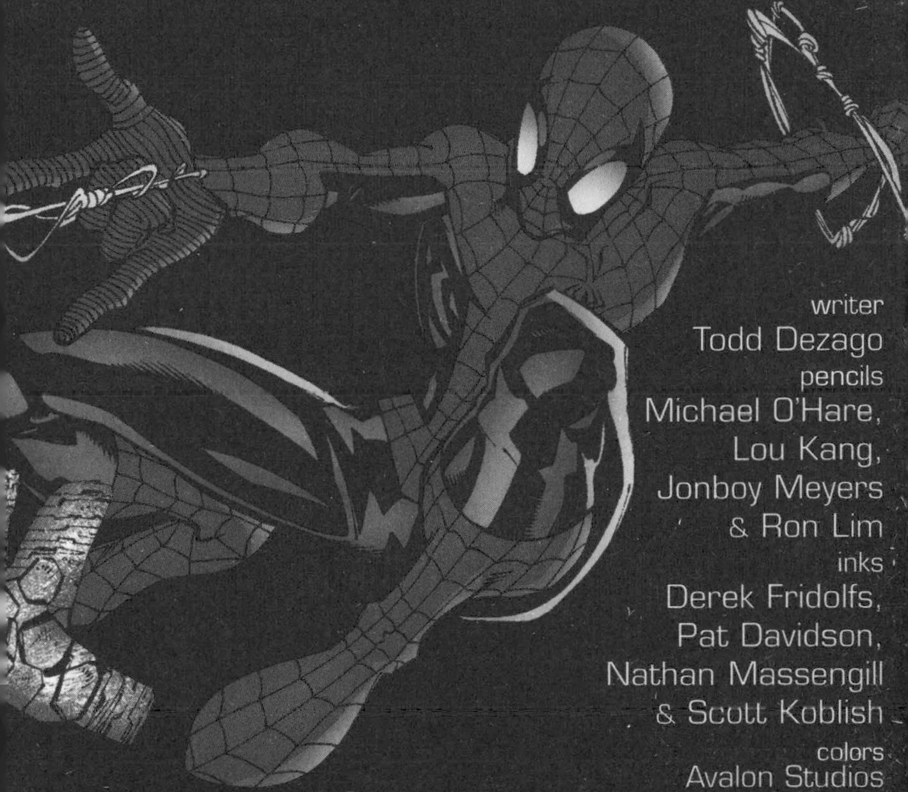

writer
Todd Dezago
pencils
Michael O'Hare,
Lou Kang,
Jonboy Meyers
& Ron Lim
inks
Derek Fridolfs,
Pat Davidson,
Nathan Massengill
& Scott Koblish
colors
Avalon Studios
covers
Randy Green, Rick Ketcham & Chris Sotomayor

editor: John Barber
consulting editors: MacKenzie Cadenhead & Ralph Macchio

Inspired by Stan Lee & Friends

collection editor: Jennifer Grünwald
senior editor, special projects: Jeff Youngquist
director of sales: David Gabriel
production: Jerry Kalinowski
book designer: Carrie Beadle
creative director: Tom Marvelli

editor in chief: Joe Quesada
publisher: Dan Buckley

A LITTLE HELP FROM MY FRIENDS

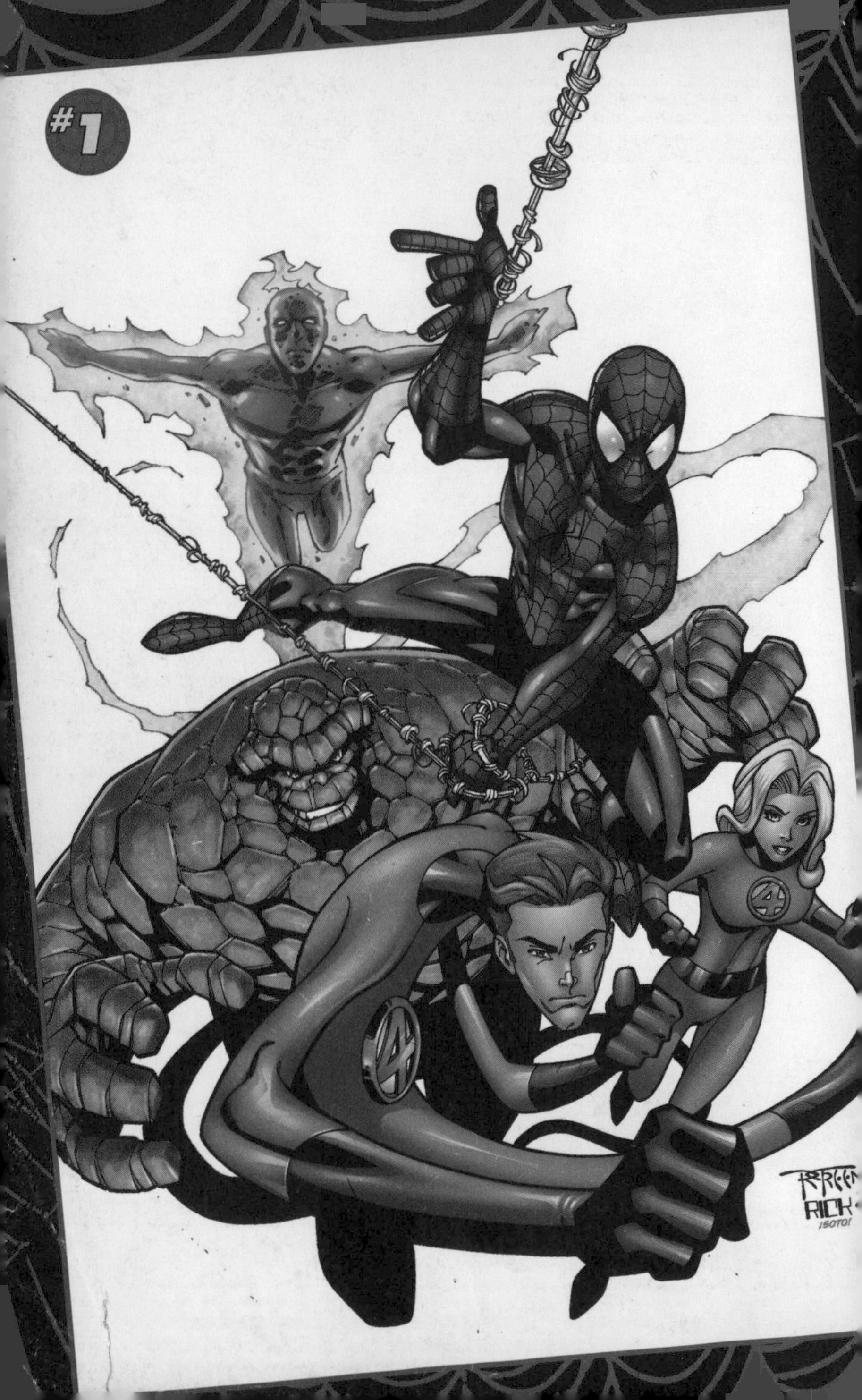
#1
RICK

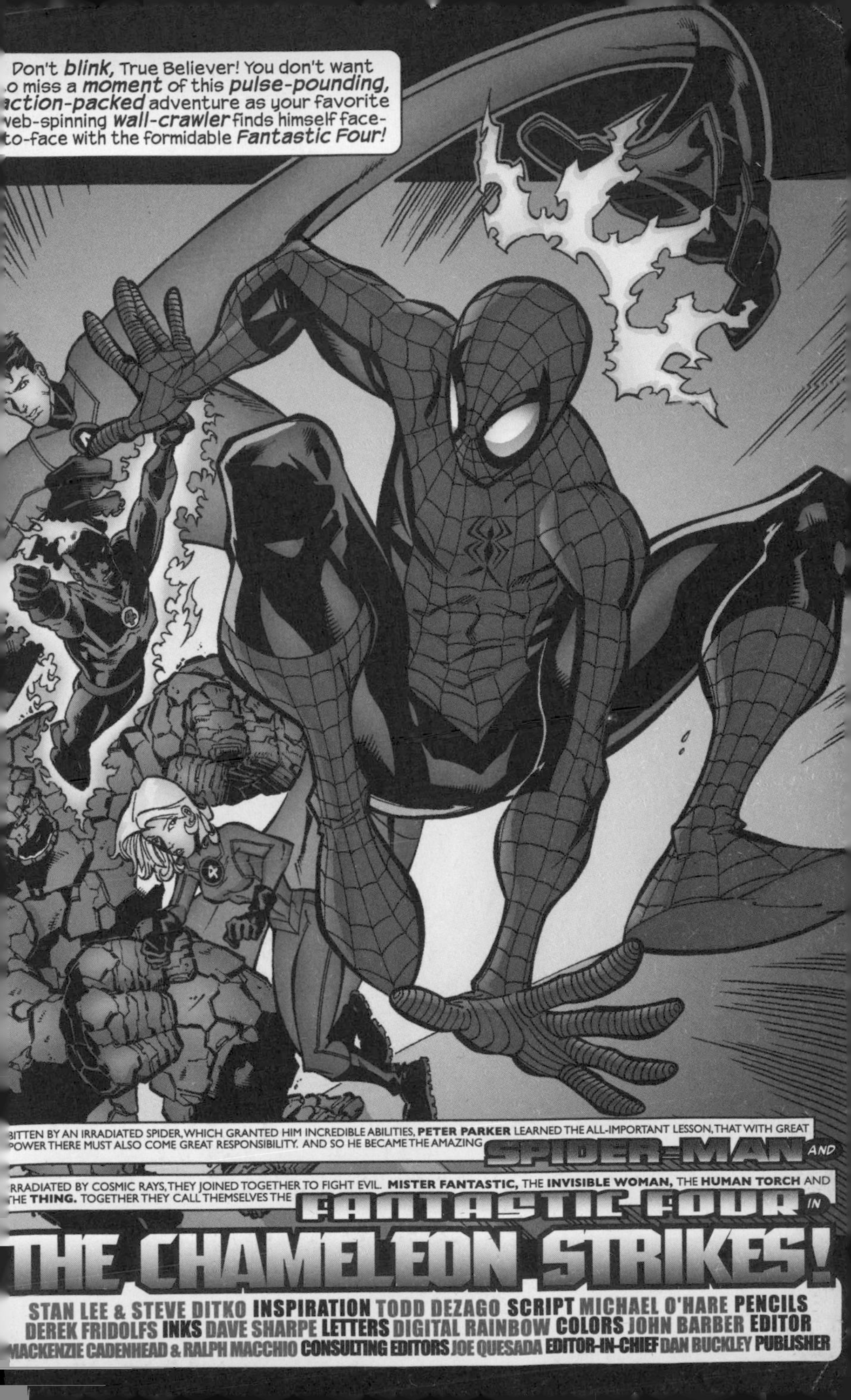
Don't blink, True Believer! You don't want o miss a moment of this pulse-pounding, action-packed adventure as your favorite veb-spinning wall-crawler finds himself face-to-face with the formidable Fantastic Four!
BITTEN BY AN IRRADIATED SPIDER, WHICH GRANTED HIM INCREDIBLE ABILITIES, PETER PARKER LEARNED THE ALL-IMPORTANT LESSON, THAT WITH GREAT POWER THERE MUST ALSO COME GREAT RESPONSIBILITY. AND SO HE BECAME THE AMAZING
SPIDER-MAN AND
IRRADIATED BY COSMIC RAYS, THEY JOINED TOGETHER TO FIGHT EVIL. MISTER FANTASTIC, THE INVISIBLE WOMAN, THE HUMAN TORCH AND THE THING. TOGETHER THEY CALL THEMSELVES THE
FANTASTIC FOUR IN
THE CHAMELEON STRIKES!
STAN LEE & STEVE DITKO INSPIRATION TODD DEZAGO SCRIPT MICHAEL O'HARE PENCILS
DEREK FRIDOLFS INKS DAVE SHARPE LETTERS DIGITAL RAINBOW COLORS JOHN BARBER EDITOR
MACKENZIE CADENHEAD & RALPH MACCHIO CONSULTING EDITORS JOE QUESADA EDITOR-IN-CHIEF DAN BUCKLEY PUBLISHER

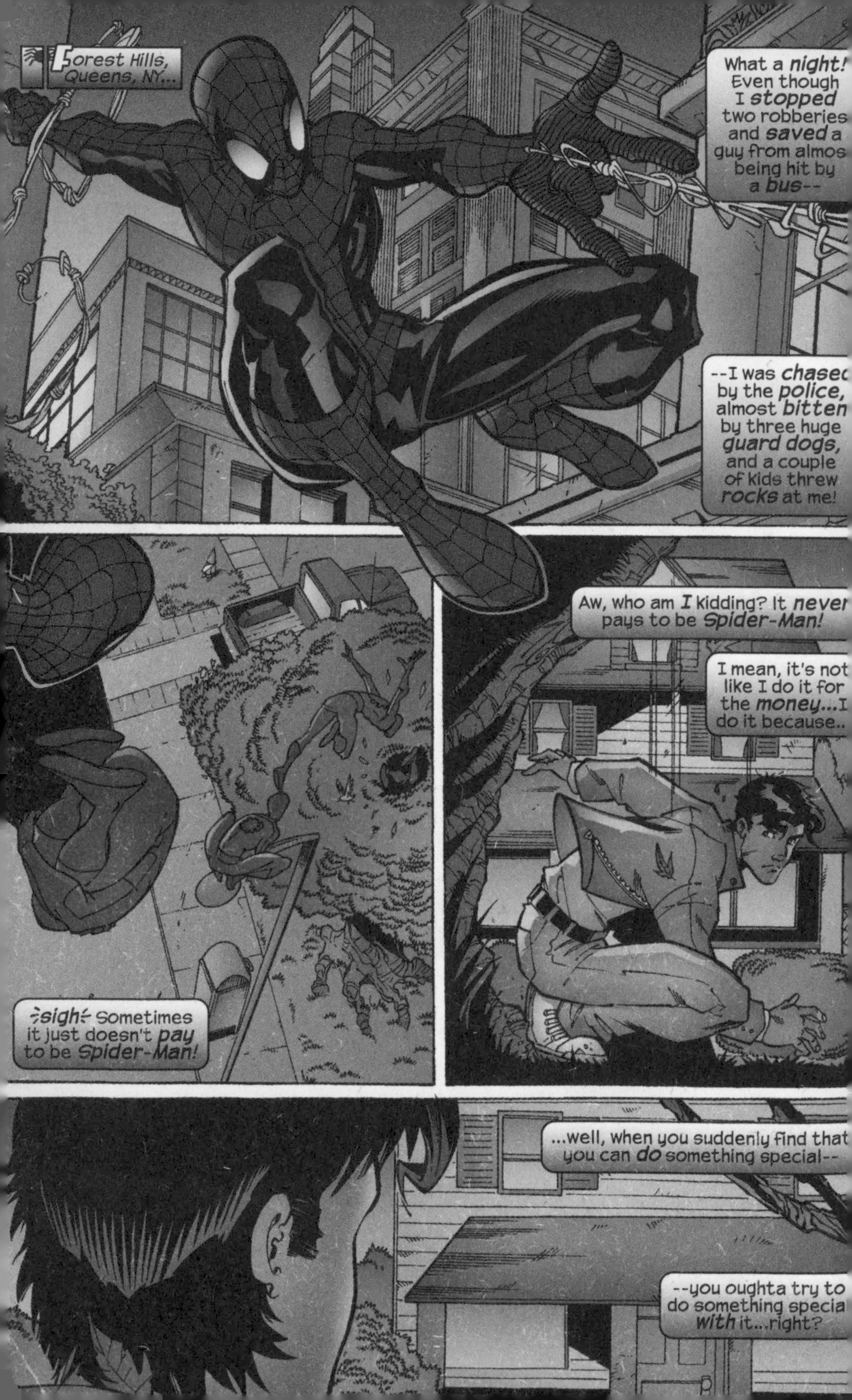
Forest Hills, Queens, NY...
What a night! Even though I stopped two robberies and saved a guy from almos being hit by a bus--
--I was chased by the police, almost bitten by three huge guard dogs, and a couple of kids threw rocks at me!
sigh Sometimes it just doesn't pay to be Spider-Man!
Aw, who am I kidding? It never pays to be Spider-Man!
I mean, it's not like I do it for the money...I do it because..
...well, when you suddenly find that you can do something special--
--you oughta try to do something specia with it...right?

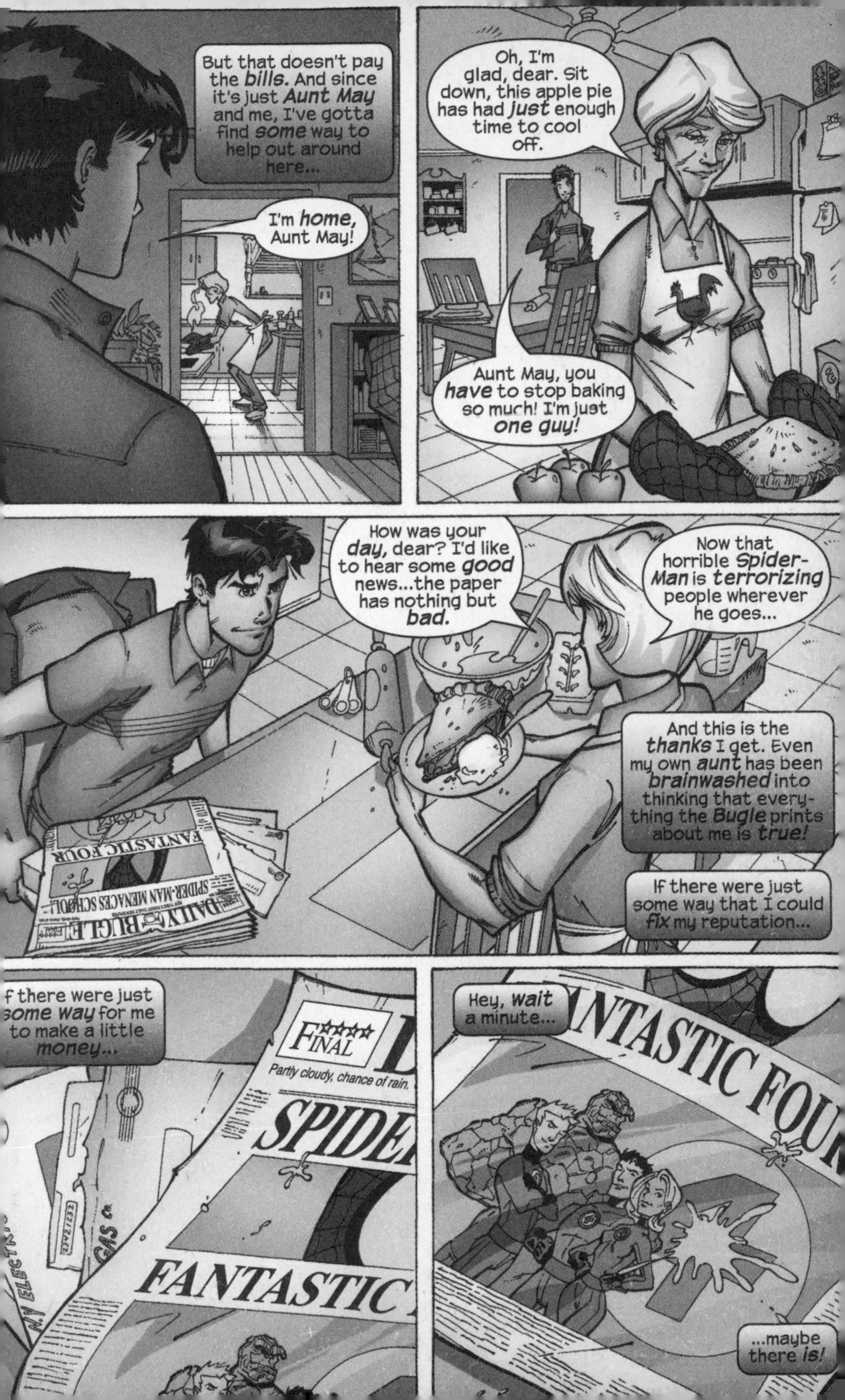
But that doesn't pay the bills. And since it's just Aunt May and me, I've gotta find some way to help out around here...
I'm home, Aunt May!
Oh, I'm glad, dear. Sit down, this apple pie has had just enough time to cool off.
Aunt May, you have to stop baking so much! I'm just one guy!
How was your day, dear? I'd like to hear some good news...the paper has nothing but bad.
Now that horrible Spider-Man is terrorizing people wherever he goes...
And this is the thanks I get. Even my own aunt has been brainwashed into thinking that everything the Bugle prints about me is true!
If there were just some way that I could fix my reputation...
DAILY BUGLE
SPIDER-MAN MENACES SCHOOL!
FANTASTIC FOUR
f there were just some way for me to make a little money...
FINAL
Partly cloudy, chance of rain.
SPIDE
FANTASTIC
Hey, wait a minute...
NTASTIC FOU
...maybe there is!

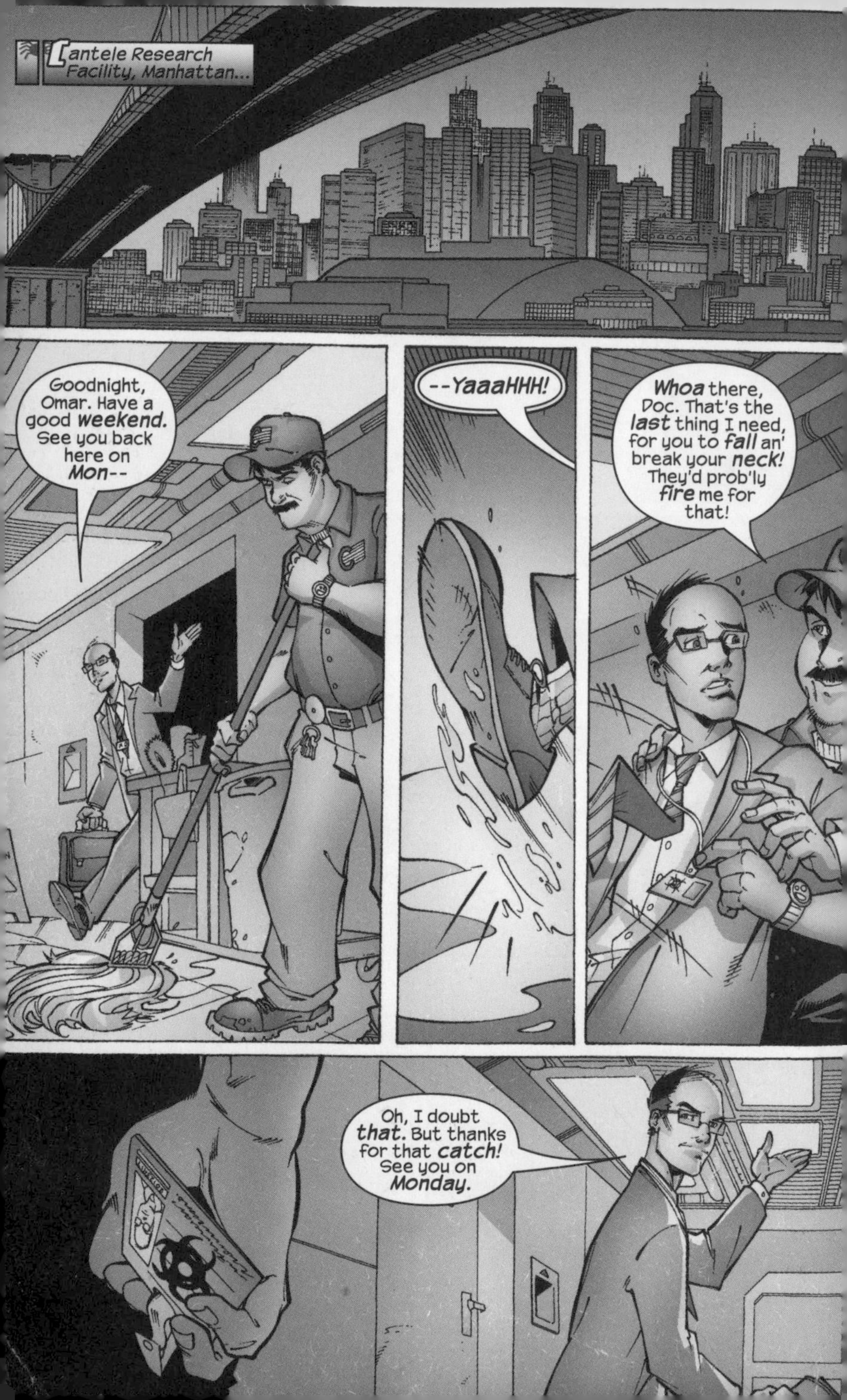
Cantele Research Facility, Manhattan...
Goodnight, Omar. Have a good weekend. See you back here on Mon--
--YaaaHHH!
Whoa there, Doc. That's the last thing I need, for you to fall an' break your neck! They'd prob'ly fire me for that!
Oh, I doubt that. But thanks for that catch! See you on Monday.

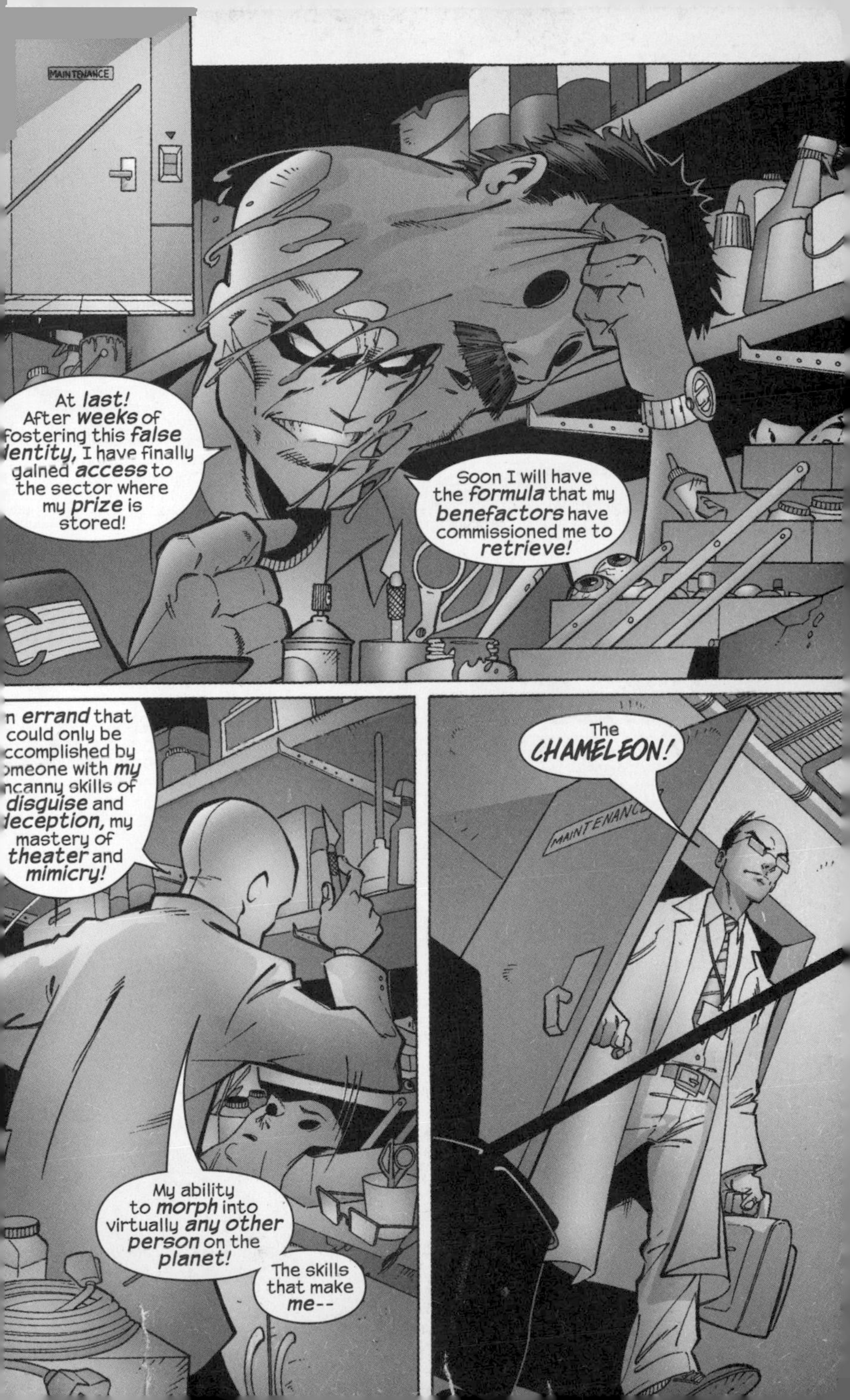
MAINTENANCE
At last! After weeks of fostering this false lentity, I have finally gained access to the sector where my prize is stored!
Soon I will have the formula that my benefactors have commissioned me to retrieve!
n errand that could only be ccomplished by omeone with my ncanny skills of disguise and leception, my mastery of theater and mimicry!
My ability to morph into virtually any other person on the planet!
The skills that make me--
MAINTENANCE
The CHAMELEON!

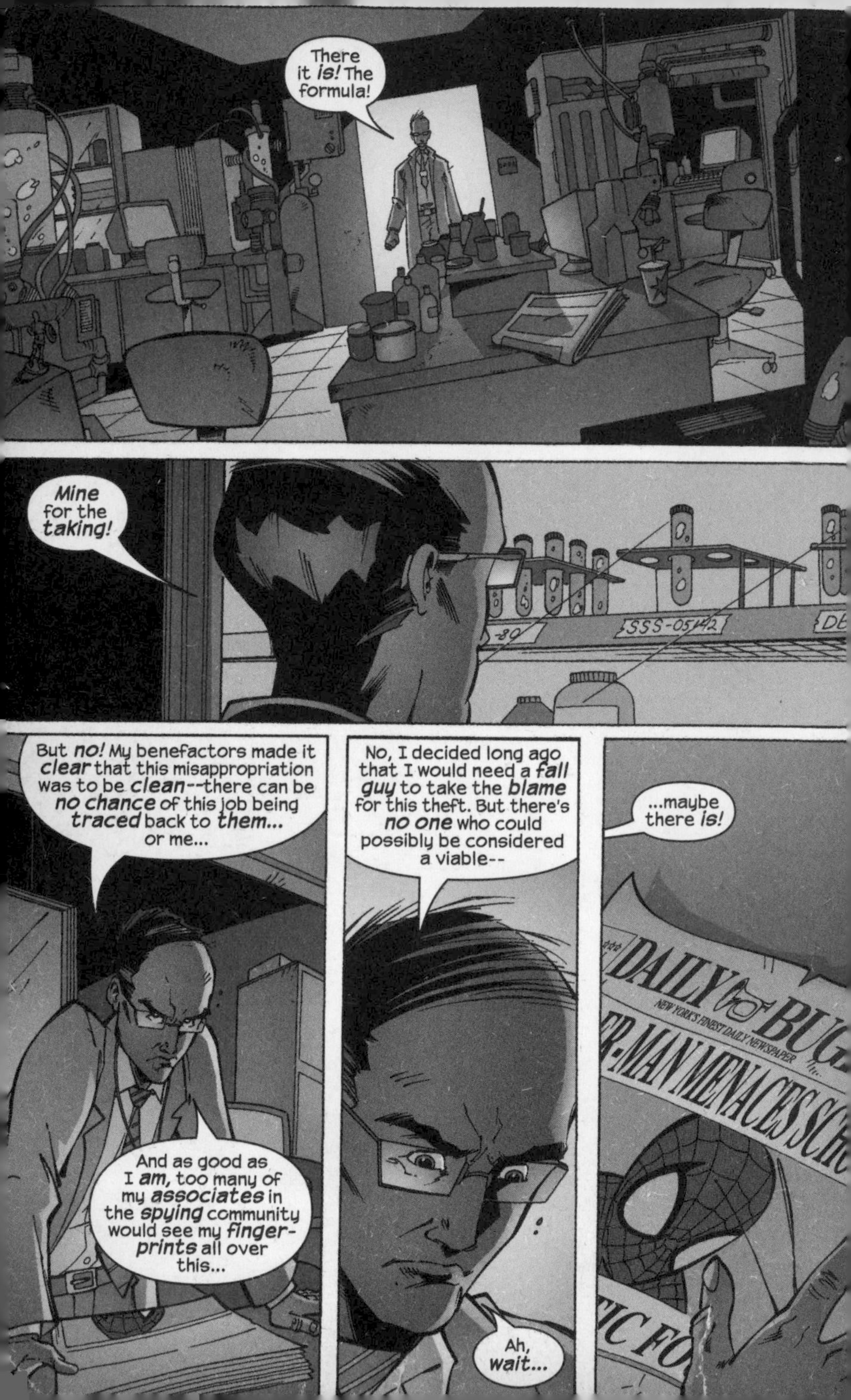
There it is! The formula!
Mine for the taking!
But no! My benefactors made it clear that this misappropriation was to be clean--there can be no chance of this job being traced back to them... or me...
And as good as I am, too many of my associates in the spying community would see my finger-prints all over this...
No, I decided long ago that I would need a fall guy to take the blame for this theft. But there's no one who could possibly be considered a viable--
Ah, wait...
...maybe there is!
NEW YORK'S FINEST DAILY NEWSPAPER

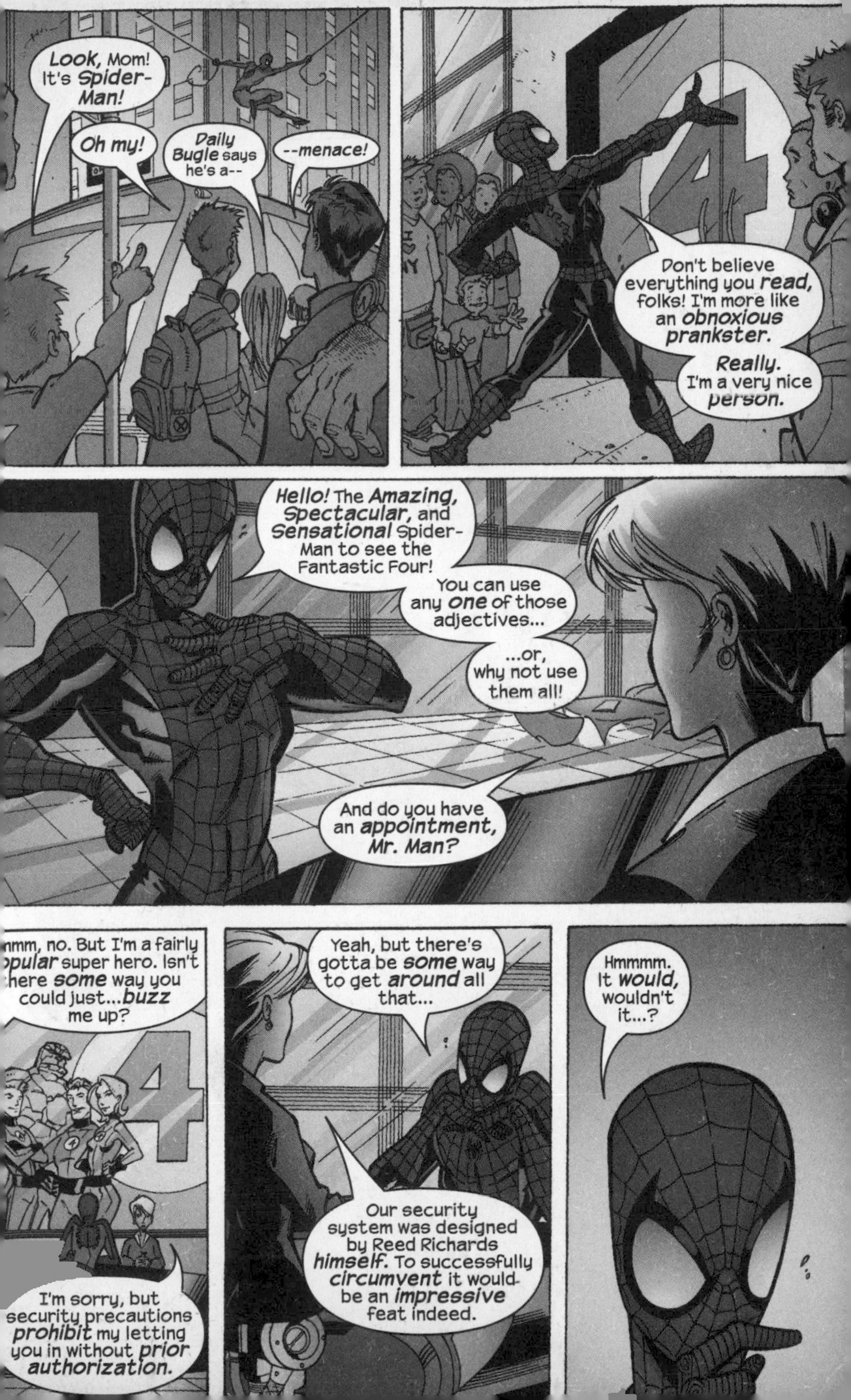
Look, Mom! It's Spider-Man!
Oh my!
Daily Bugle says he's a--
--menace!
Don't believe everything you read, folks! I'm more like an obnoxious prankster.
Really. I'm a very nice person.
Hello! The Amazing, Spectacular, and Sensational Spider-Man to see the Fantastic Four!
You can use any one of those adjectives...
...or, why not use them all!
And do you have an appointment, Mr. Man?
mmm, no. But I'm a fairly opular super hero. Isn't here some way you could just...buzz me up?
I'm sorry, but security precautions prohibit my letting you in without prior authorization.
Yeah, but there's gotta be some way to get around all that...
Our security system was designed by Reed Richards himself. To successfully circumvent it would be an impressive feat indeed.
Hmmmm. It would, wouldn't it...?

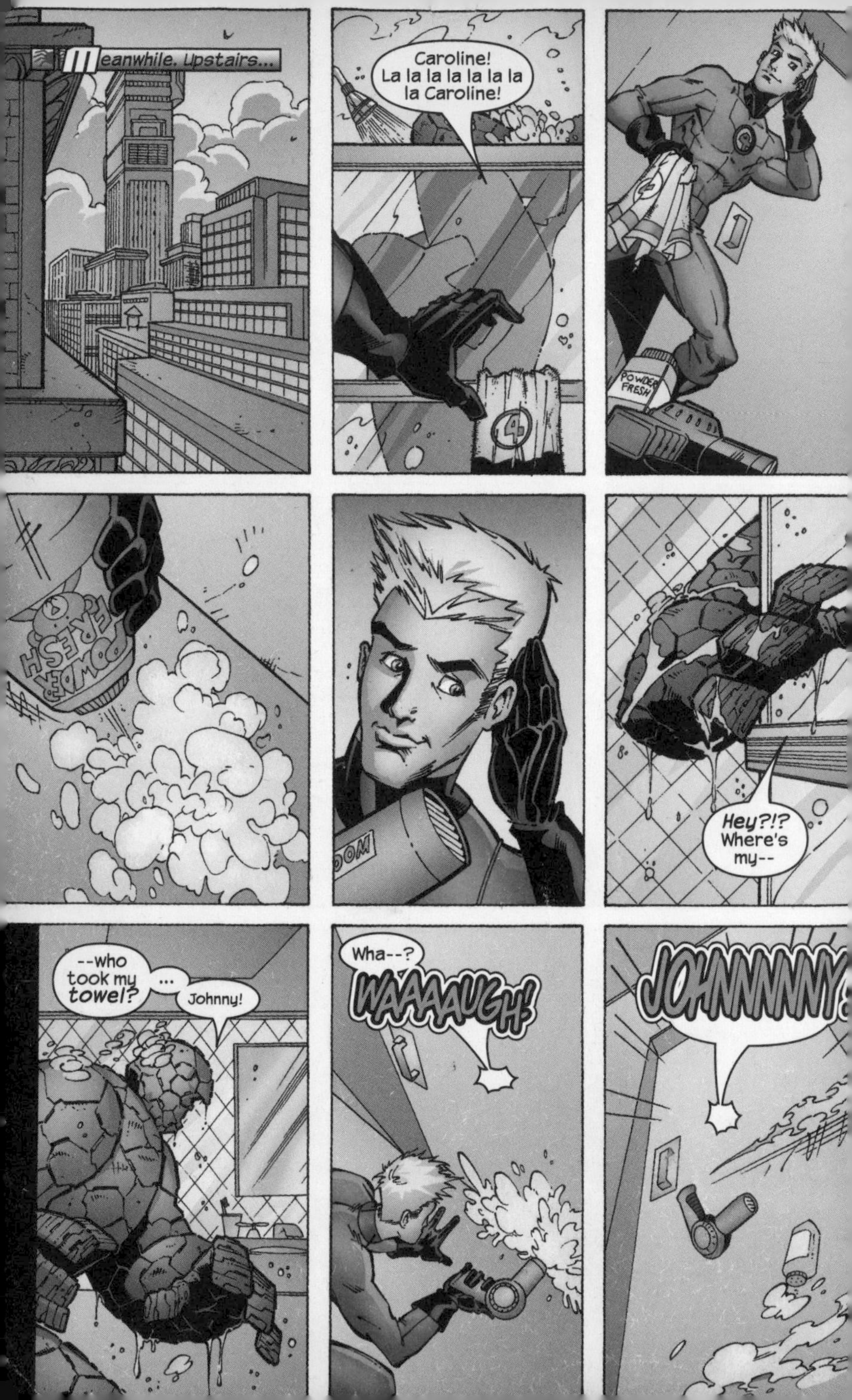
Meanwhile, Upstairs...
Caroline! La la la la la la la la Caroline!
POWDER FRESH
POWDER FRESH
Hey?!? Where's my--
--who took my towel?
...
Johnny!
Wha--?
WAAAAUGH!
JOHNNNNNY!

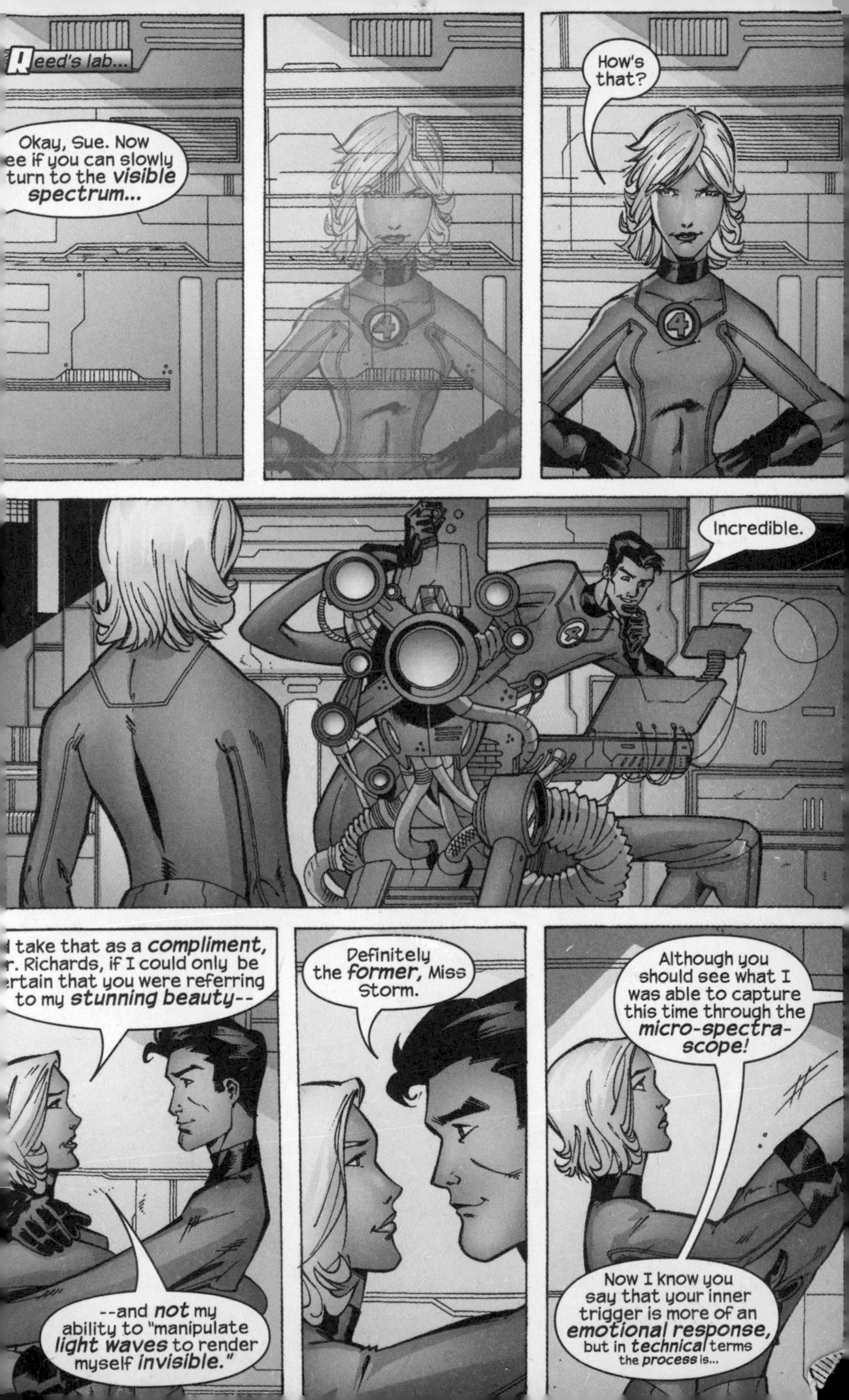
Reed's lab...
Okay, Sue. Now see if you can slowly turn to the visible spectrum...
How's that?
Incredible.
I take that as a compliment, Mr. Richards, if I could only be certain that you were referring to my stunning beauty--
--and not my ability to "manipulate light waves to render myself invisible."
Definitely the former, Miss Storm.
Although you should see what I was able to capture this time through the micro-spectra-scope!
Now I know you say that your inner trigger is more of an emotional response, but in technical terms the process is...

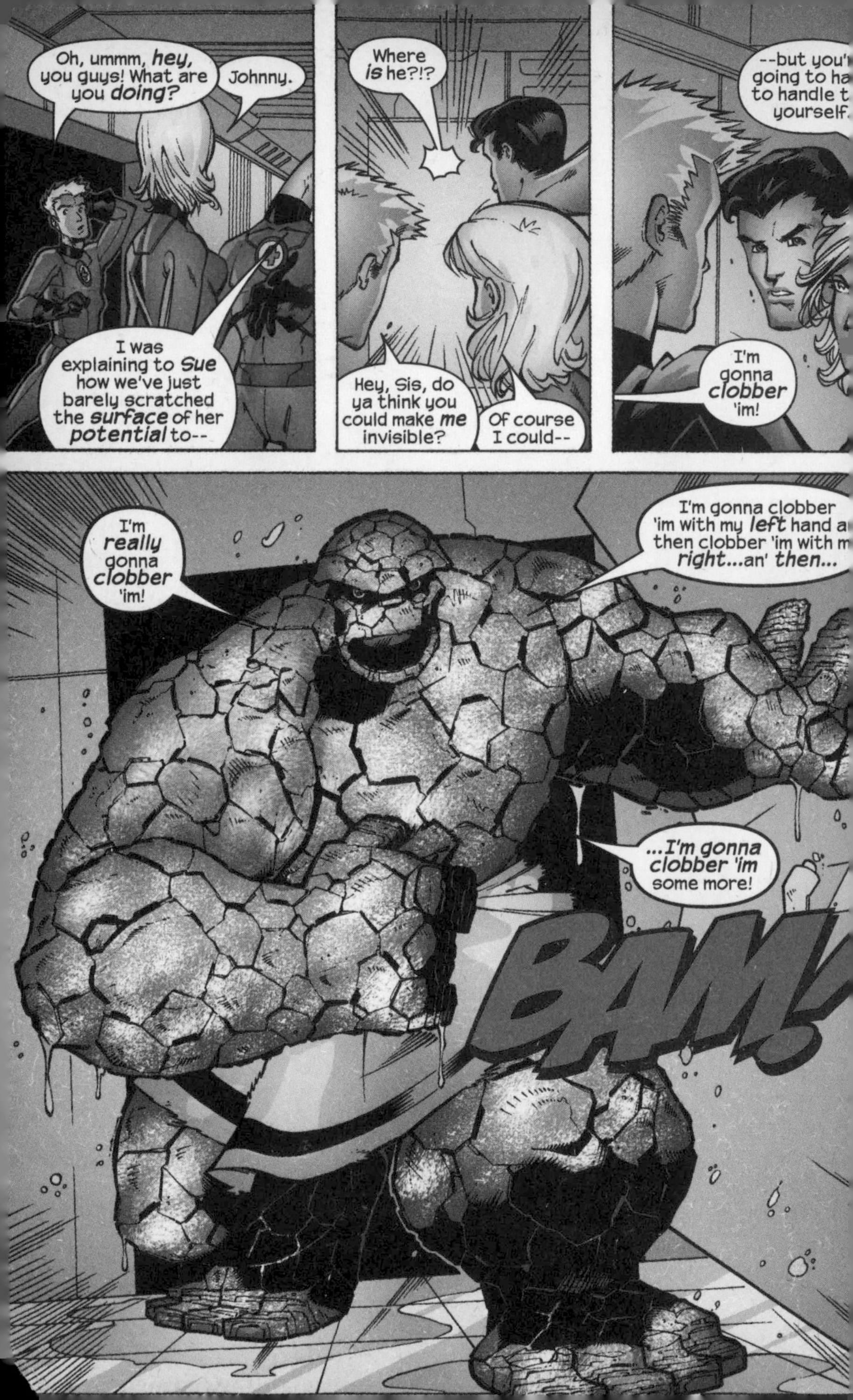
Oh, ummm, hey, you guys! What are you doing?
Johnny.
I was explaining to Sue how we've just barely scratched the surface of her potential to--
Where is he?!?
Hey, Sis, do ya think you could make me invisible?
Of course I could--
--but you' going to ha to handle t yourself.
I'm gonna clobber 'im!
I'm really gonna clobber 'im!
I'm gonna clobber 'im with my left hand a then clobber 'im with m right...an' then...
...I'm gonna clobber 'im some more!
BAM!

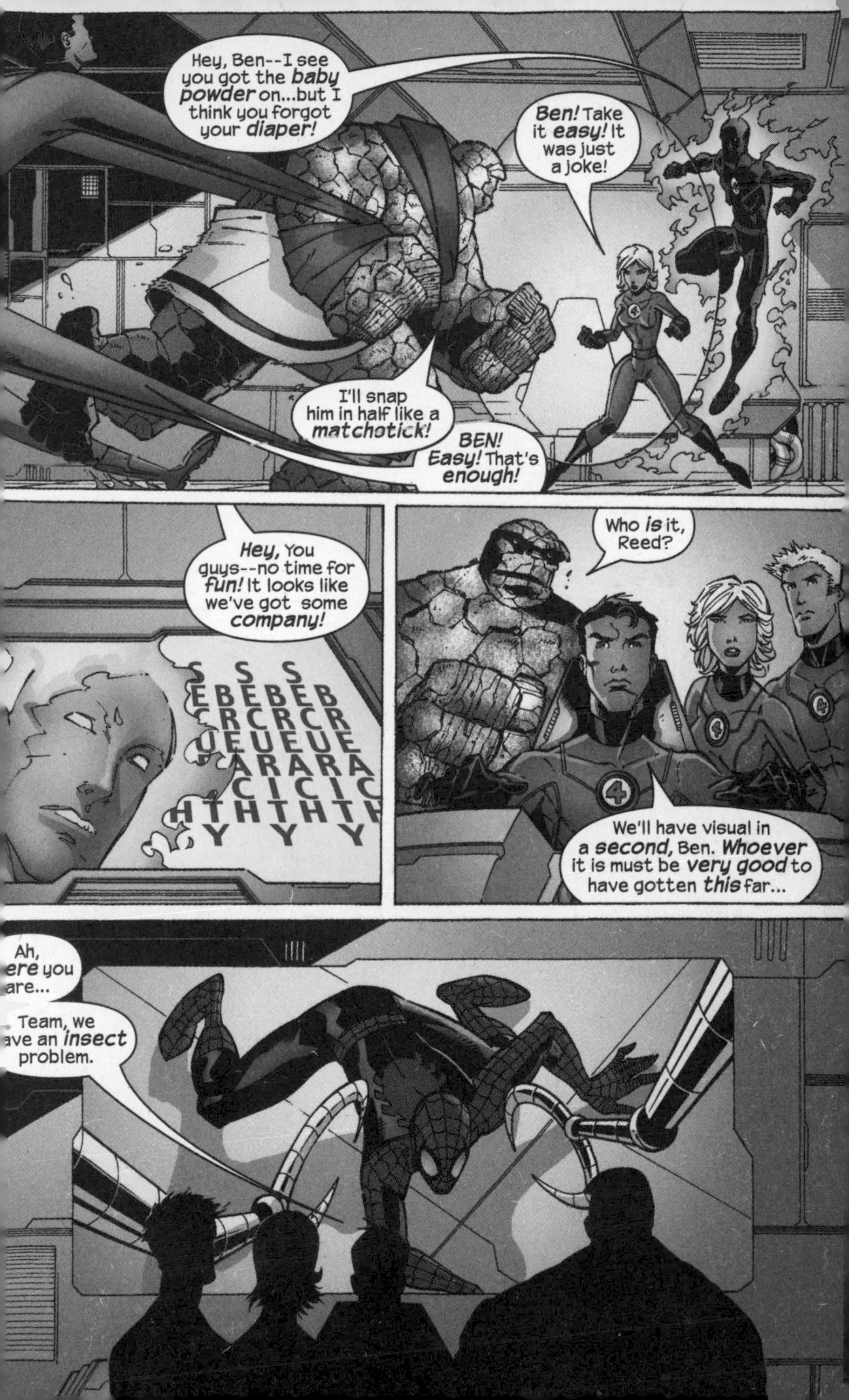
Hey, Ben--I see you got the baby powder on...but I think you forgot your diaper!
Ben! Take it easy! It was just a joke!
I'll snap him in half like a matchstick!
BEN! Easy! That's enough!
Hey, You guys--no time for fun! It looks like we've got some company!
SECURITY
Who is it, Reed?
We'll have visual in a second, Ben. Whoever it is must be very good to have gotten this far...
Ah, ere you are...
Team, we ave an insect problem.

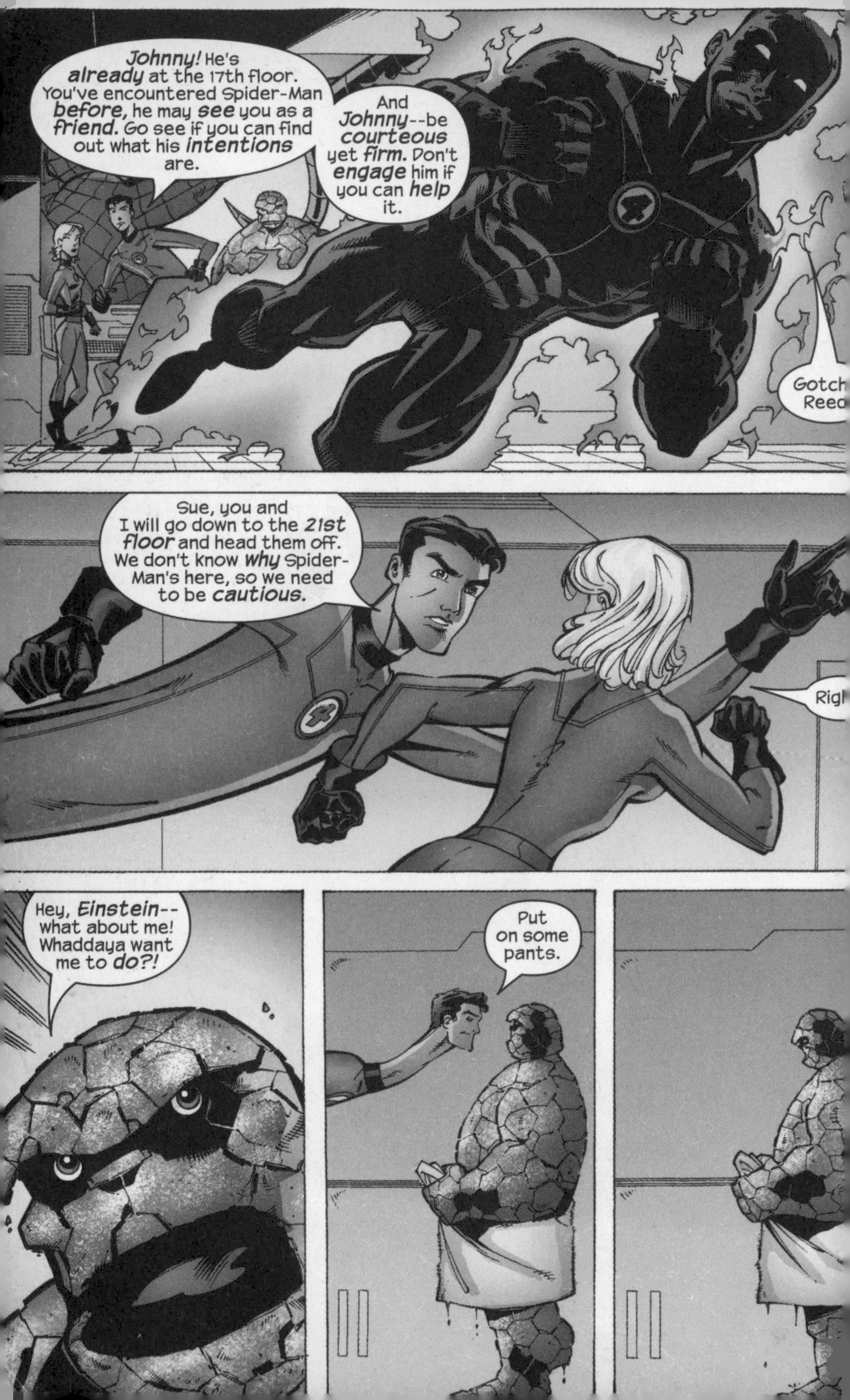
Johnny! He's already at the 17th floor. You've encountered Spider-Man before, he may see you as a friend. Go see if you can find out what his intentions are.
And Johnny--be courteous yet firm. Don't engage him if you can help it.
Sue, you and I will go down to the 21st floor and head them off. We don't know why Spider-Man's here, so we need to be cautious.
Hey, Einstein--what about me! Whaddaya want me to do?!
Put on some pants.

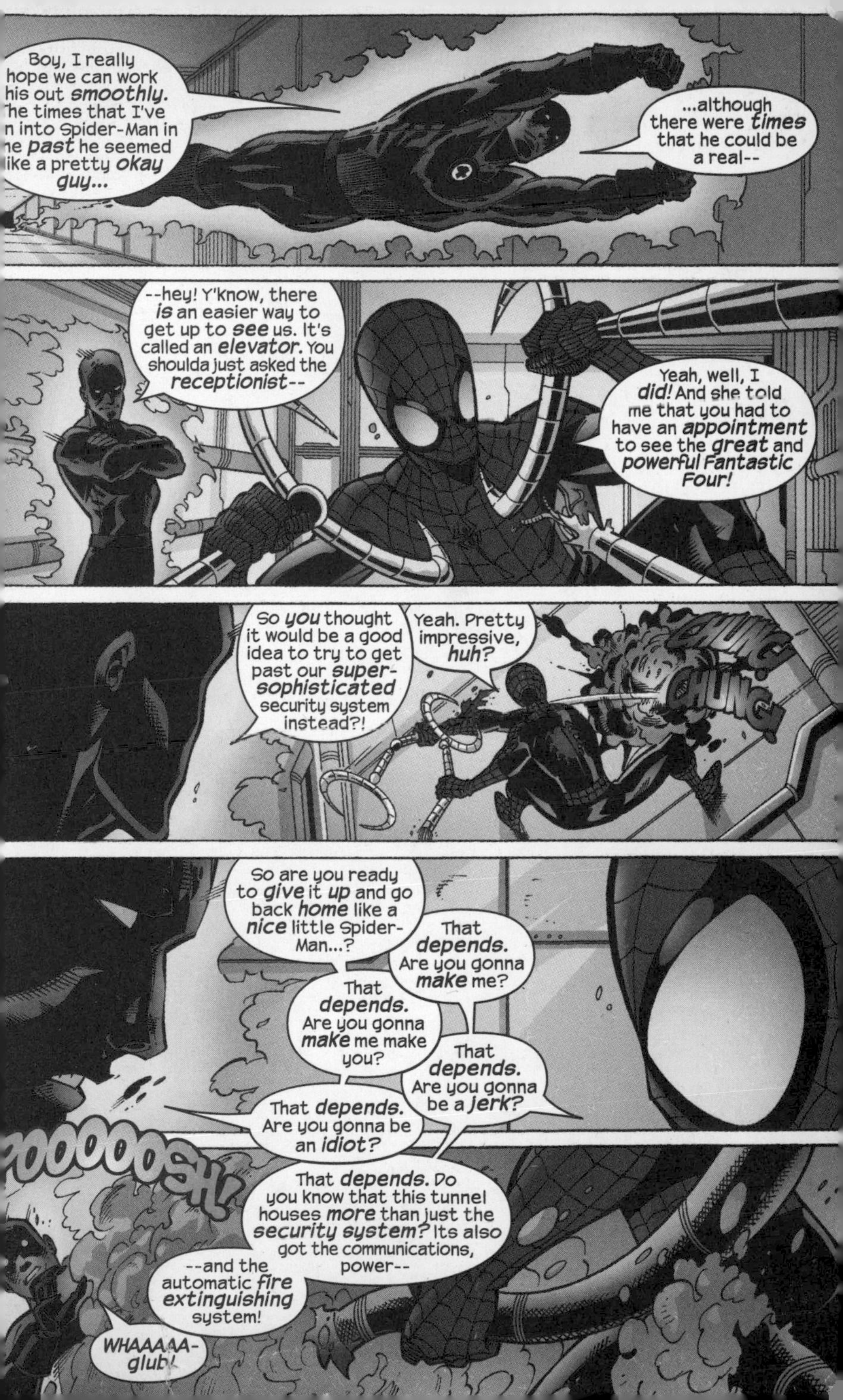

Boy, I really hope we can work his out smoothly. he times that I've n into Spider-Man in e past he seemed like a pretty okay guy...
...although there were times that he could be a real--
--hey! Y'know, there is an easier way to get up to see us. It's called an elevator. You shoulda just asked the receptionist--
Yeah, well, I did! And she told me that you had to have an appointment to see the great and powerful Fantastic Four!
So you thought it would be a good idea to try to get past our super-sophisticated security system instead?!
Yeah. Pretty impressive, huh?
CHUNG
CHUNG
So are you ready to give it up and go back home like a nice little Spider-Man...?
That depends. Are you gonna make me?
That depends. Are you gonna make me make you?
That depends. Are you gonna be a jerk?
That depends. Are you gonna be an idiot?
That depends. Do you know that this tunnel houses more than just the security system? Its also got the communications, power--
POOOOOSH!
--and the automatic fire extinguishing system!
WHAAAAA-glub!

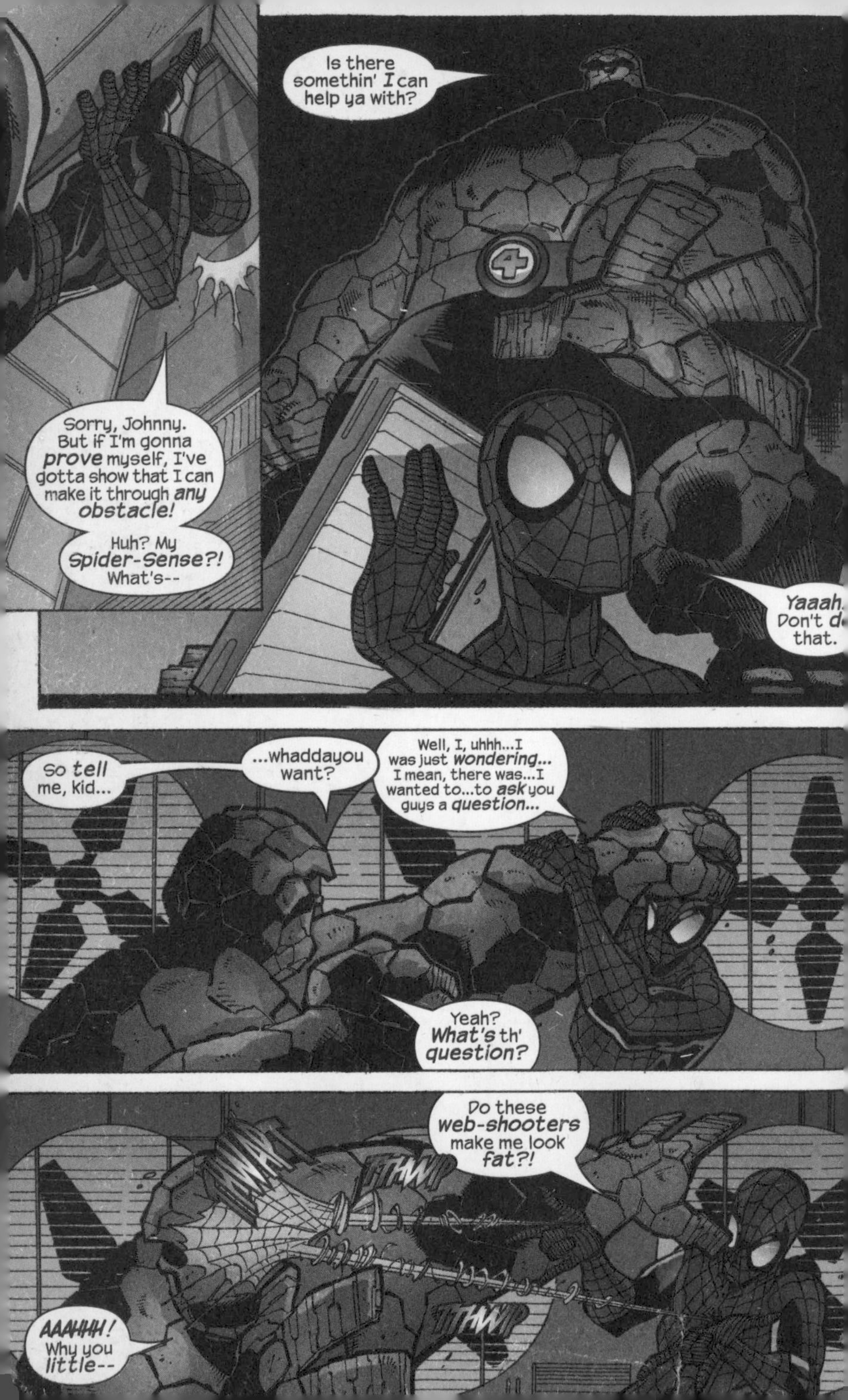
Sorry, Johnny. But if I'm gonna prove myself, I've gotta show that I can make it through any obstacle!
Huh? My Spider-Sense?! What's--
Is there somethin' I can help ya with?
Yaaah. Don't do that.
So tell me, kid...
...whaddayou want?
Well, I, uhhh...I was just wondering... I mean, there was...I wanted to...to ask you guys a question...
Yeah? What's th' question?
Do these web-shooters make me look fat?!
THWIP
THWIP
AAAHHH! Why you little--

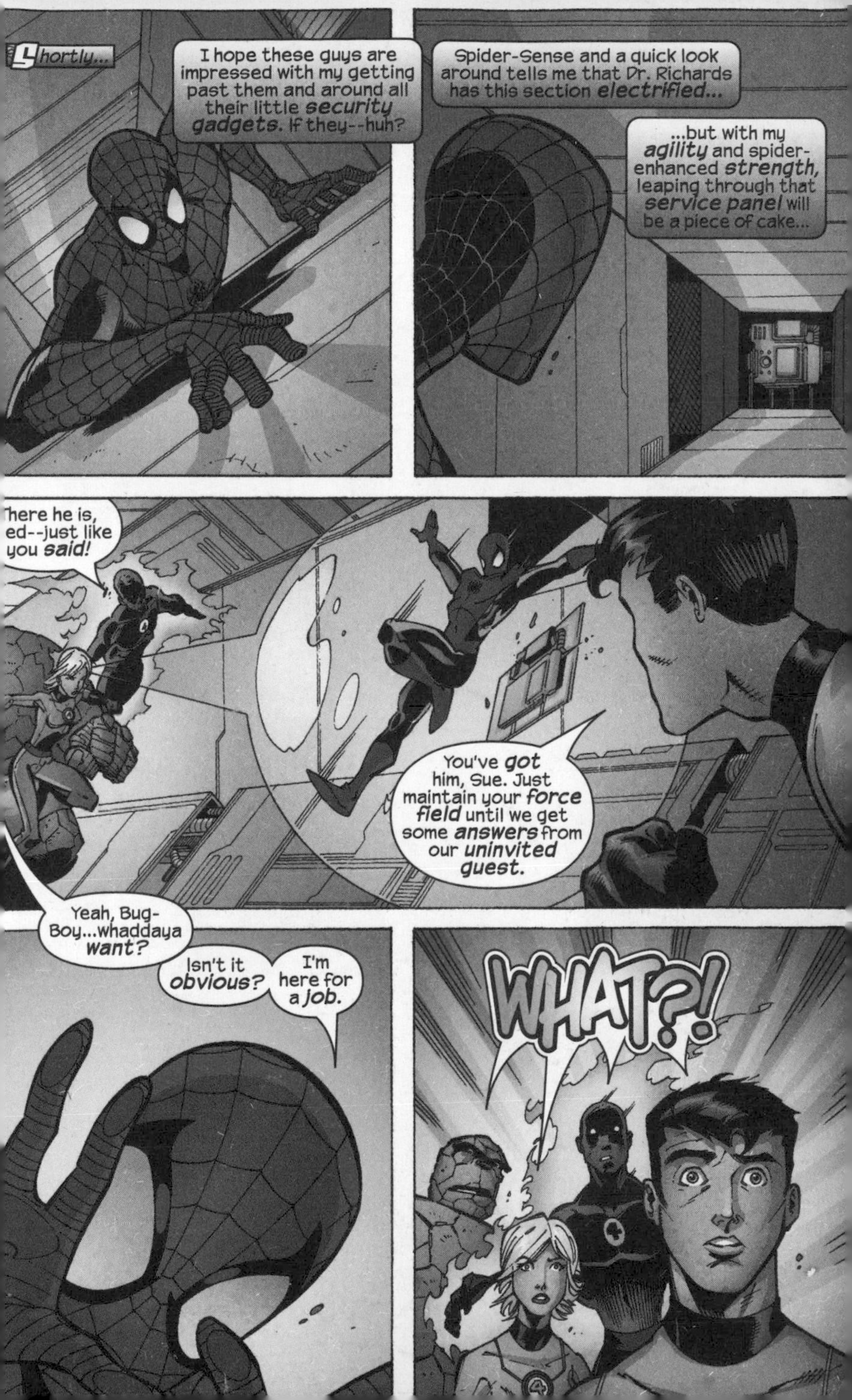
Shortly...
I hope these guys are impressed with my getting past them and around all their little security gadgets. If they--huh?
Spider-Sense and a quick look around tells me that Dr. Richards has this section electrified...
...but with my agility and spider-enhanced strength, leaping through that service panel will be a piece of cake...
here he is, ed--just like you said!
You've got him, Sue. Just maintain your force field until we get some answers from our uninvited guest.
Yeah, Bug-Boy...whaddaya want?
Isn't it obvious?
I'm here for a job.
WHAT?!

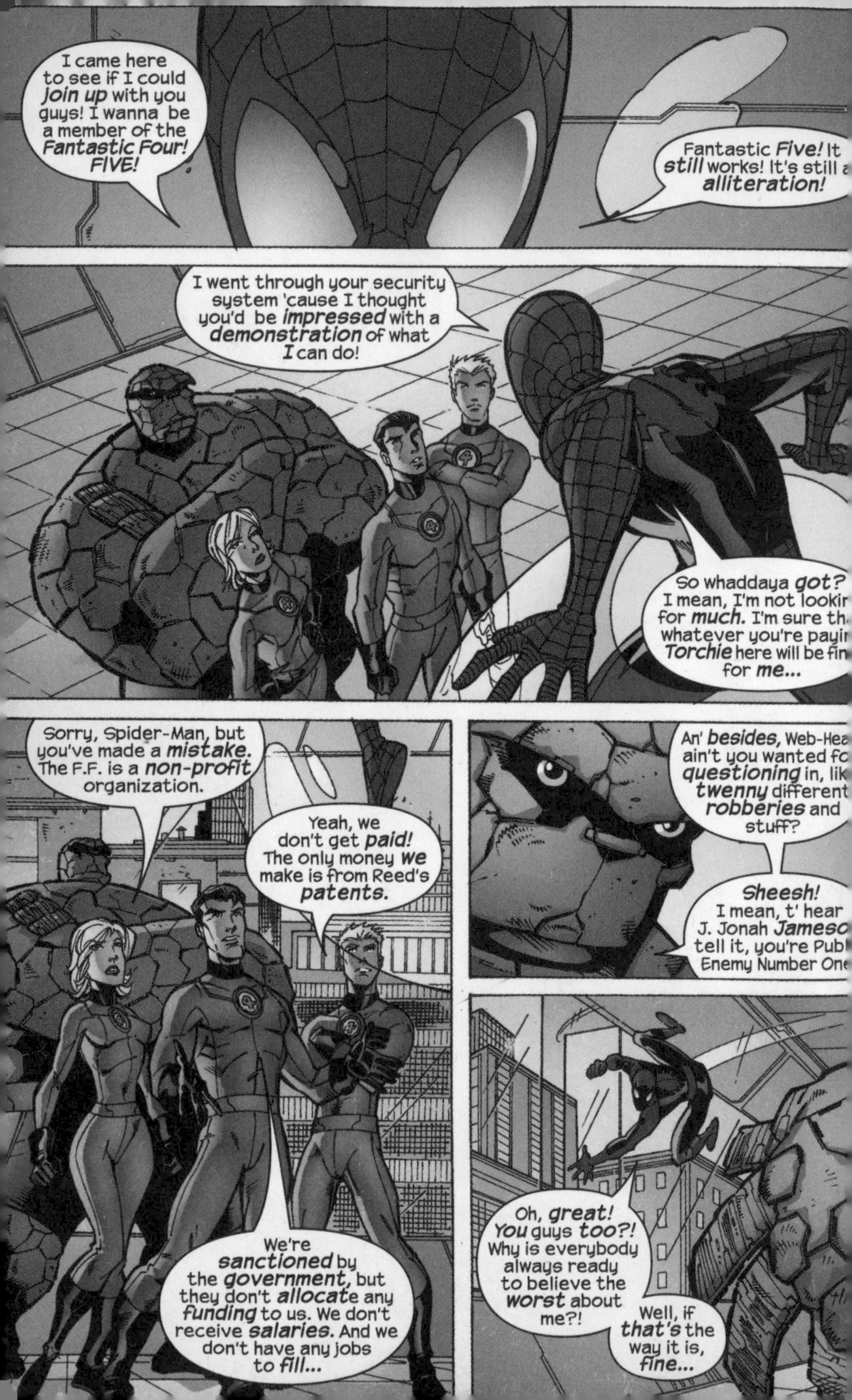
I came here to see if I could join up with you guys! I wanna be a member of the Fantastic Four! FIVE!
Fantastic Five! It still works! It's still a alliteration!
I went through your security system 'cause I thought you'd be impressed with a demonstration of what I can do!
So whaddaya got? I mean, I'm not lookin for much. I'm sure th whatever you're payin Torchie here will be fin for me...
Sorry, Spider-Man, but you've made a mistake. The F.F. is a non-profit organization.
Yeah, we don't get paid! The only money we make is from Reed's patents.
We're sanctioned by the government, but they don't allocate any funding to us. We don't receive salaries. And we don't have any jobs to fill...
An' besides, Web-Hea ain't you wanted fo questioning in, lik twenny different robberies and stuff?
Sheesh! I mean, t' hear J. Jonah Jameso tell it, you're Publ Enemy Number One
Oh, great! You guys too?! Why is everybody always ready to believe the worst about me?!
Well, if that's the way it is, fine...

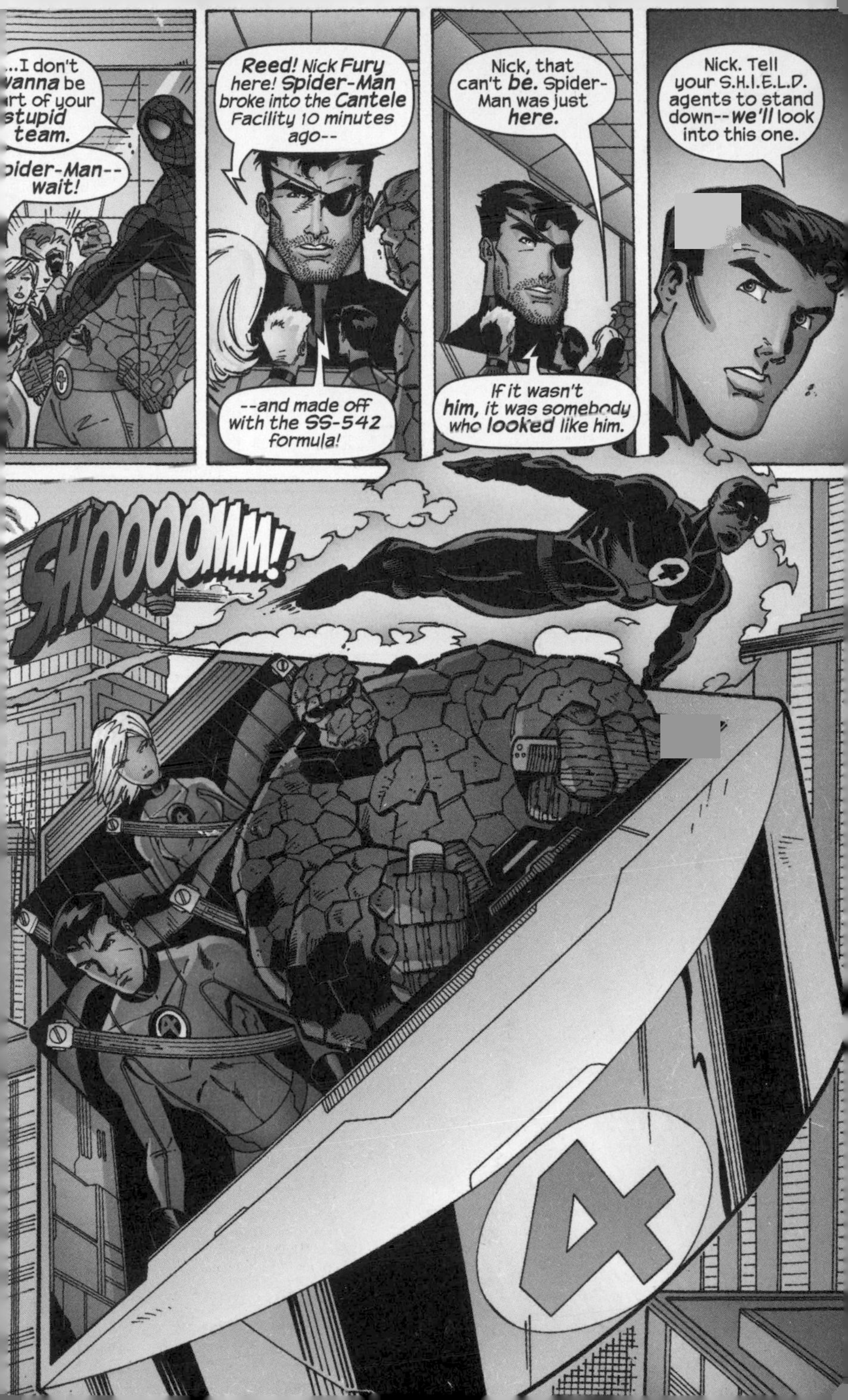

...I don't vanna be rt of your stupid team.
pider-Man-- wait!
Reed! Nick Fury here! Spider-Man broke into the Cantele Facility 10 minutes ago--
--and made off with the SS-542 formula!
Nick, that can't be. Spider-Man was just here.
If it wasn't him, it was somebody who looked like him.
Nick. Tell your S.H.I.E.L.D. agents to stand down--we'll look into this one.
SHOOOOMM!

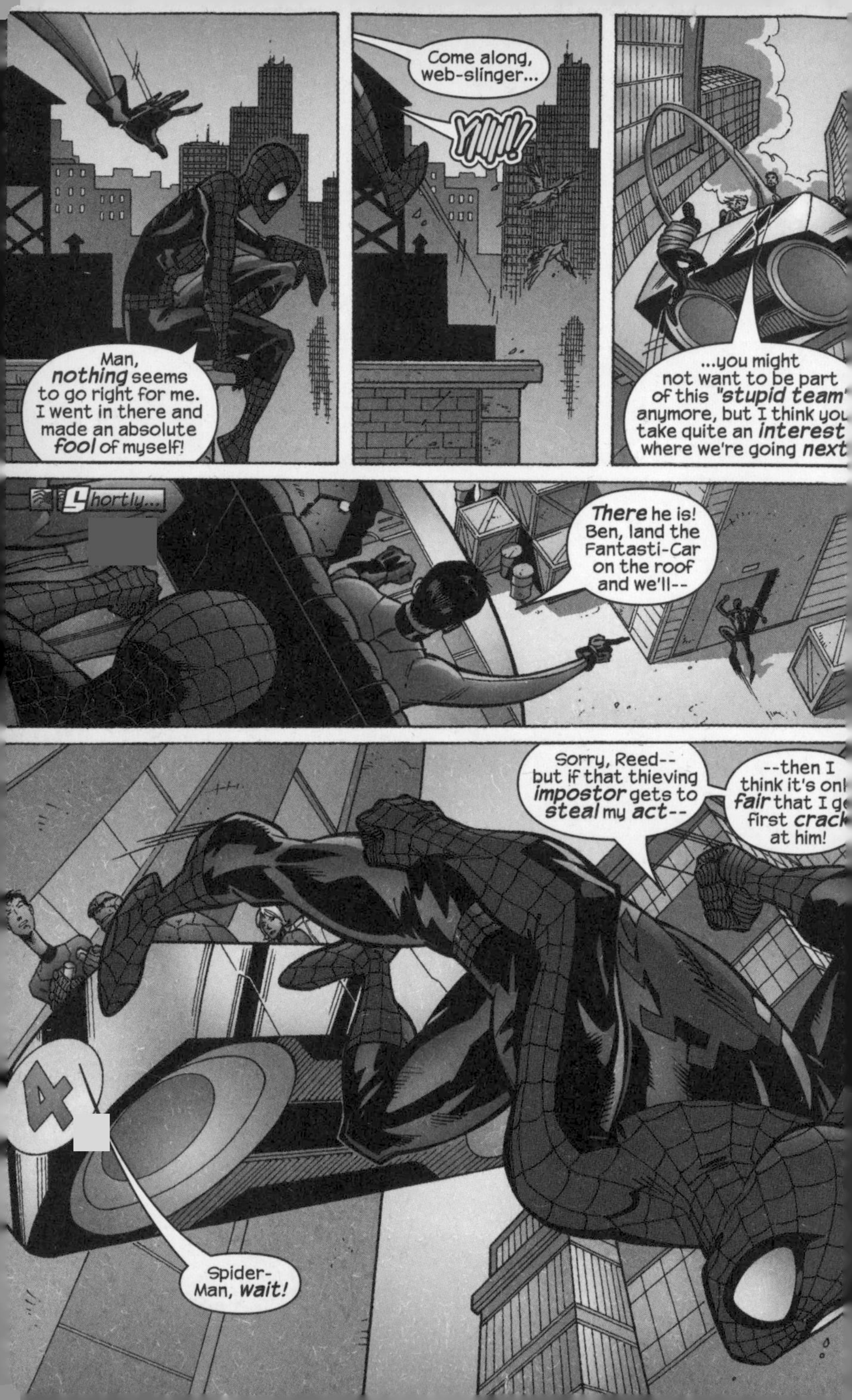

Man, *nothing* seems to go right for me. I went in there and made an absolute *fool* of myself!
Come along, web-slinger...
YAAA!!
...you might not want to be part of this *"stupid team"* anymore, but I think you take quite an *interest* where we're going *next*
Shortly...
There he is! Ben, land the Fantasti-Car on the roof and we'll--
Sorry, Reed-- but if that thieving *impostor* gets to *steal* my *act*--
--then I think it's onl *fair* that I g first *crack* at him!
Spider-Man, *wait!*

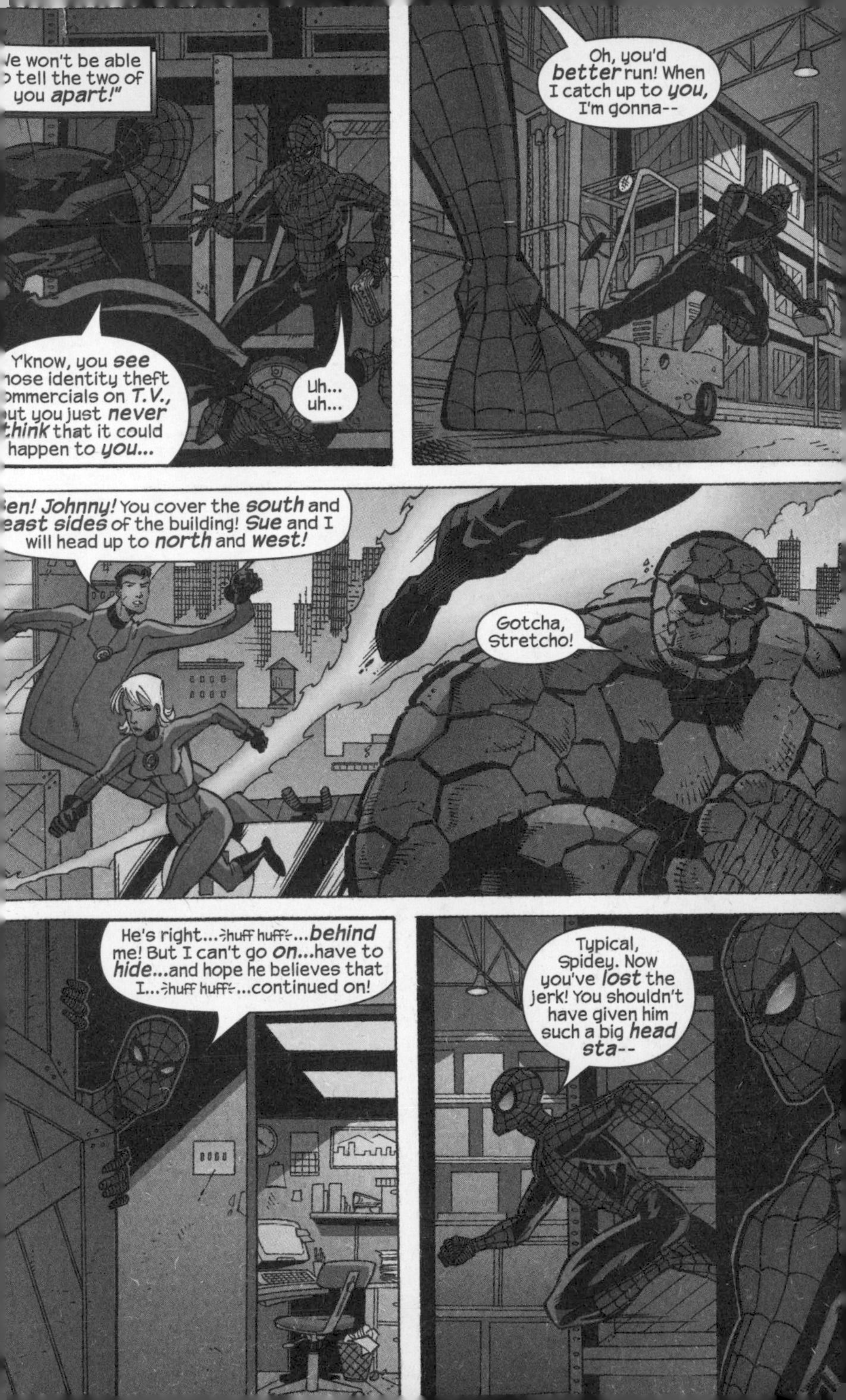

/e won't be able
o tell the two of
you apart!"
Y'know, you see
nose identity theft
ommercials on T.V.,
ut you just never
think that it could
happen to you...
Uh...
uh...
Oh, you'd better run! When I catch up to you, I'm gonna--
en! Johnny! You cover the south and
east sides of the building! Sue and I
will head up to north and west!
Gotcha, Stretcho!
He's right...huff huff...behind me! But I can't go on...have to hide...and hope he believes that I...huff huff...continued on!
Typical, Spidey. Now you've lost the jerk! You shouldn't have given him such a big head sta--

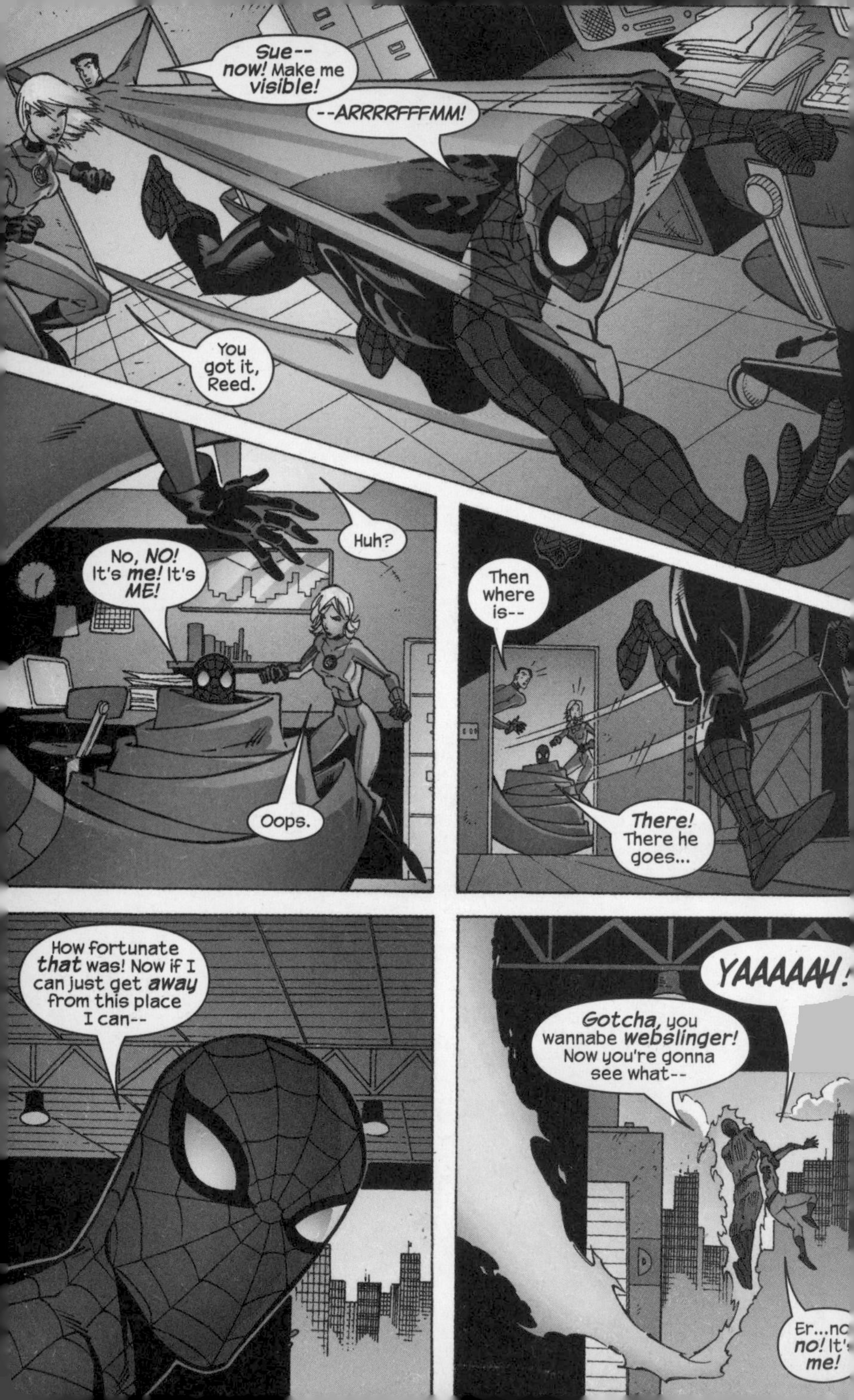
Sue--
now! Make me visible!
--ARRRRFFFMM!
You got it, Reed.
Huh?
No, NO! It's me! It's ME!
Oops.
Then where is--
There! There he goes...
How fortunate that was! Now if I can just get away from this place I can--
YAAAAAH!
Gotcha, you wannabe webslinger! Now you're gonna see what--
Er...no no! It's me!

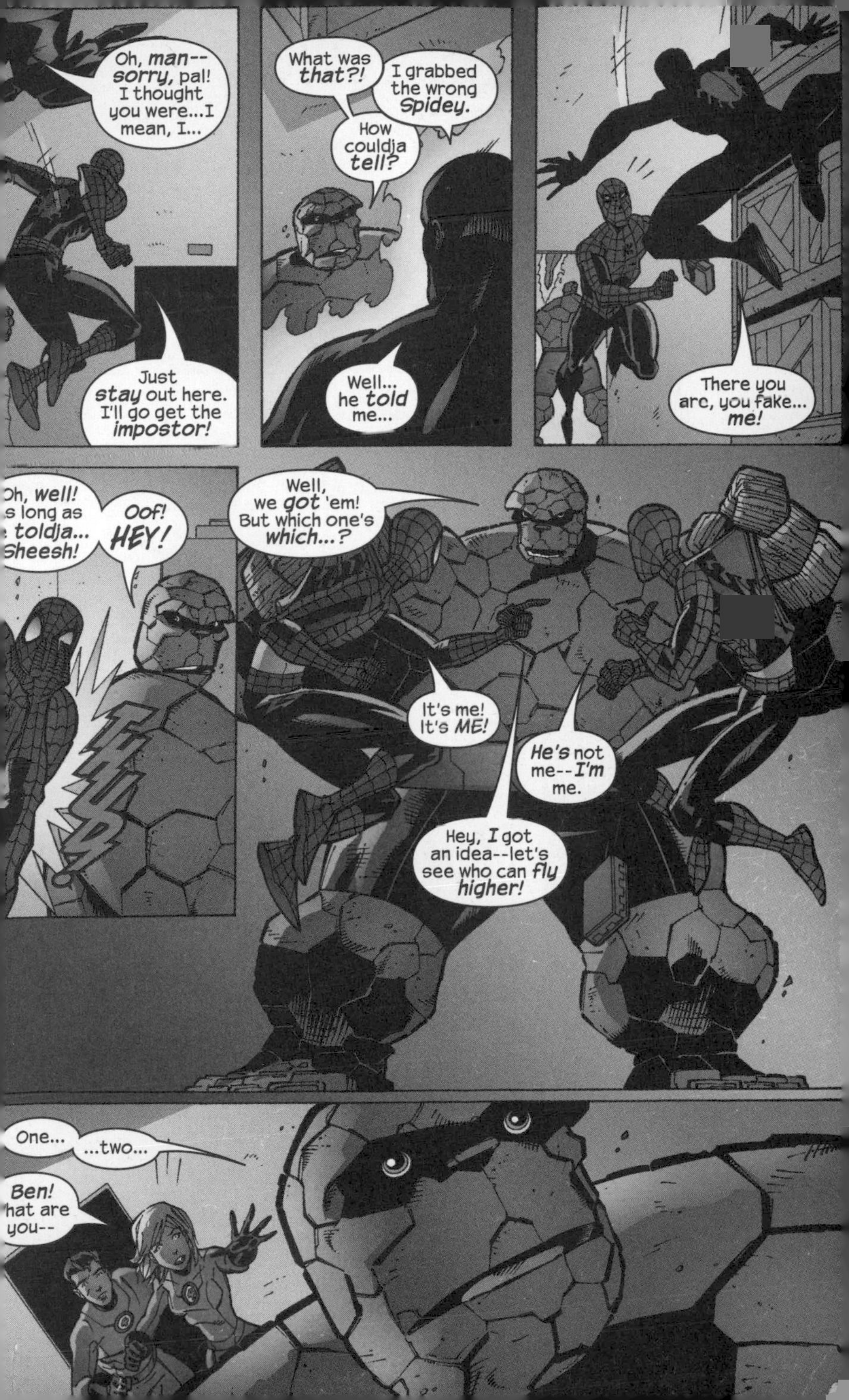

Oh, man--sorry, pal! I thought you were...I mean, I...
Just stay out here. I'll go get the impostor!
What was that?!
I grabbed the wrong Spidey.
How couldja tell?
Well... he told me...
There you arc, you fake... me!
Oh, well! s long as toldja... Sheesh!
Oof! HEY!
Well, we got 'em! But which one's which...?
It's me! It's ME!
He's not me--I'm me.
Hey, I got an idea--let's see who can fly higher!
One...
...two...
Ben! hat are you--

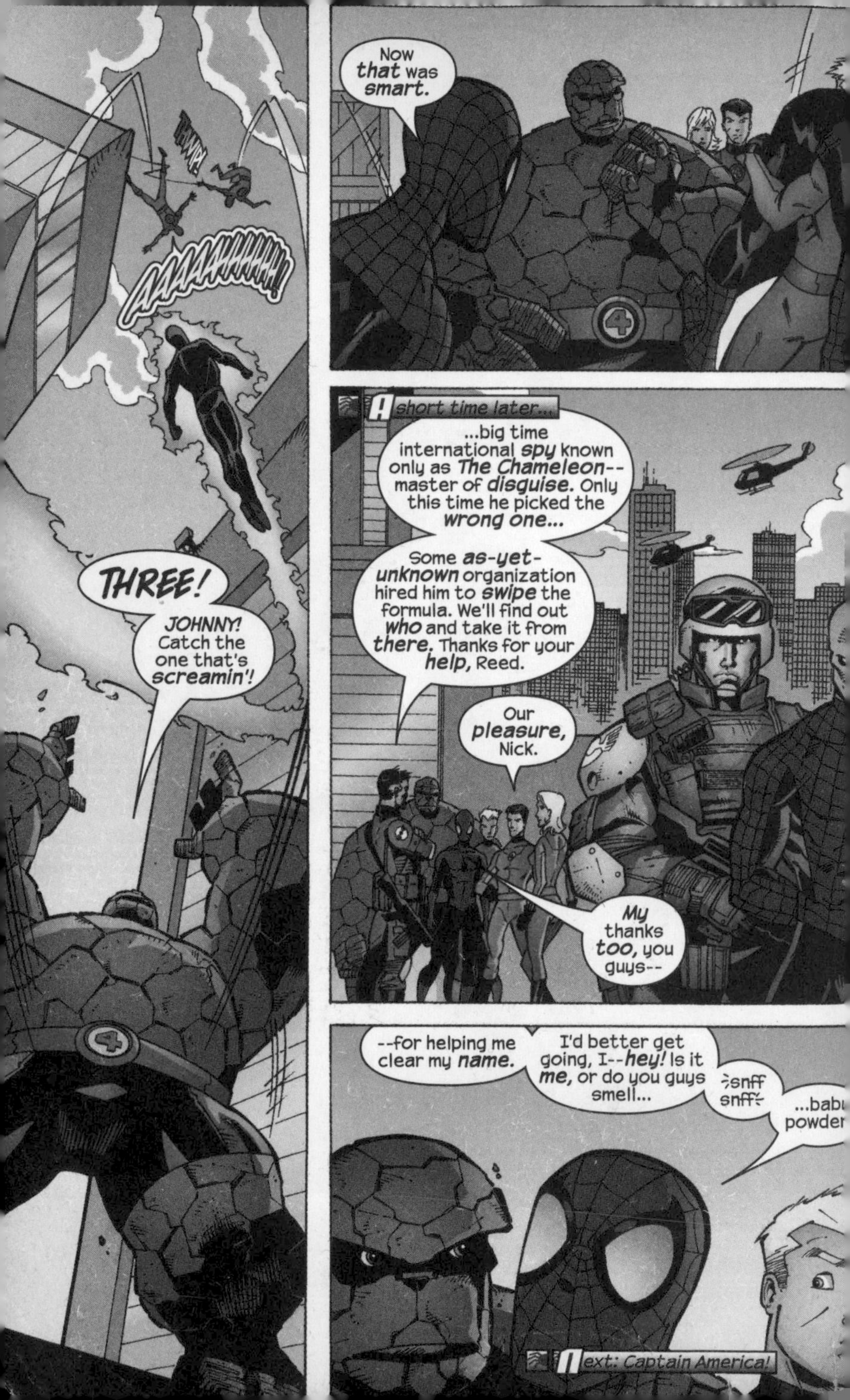
THWIP!
AAAAAAHHHHHH!
THREE!
JOHNNY! Catch the one that's screamin'!
Now that was smart.
A short time later...
...big time international spy known only as The Chameleon--master of disguise. Only this time he picked the wrong one...
Some as-yet-unknown organization hired him to swipe the formula. We'll find out who and take it from there. Thanks for your help, Reed.
Our pleasure, Nick.
My thanks too, you guys--
--for helping me clear my name.
I'd better get going, I--hey! Is it me, or do you guys smell...
snff snff
...bab powder
Next: Captain America!

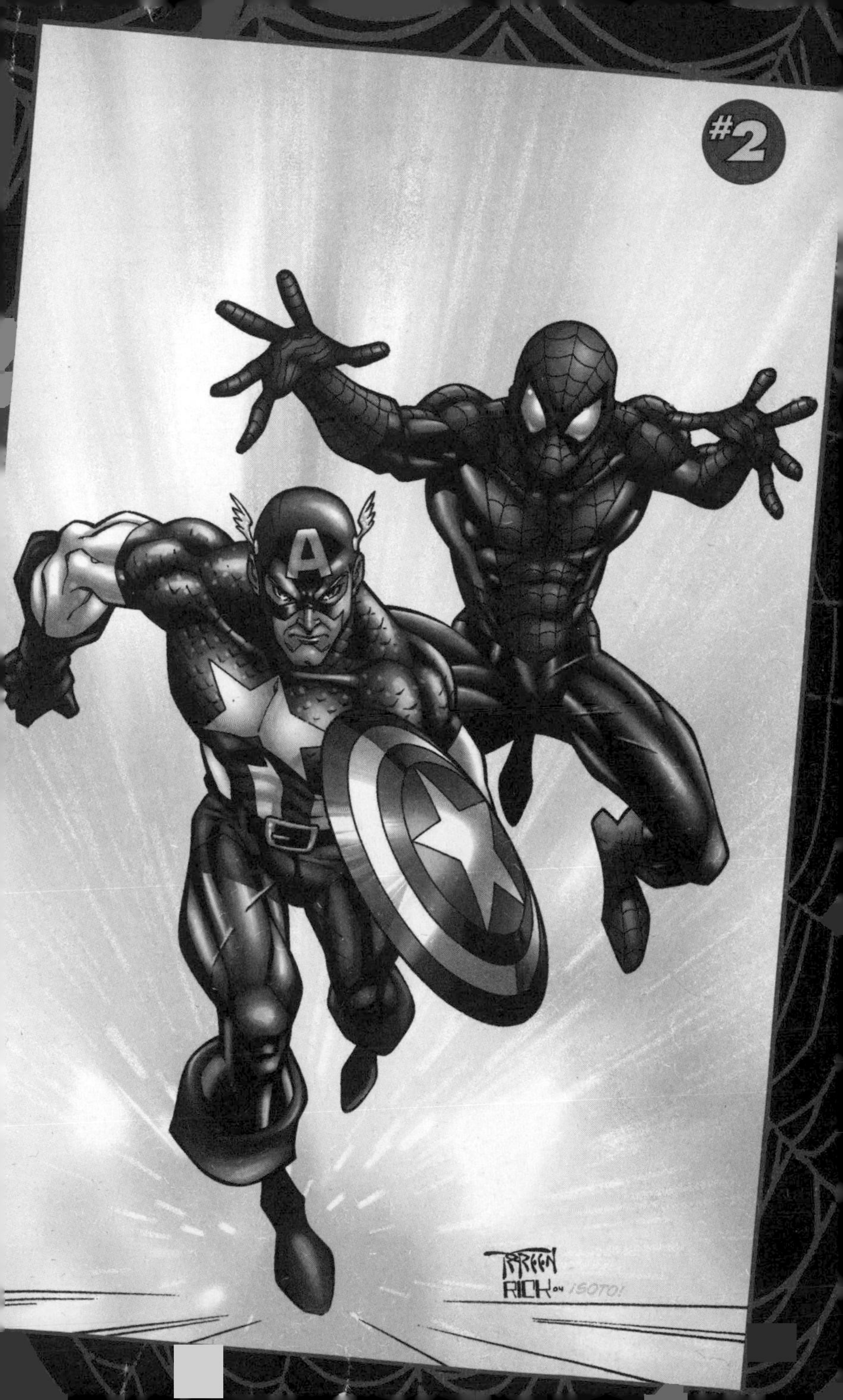

#2
RICK 04 ¡SOTO!

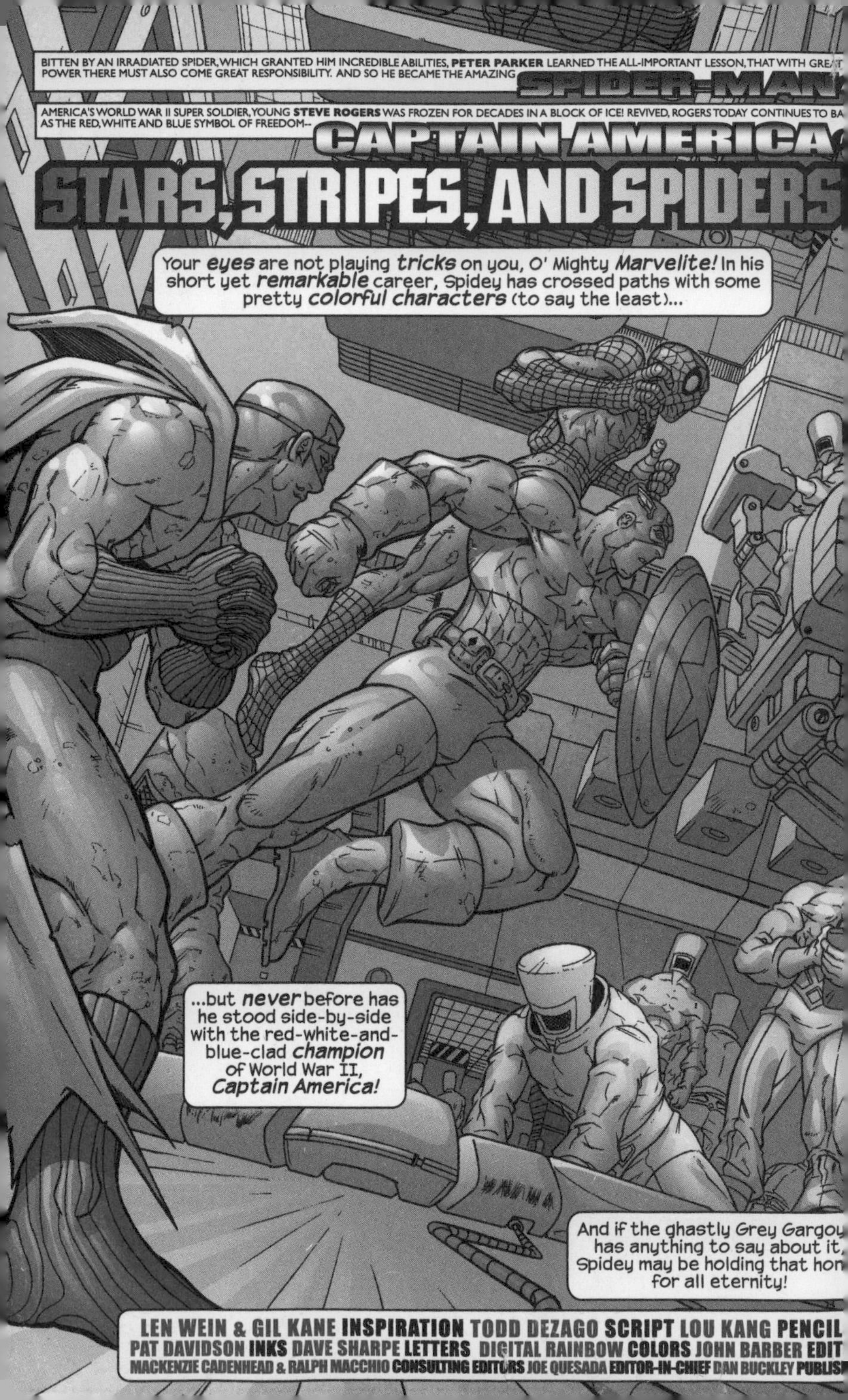
BITTEN BY AN IRRADIATED SPIDER, WHICH GRANTED HIM INCREDIBLE ABILITIES, PETER PARKER LEARNED THE ALL-IMPORTANT LESSON, THAT WITH GREAT POWER THERE MUST ALSO COME GREAT RESPONSIBILITY. AND SO HE BECAME THE AMAZING
SPIDER-MAN
AMERICA'S WORLD WAR II SUPER SOLDIER, YOUNG STEVE ROGERS WAS FROZEN FOR DECADES IN A BLOCK OF ICE! REVIVED, ROGERS TODAY CONTINUES TO BA AS THE RED, WHITE AND BLUE SYMBOL OF FREEDOM--
CAPTAIN AMERICA
STARS, STRIPES, AND SPIDERS
Your eyes are not playing tricks on you, O' Mighty Marvelite! In his short yet remarkable career, Spidey has crossed paths with some pretty colorful characters (to say the least)...
...but never before has he stood side-by-side with the red-white-and-blue-clad champion of World War II, Captain America!
And if the ghastly Grey Gargoy has anything to say about it, Spidey may be holding that hon for all eternity!
LEN WEIN & GIL KANE INSPIRATION TODD DEZAGO SCRIPT LOU KANG PENCIL
PAT DAVIDSON INKS DAVE SHARPE LETTERS DIGITAL RAINBOW COLORS JOHN BARBER EDIT
MACKENZIE CADENHEAD & RALPH MACCHIO CONSULTING EDITORS JOE QUESADA EDITOR-IN-CHIEF DAN BUCKLEY PUBLISH

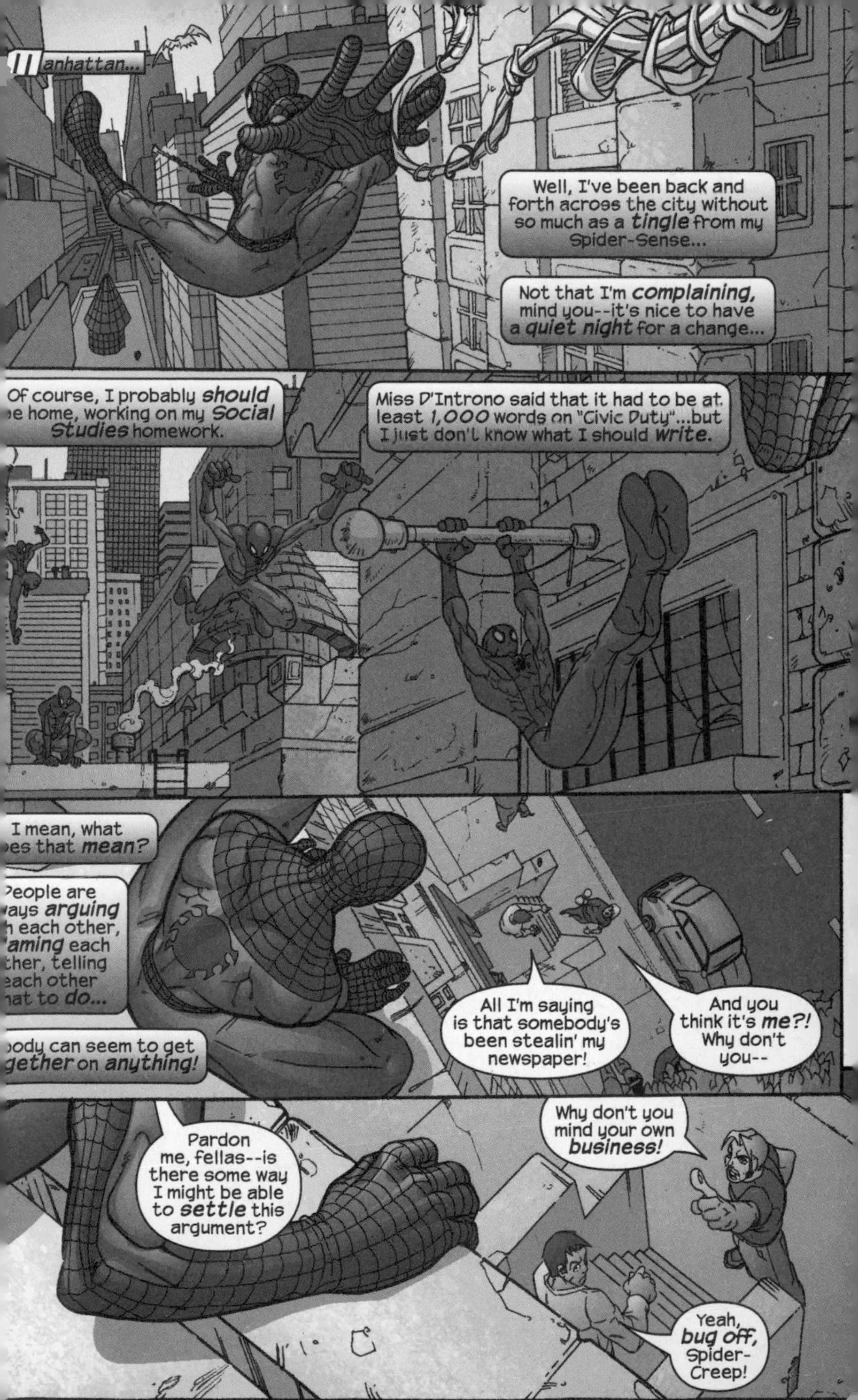

Manhattan...
Well, I've been back and forth across the city without so much as a tingle from my Spider-Sense...
Not that I'm complaining, mind you--it's nice to have a quiet night for a change...
Of course, I probably should e home, working on my Social Studies homework.
Miss D'Introno said that it had to be at least 1,000 words on "Civic Duty"...but I just don't know what I should write.
I mean, what es that mean?
eople are ays arguing h each other, aming each ther, telling each other hat to do...
ody can seem to get gether on anything!
All I'm saying is that somebody's been stealin' my newspaper!
And you think it's me?! Why don't you--
Pardon me, fellas--is there some way I might be able to settle this argument?
Why don't you mind your own business!
Yeah, bug off, Spider-Creep!

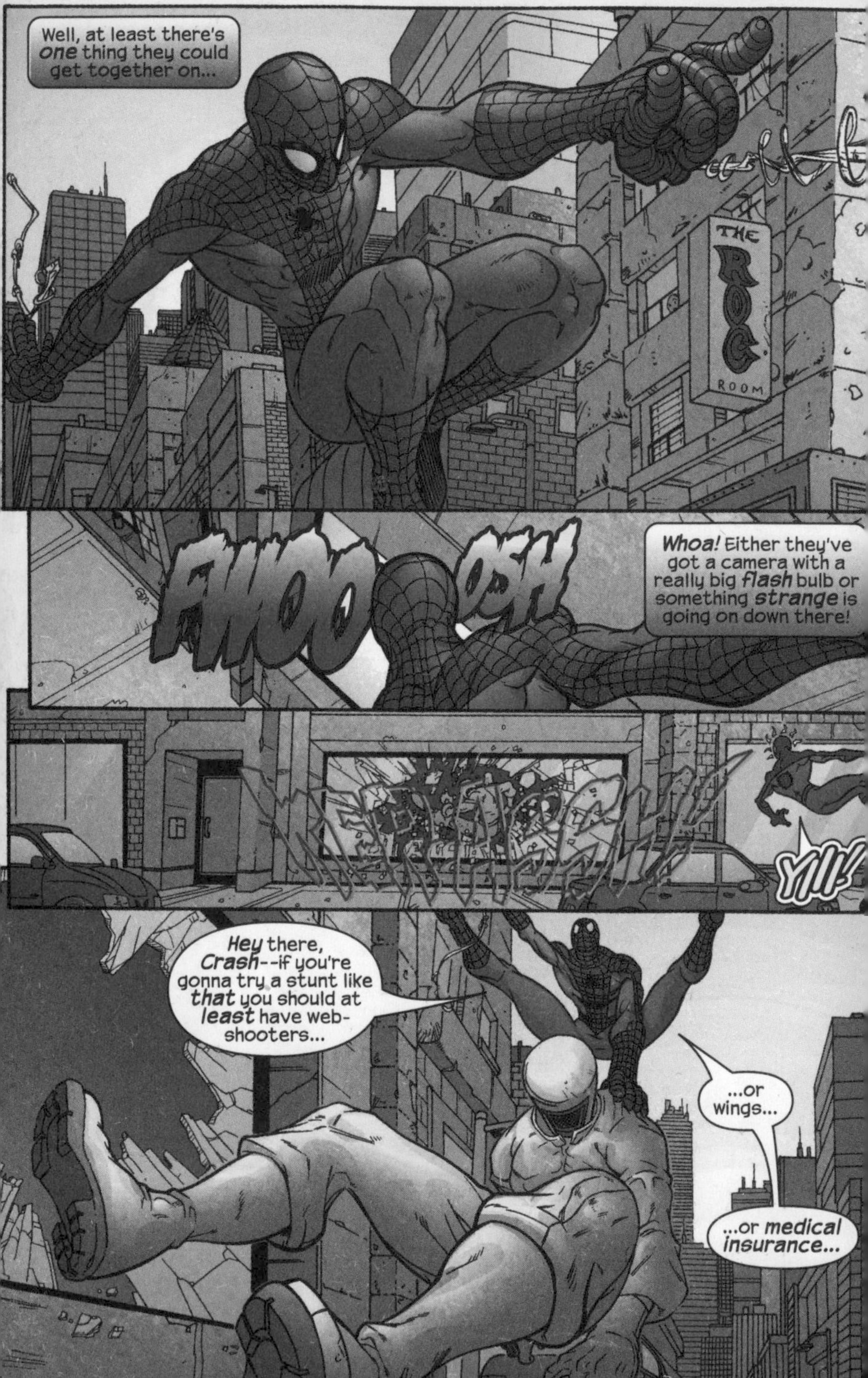
Well, at least there's one thing they could get together on...
THE ROC. ROOM
FWOOOOSH
Whoa! Either they've got a camera with a really big flash bulb or something strange is going on down there!
YIII!
Hey there, Crash--if you're gonna try a stunt like that you should at least have web-shooters...
...or wings...
...or medical insurance...

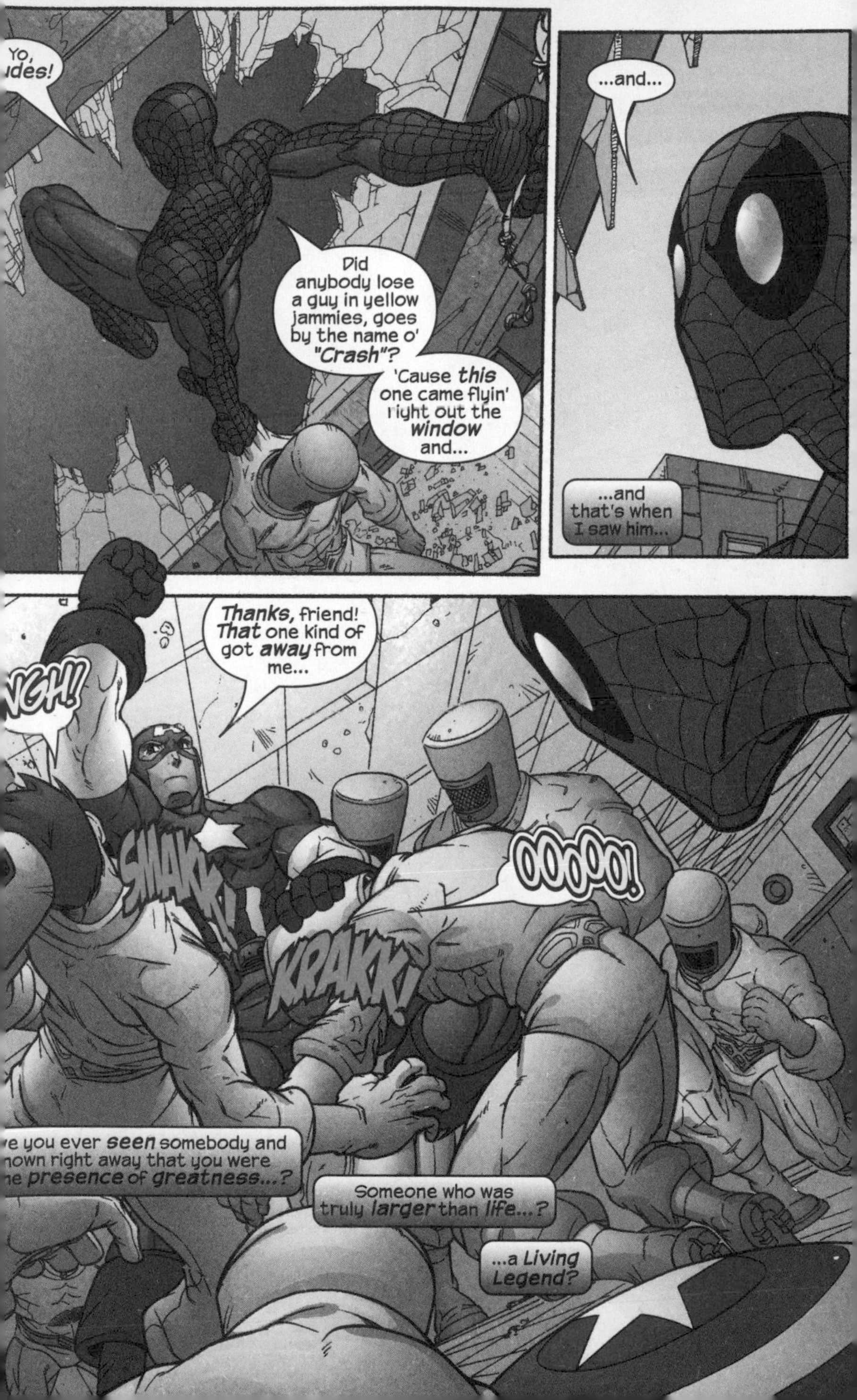
Yo,
udes!
Did anybody lose a guy in yellow jammies, goes by the name o' "Crash"?
'Cause this one came flyin' right out the window and...
...and...
...and that's when I saw him...
Thanks, friend! That one kind of got away from me...
NGH!!
SMAKK!
KRAKK!
OOOOO!
e you ever seen somebody and
nown right away that you were
e presence of greatness...?
Someone who was truly larger than life...?
...a Living Legend?

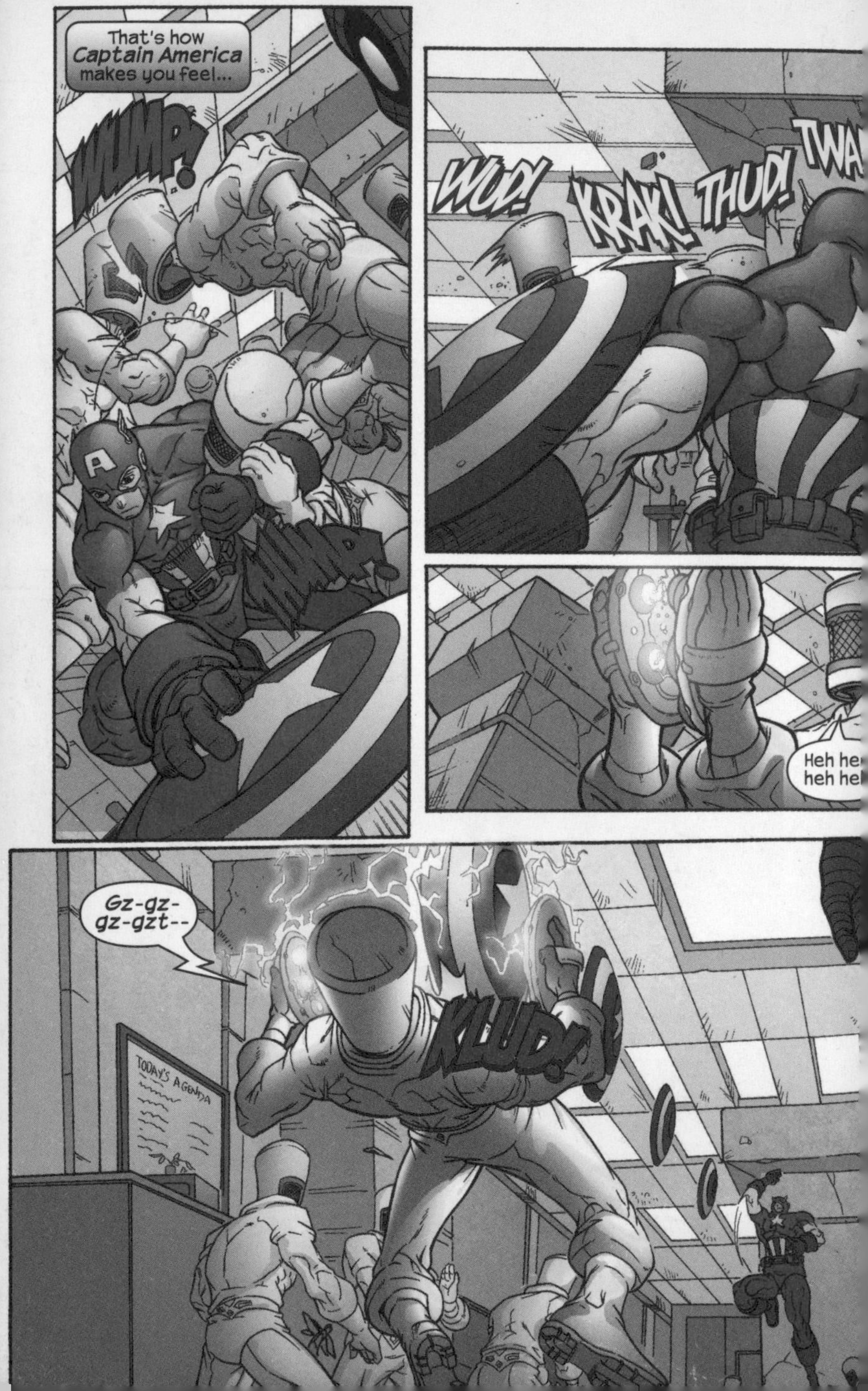
That's how Captain America makes you feel...
WUMP!
WUMP!
WUD!
KRAK!
THUD!
Heh he
heh he
Gz-gz-
gz-gzt--
KLUD!
TODAY'S AGENDA

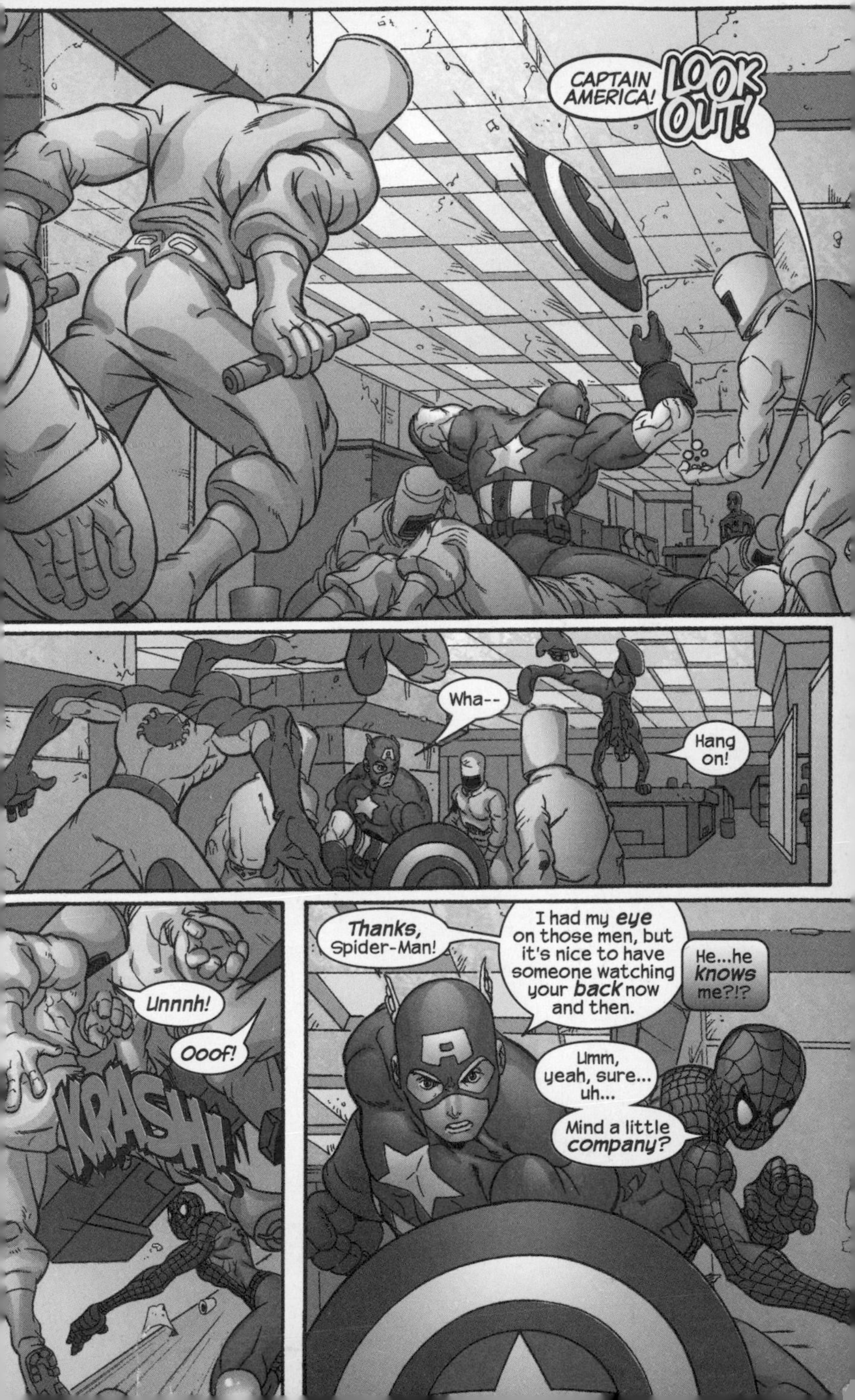

CAPTAIN AMERICA! LOOK OUT!
Wha--
Hang on!
Unnnh!
Ooof!
KRASH!
Thanks, Spider-Man!
I had my eye on those men, but it's nice to have someone watching your back now and then.
He...he knows me?!?
Umm, yeah, sure... uh...
Mind a little company?

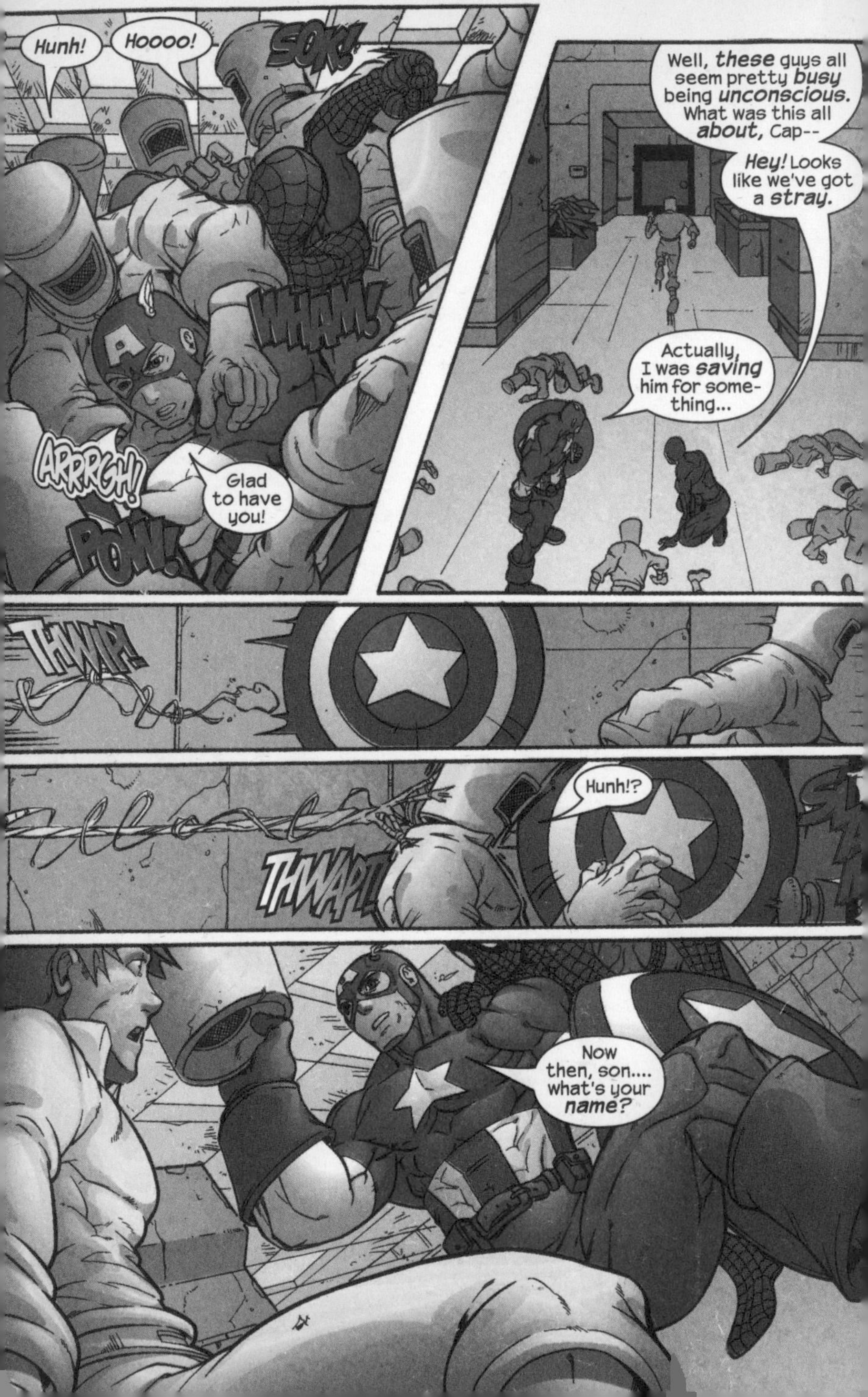
Hunh!
Hoooo!
SOK!
WHAM!
ARRRGH!
Glad to have you!
POW!
Well, these guys all seem pretty busy being unconscious. What was this all about, Cap--
Hey! Looks like we've got a stray.
Actually, I was saving him for some-thing...
THWIP!
Hunh!?
THWAP!
Now then, son.... what's your name?

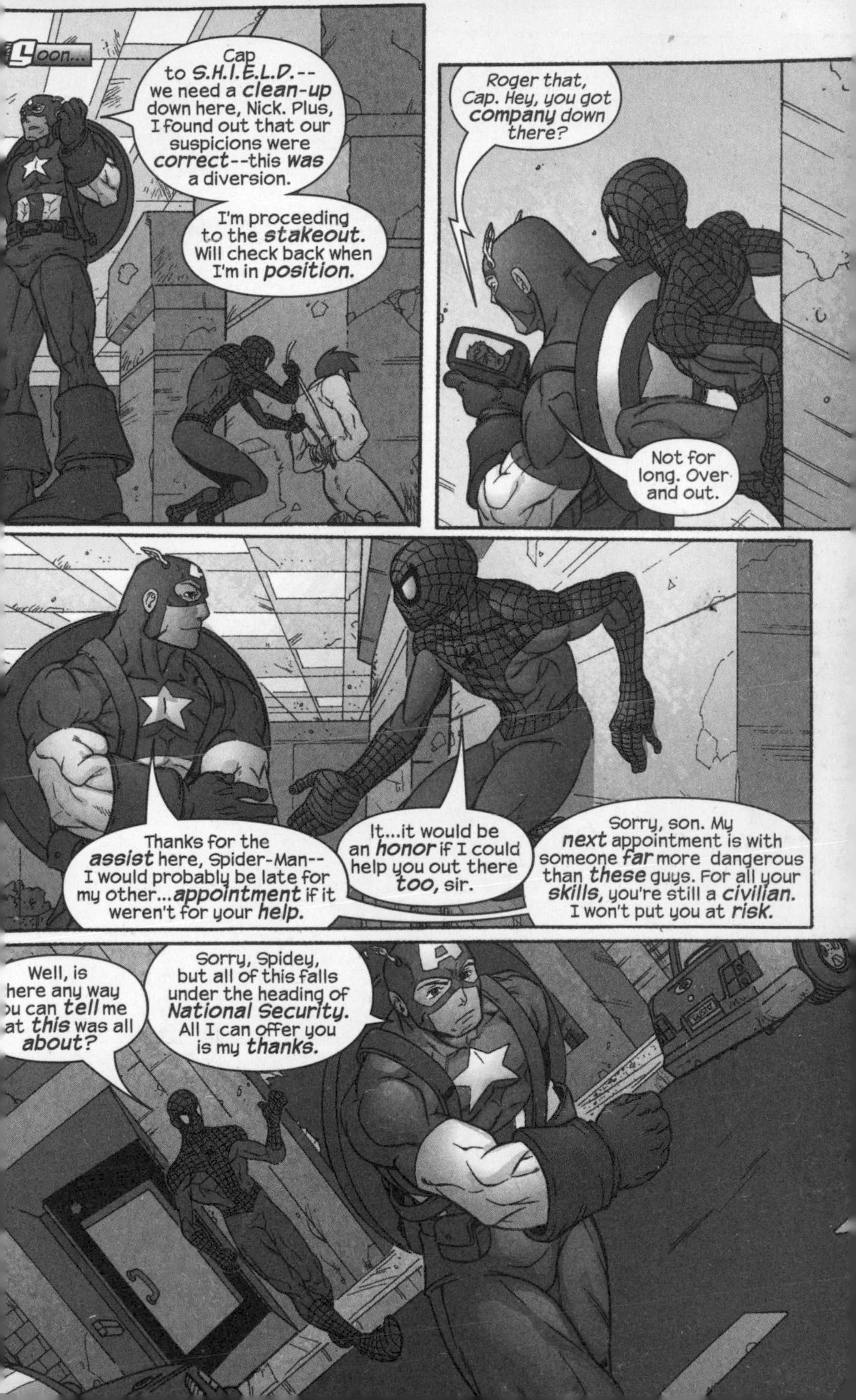
Soon...
Cap to S.H.I.E.L.D.-- we need a clean-up down here, Nick. Plus, I found out that our suspicions were correct--this was a diversion.
I'm proceeding to the stakeout. Will check back when I'm in position.
Roger that, Cap. Hey, you got company down there?
Not for long. Over and out.
Thanks for the assist here, Spider-Man-- I would probably be late for my other...appointment if it weren't for your help.
It...it would be an honor if I could help you out there too, sir.
Sorry, son. My next appointment is with someone far more dangerous than these guys. For all your skills, you're still a civilian. I won't put you at risk.
Well, is here any way ou can tell me at this was all about?
Sorry, Spidey, but all of this falls under the heading of National Security. All I can offer you is my thanks.

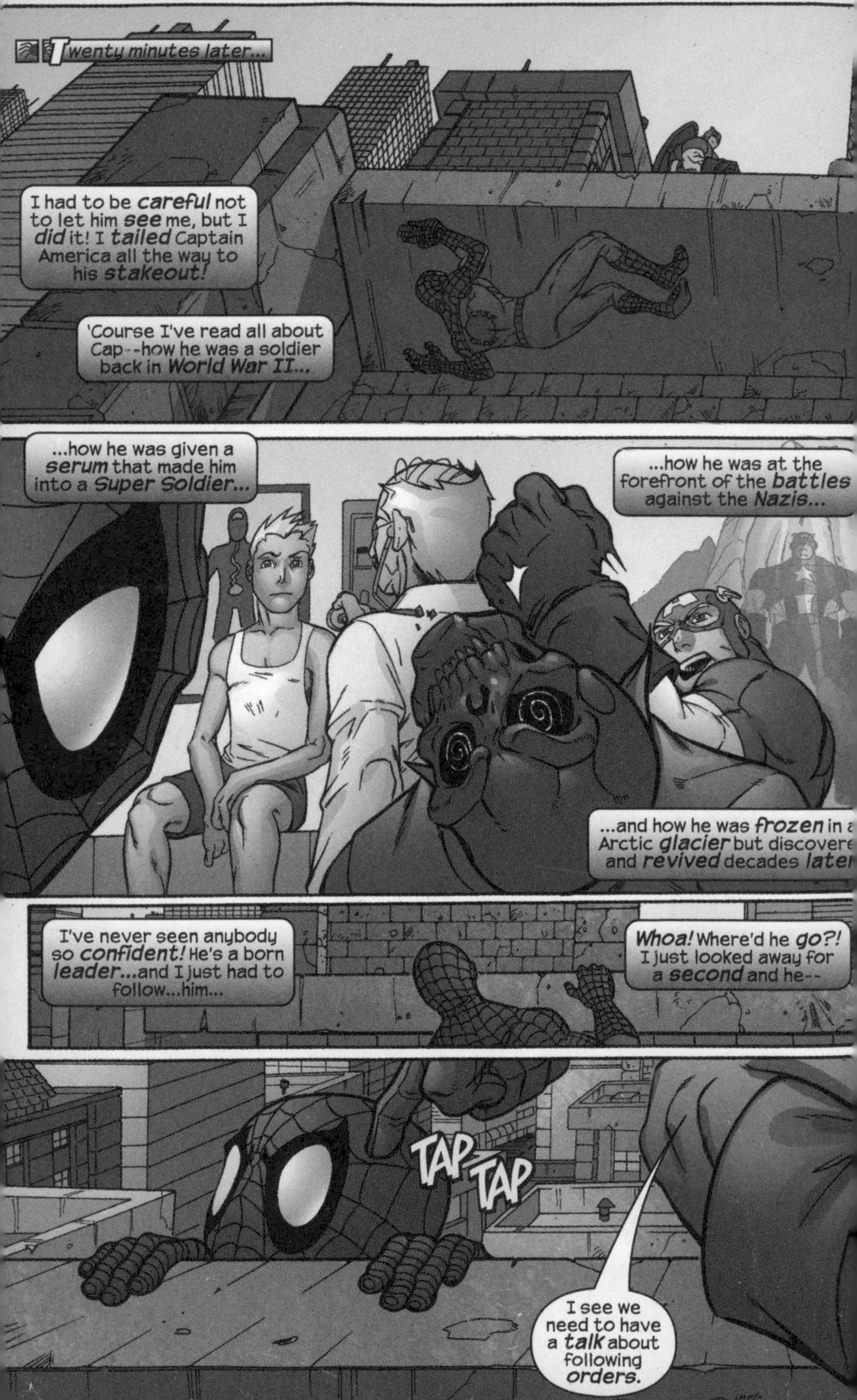
Twenty minutes later...
I had to be careful not to let him see me, but I did it! I tailed Captain America all the way to his stakeout!
'Course I've read all about Cap--how he was a soldier back in World War II...
...how he was given a serum that made him into a Super Soldier...
...how he was at the forefront of the battles against the Nazis...
...and how he was frozen in a Arctic glacier but discovere and revived decades late
I've never seen anybody so confident! He's a born leader...and I just had to follow...him...
Whoa! Where'd he go?! I just looked away for a second and he--
TAP TAP
I see we need to have a talk about following orders.

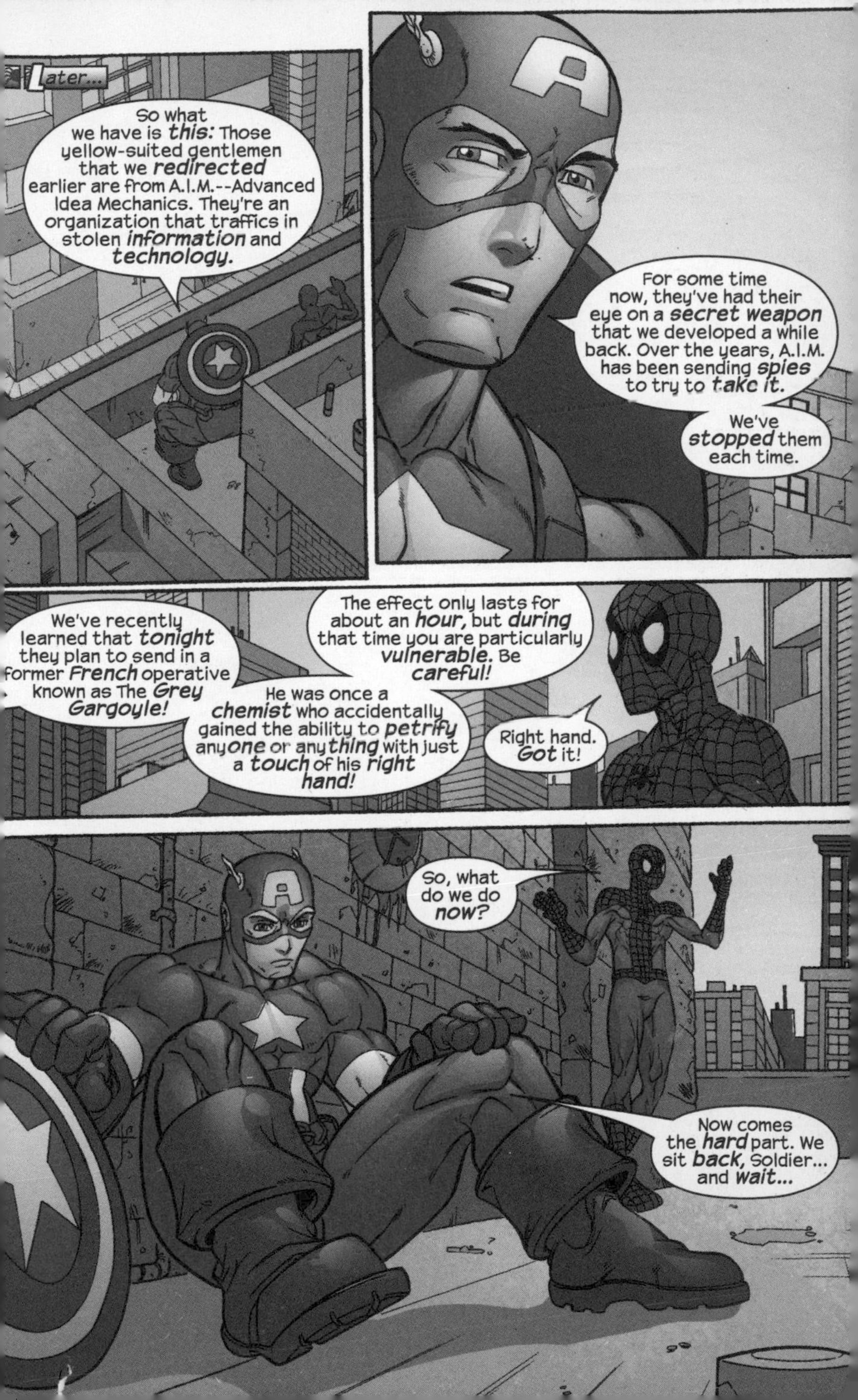

Later...
So what we have is this: Those yellow-suited gentlemen that we redirected earlier are from A.I.M.--Advanced Idea Mechanics. They're an organization that traffics in stolen information and technology.
For some time now, they've had their eye on a secret weapon that we developed a while back. Over the years, A.I.M. has been sending spies to try to take it.
We've stopped them each time.
We've recently learned that tonight they plan to send in a former French operative known as The Grey Gargoyle!
He was once a chemist who accidentally gained the ability to petrify anyone or anything with just a touch of his right hand!
The effect only lasts for about an hour, but during that time you are particularly vulnerable. Be careful!
Right hand. Got it!
So, what do we do now?
Now comes the hard part. We sit back, Soldier... and wait...

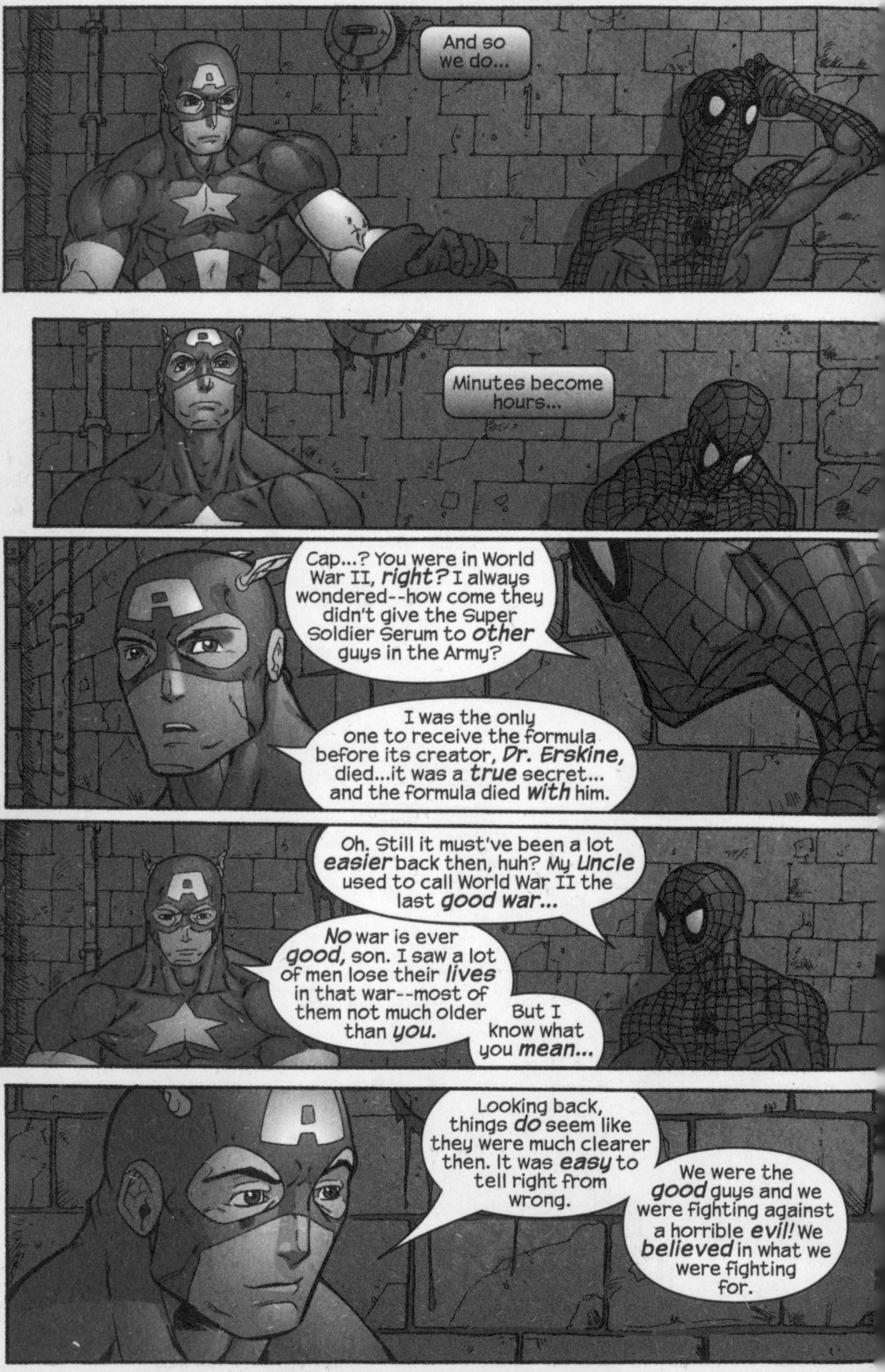
And so we do...
Minutes become hours...
Cap...? You were in World War II, right? I always wondered--how come they didn't give the Super Soldier Serum to other guys in the Army?
I was the only one to receive the formula before its creator, Dr. Erskine, died...it was a true secret... and the formula died with him.
Oh. Still it must've been a lot easier back then, huh? My Uncle used to call World War II the last good war...
No war is ever good, son. I saw a lot of men lose their lives in that war--most of them not much older than you.
But I know what you mean...
Looking back, things do seem like they were much clearer then. It was easy to tell right from wrong.
We were the good guys and we were fighting against a horrible evil! We believed in what we were fighting for.

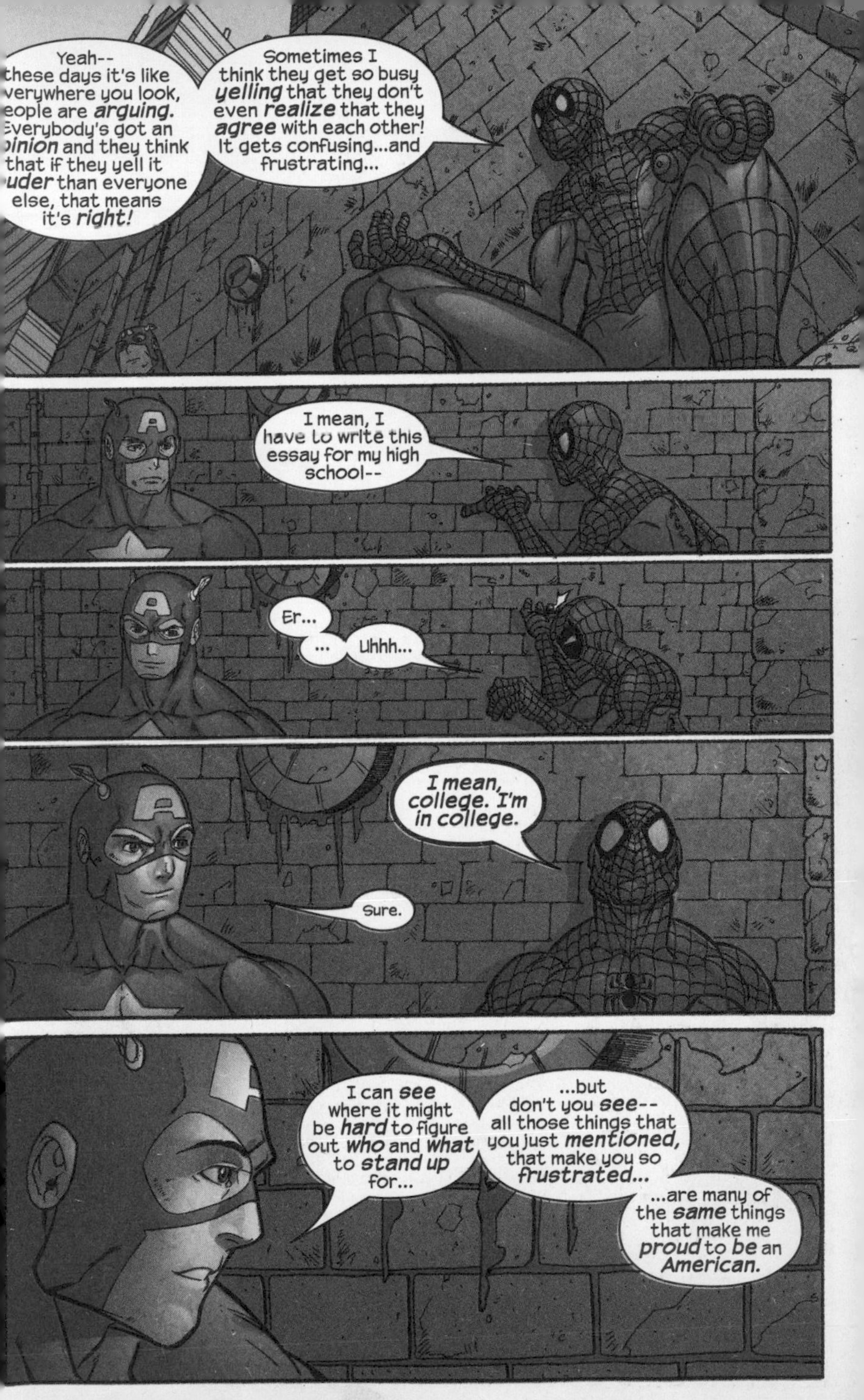
Yeah-- these days it's like verywhere you look, eople are arguing. verybody's got an inion and they think that if they yell it uder than everyone else, that means it's right!
Sometimes I think they get so busy yelling that they don't even realize that they agree with each other! It gets confusing...and frustrating...
I mean, I have to write this essay for my high school--
Er...
...
Uhhh...
I mean, college. I'm in college.
Sure.
I can see where it might be hard to figure out who and what to stand up for...
...but don't you see-- all those things that you just mentioned, that make you so frustrated...
...are many of the same things that make me proud to be an American.

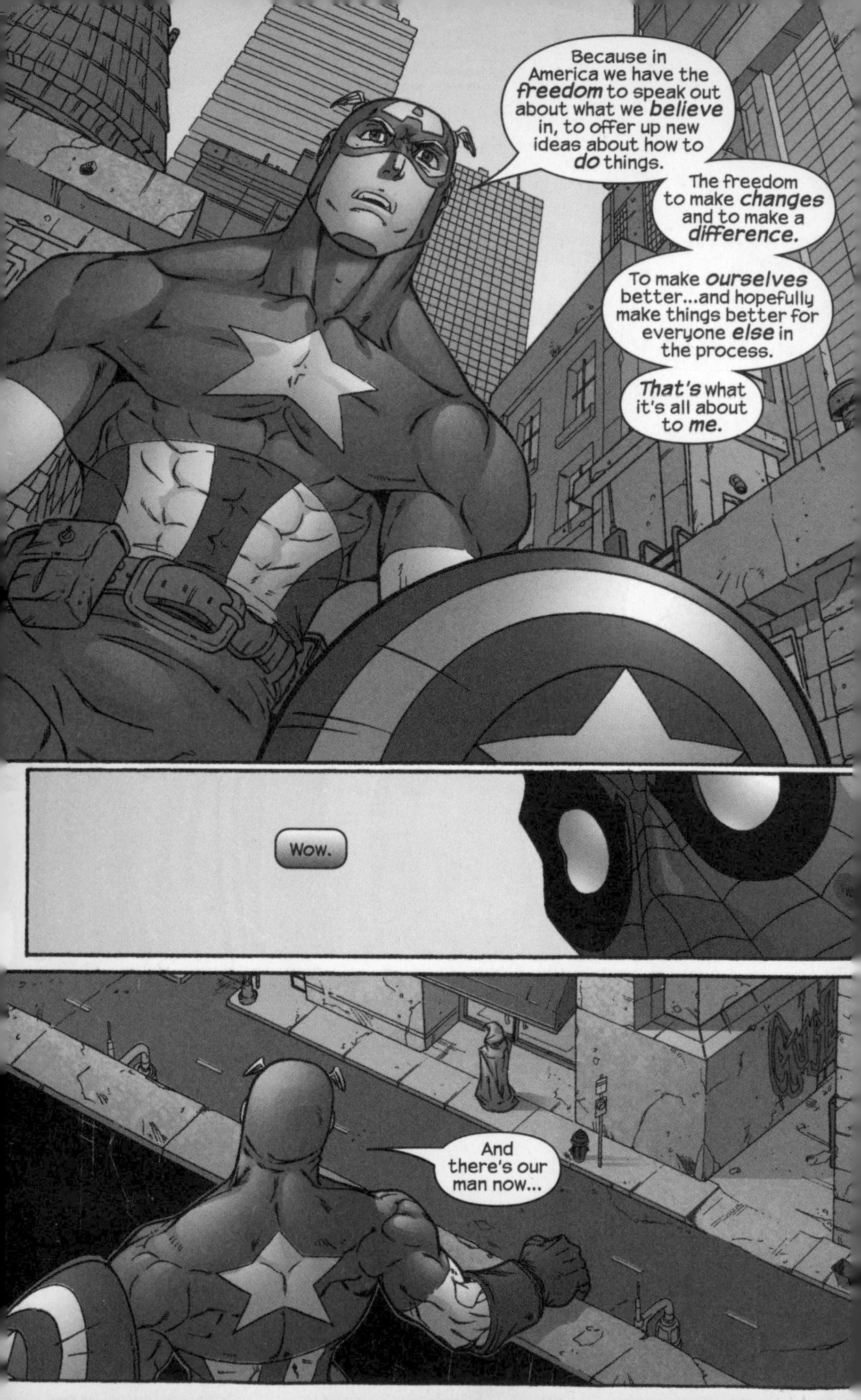
Because in America we have the freedom to speak out about what we believe in, to offer up new ideas about how to do things.
The freedom to make changes and to make a difference.
To make ourselves better...and hopefully make things better for everyone else in the process.
That's what it's all about to me.
Wow.
And there's our man now...

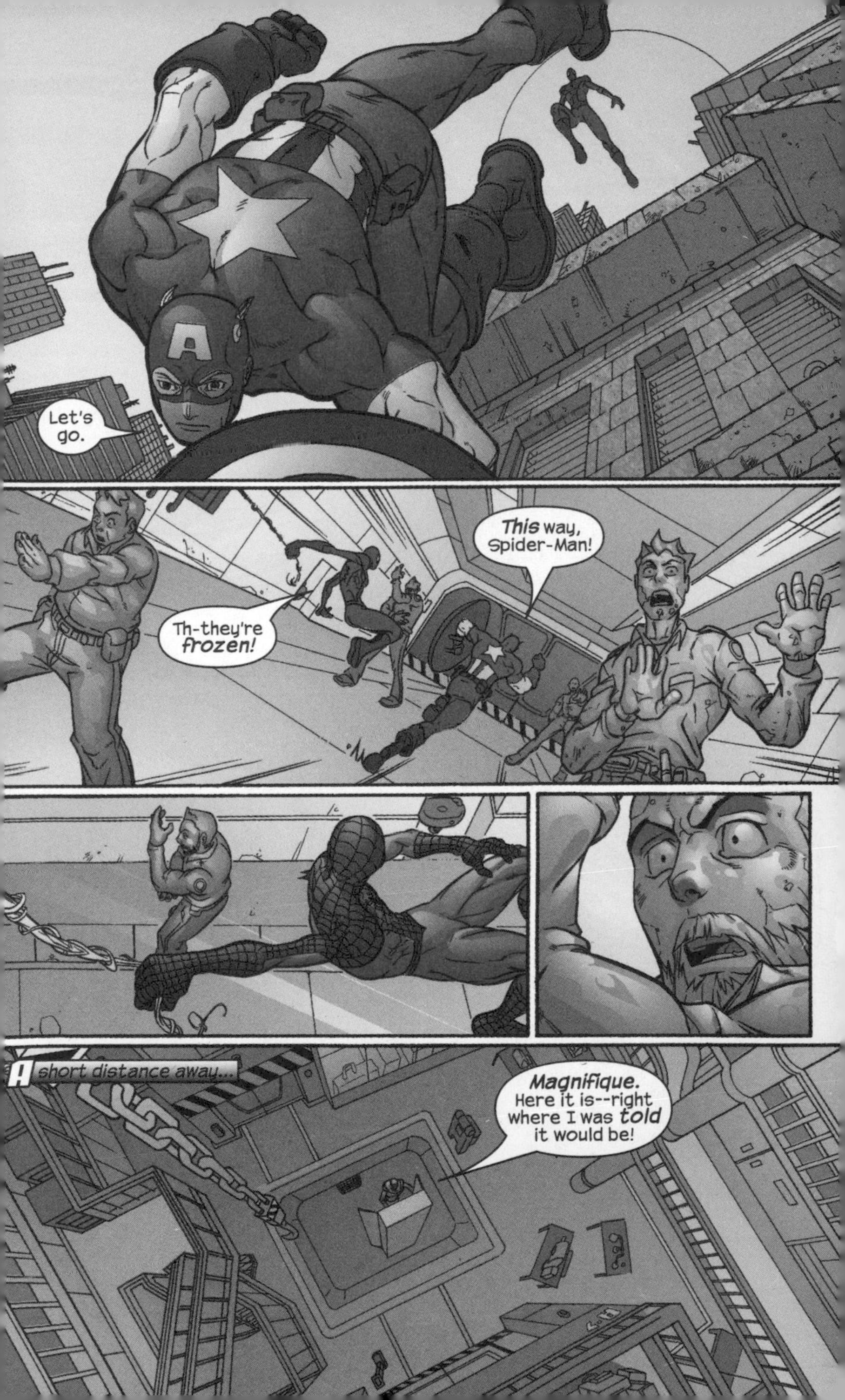
Let's go.
This way, Spider-Man!
Th-they're frozen!
A short distance away...
Magnifique. Here it is--right where I was told it would be!

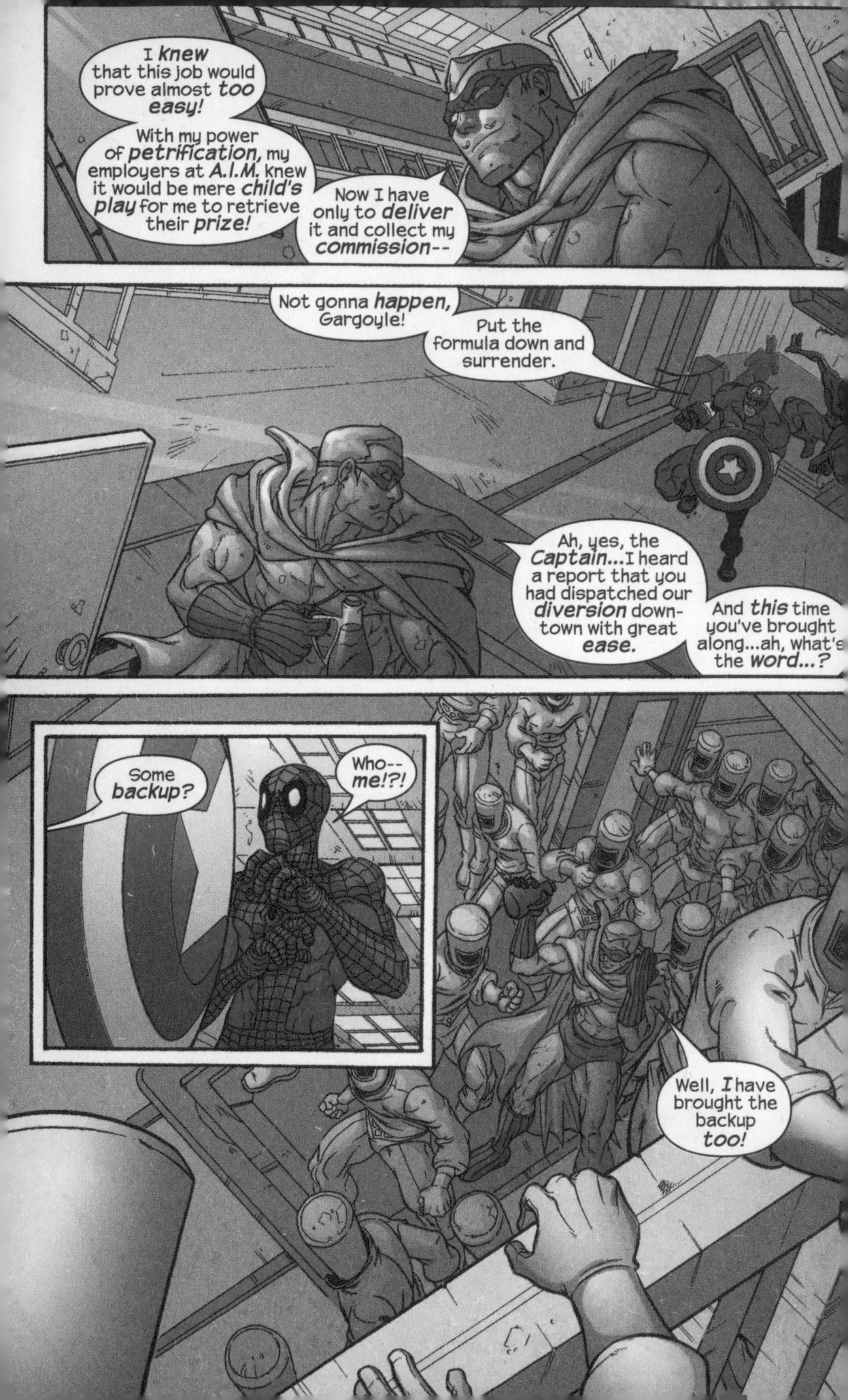
I knew that this job would prove almost too easy!
With my power of petrification, my employers at A.I.M. knew it would be mere child's play for me to retrieve their prize!
Now I have only to deliver it and collect my commission--
Not gonna happen, Gargoyle!
Put the formula down and surrender.
Ah, yes, the Captain...I heard a report that you had dispatched our diversion down-town with great ease.
And this time you've brought along...ah, what's the word...?
Some backup?
Who-- me!?!
Well, I have brought the backup too!

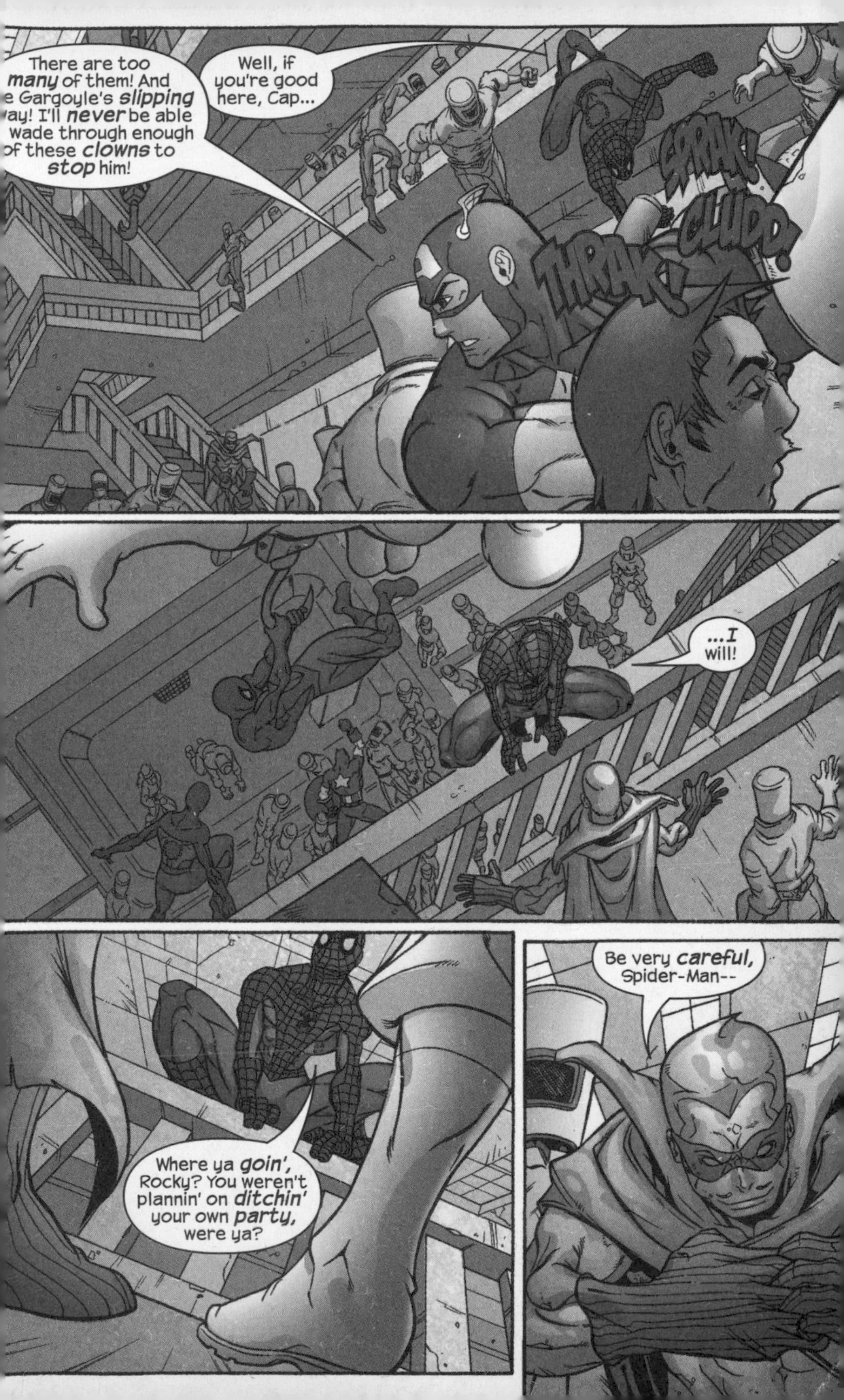
There are too many of them! And e Gargoyle's slipping ay! I'll never be able wade through enough of these clowns to stop him!
Well, if you're good here, Cap...
SPRAK!
CLUDD!
THRAK!
...I will!
Where ya goin', Rocky? You weren't plannin' on ditchin' your own party, were ya?
Be very careful, Spider-Man--

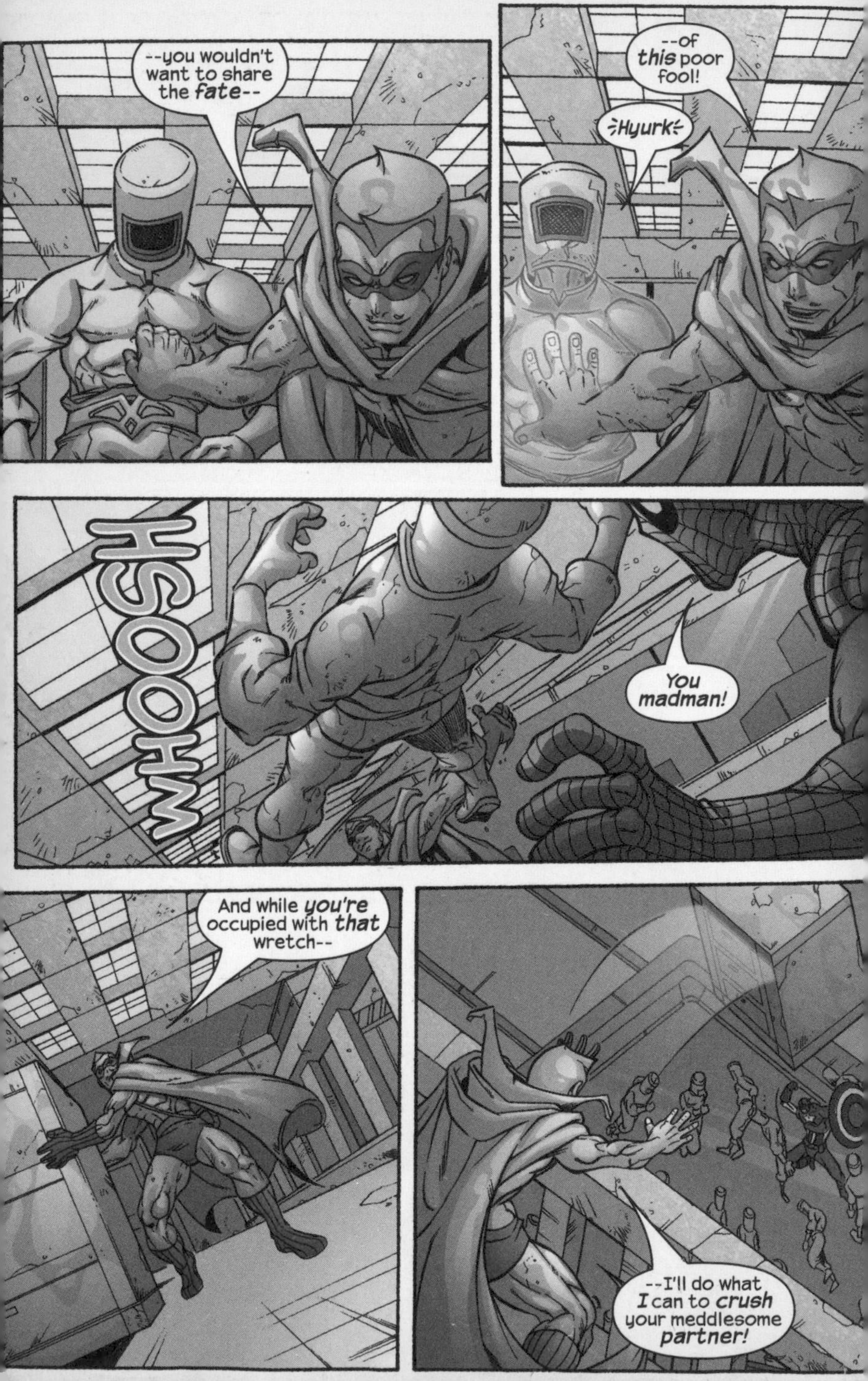
--you wouldn't want to share the *fate*--
--of *this* poor fool!
Hyurk
WHOOSH
You madman!
And while *you're* occupied with *that* wretch--
--I'll do what *I* can to *crush* your meddlesome *partner!*

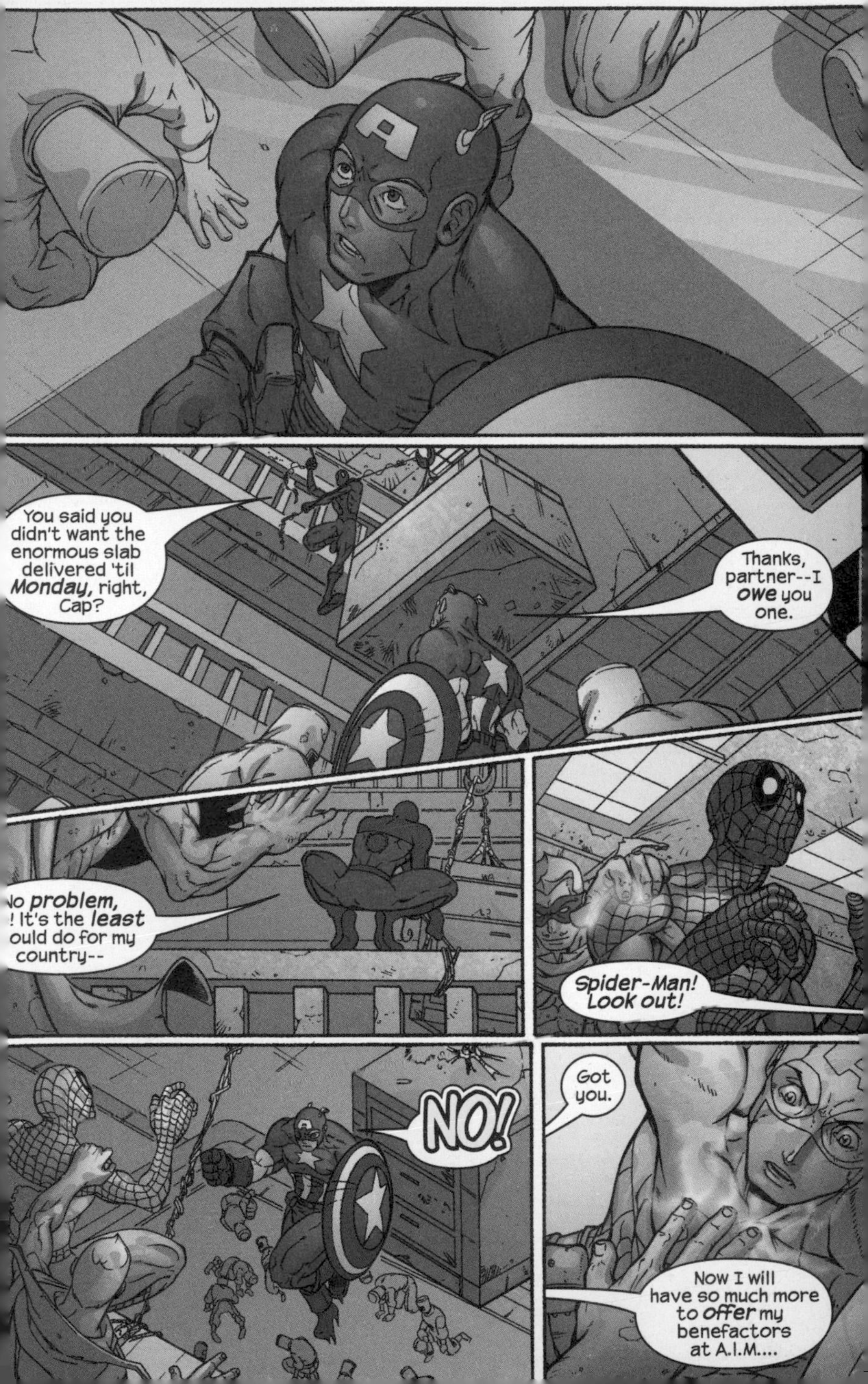

You said you didn't want the enormous slab delivered 'til Monday, right, Cap?
Thanks, partner--I owe you one.
No problem, ! It's the least ould do for my country--
Spider-Man! Look out!
NO!
Got you.
Now I will have so much more to offer my benefactors at A.I.M....

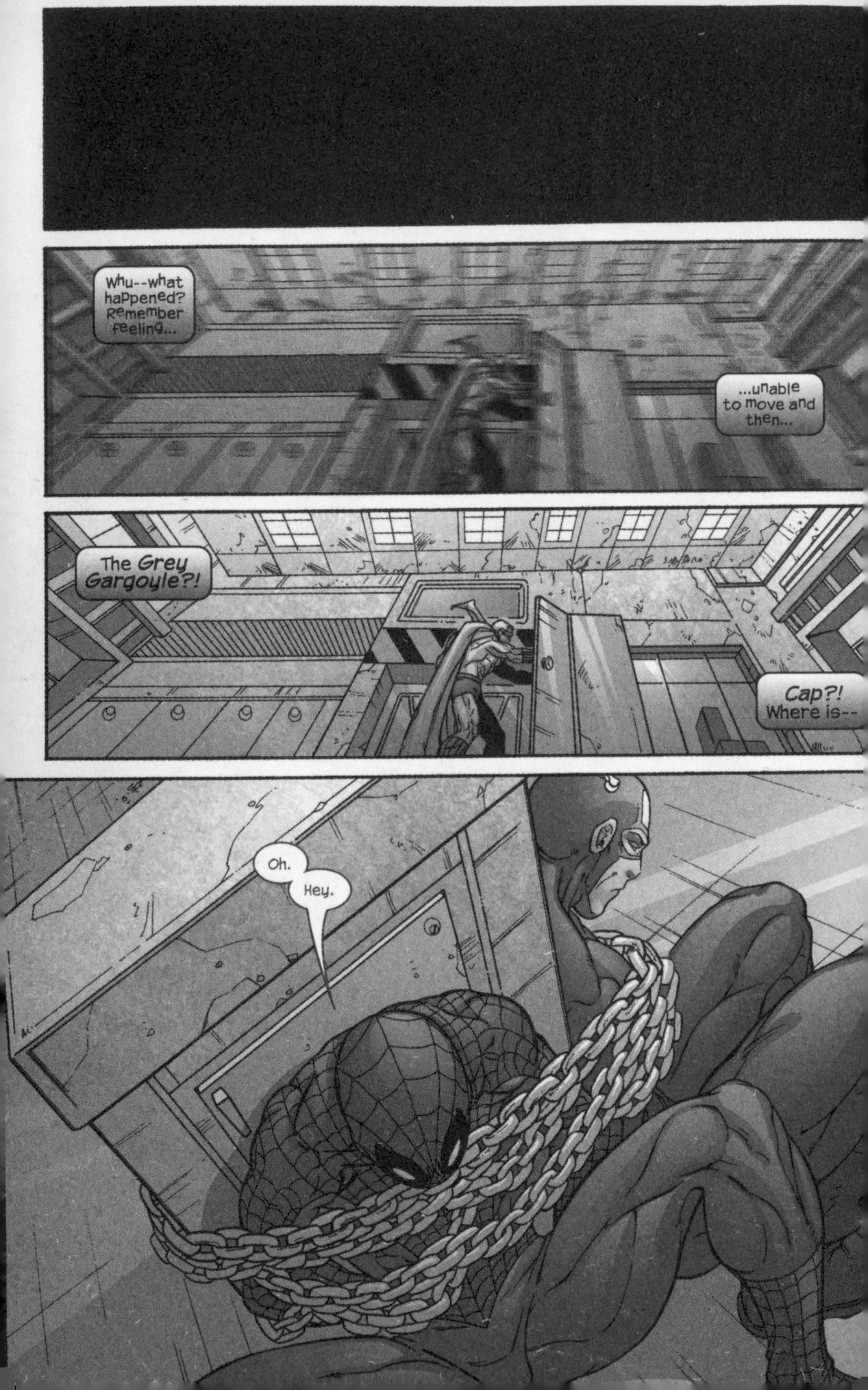
Whu--what happened? Remember feeling...
...unable to move and then...
The Grey Gargoyle?!
Cap?! Where is--
Oh.
Hey.

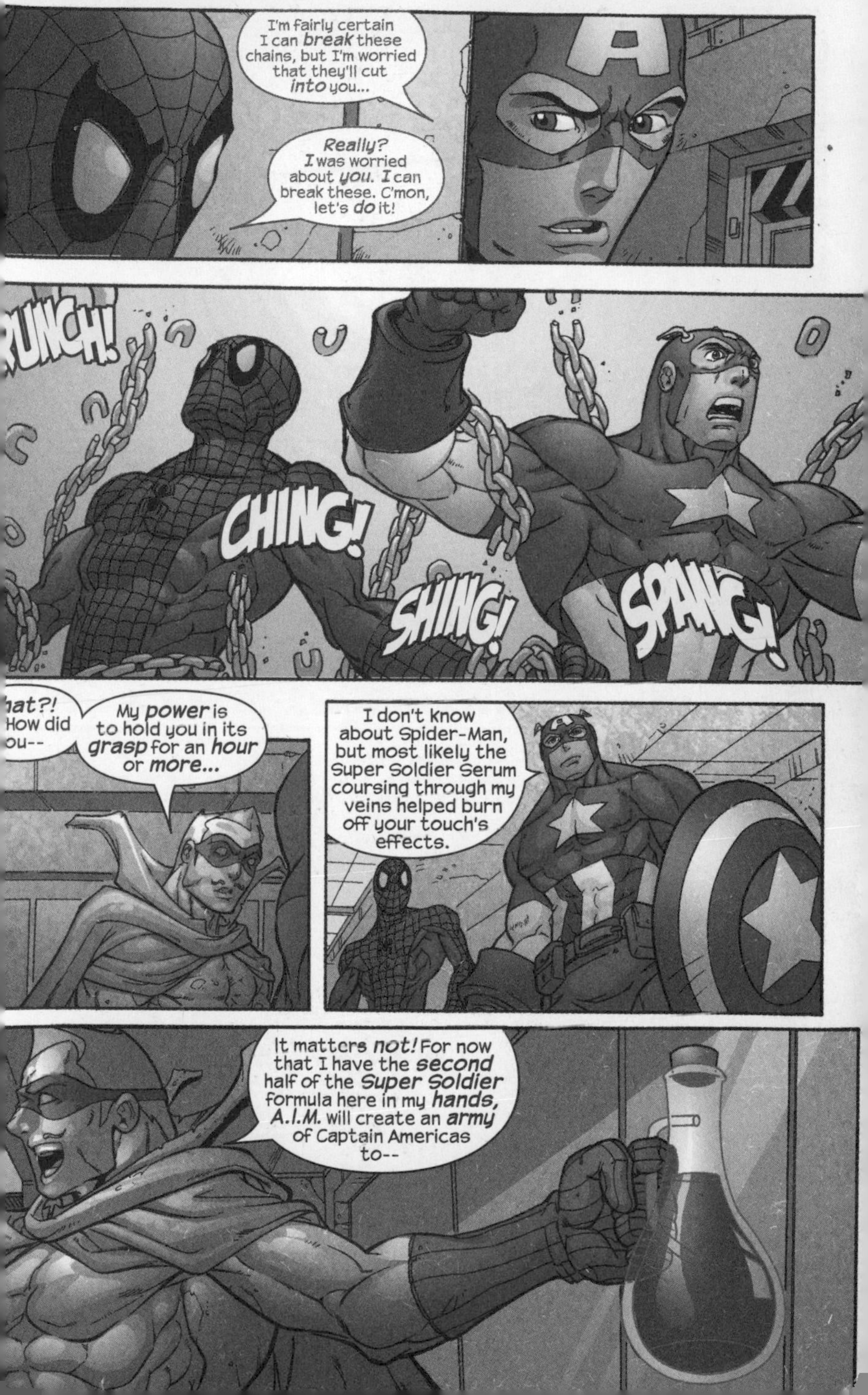
I'm fairly certain I can break these chains, but I'm worried that they'll cut into you...
Really? I was worried about you. I can break these. C'mon, let's do it!
RUNCH!
CHING!
SHING!
SPANG!
hat?! How did ou--
My power is to hold you in its grasp for an hour or more...
I don't know about Spider-Man, but most likely the Super Soldier Serum coursing through my veins helped burn off your touch's effects.
It matters not! For now that I have the second half of the Super Soldier formula here in my hands, A.I.M. will create an army of Captain Americas to--

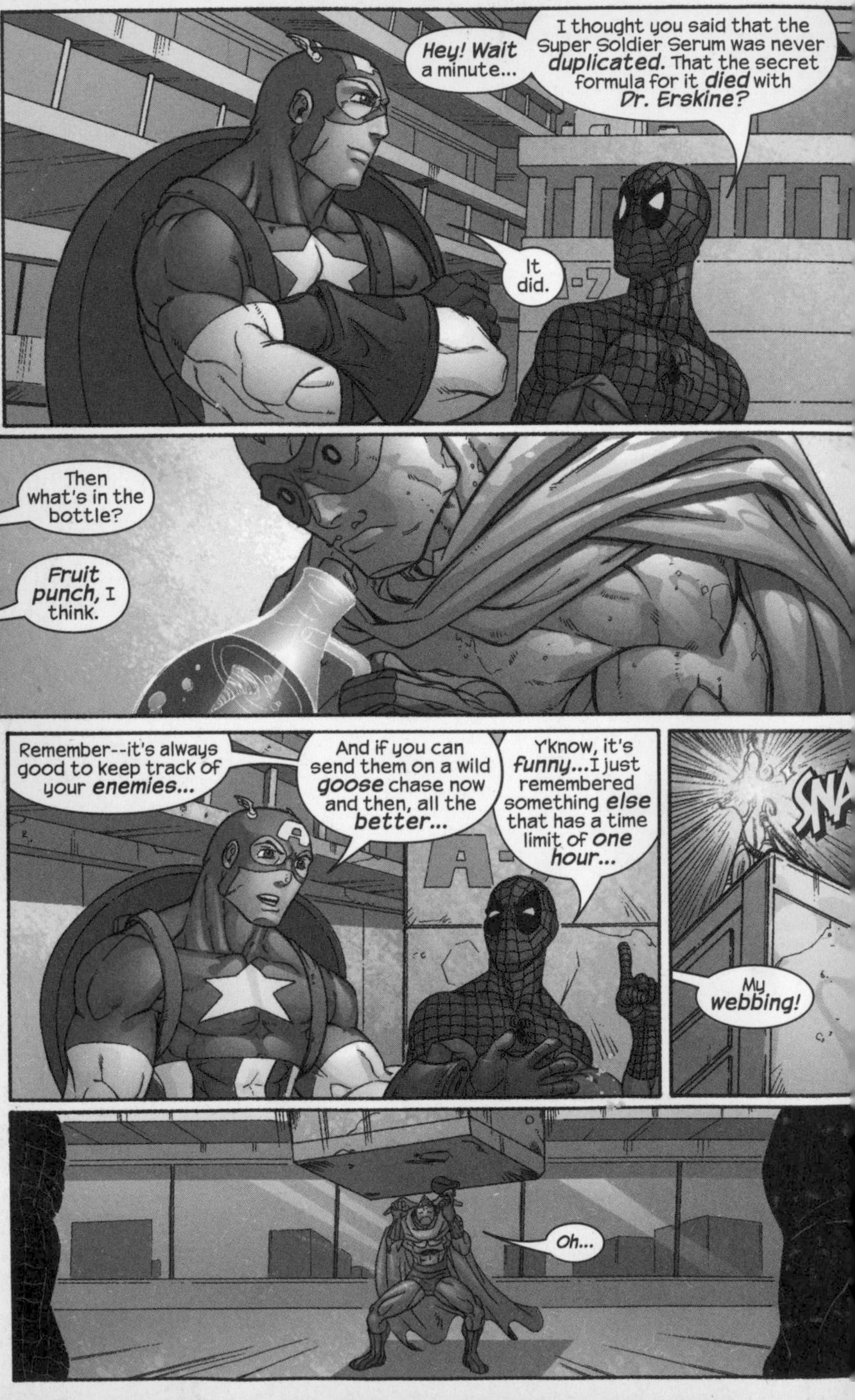
Hey! Wait a minute...
I thought you said that the Super Soldier Serum was never duplicated. That the secret formula for it died with Dr. Erskine?
It did.
Then what's in the bottle?
Fruit punch, I think.
Remember--it's always good to keep track of your enemies...
And if you can send them on a wild goose chase now and then, all the better...
Y'know, it's funny...I just remembered something else that has a time limit of one hour...
My webbing!
Oh...

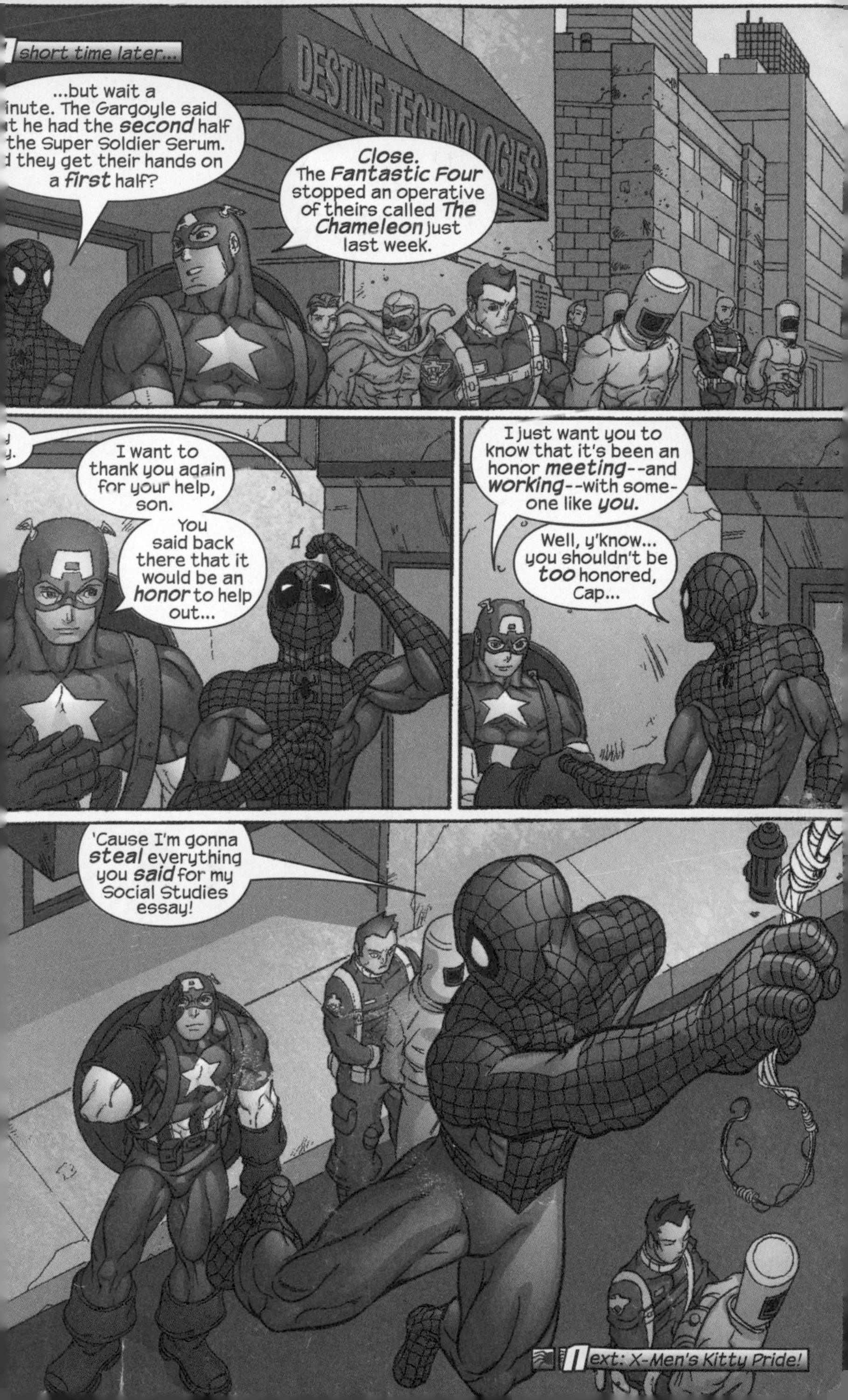
short time later...
DESTINE TECHNOLOGIES
...but wait a inute. The Gargoyle said t he had the second half the Super Soldier Serum. d they get their hands on a first half?
Close. The Fantastic Four stopped an operative of theirs called The Chameleon just last week.
I want to thank you again for your help, son.
You said back there that it would be an honor to help out...
I just want you to know that it's been an honor meeting--and working--with some-one like you.
Well, y'know... you shouldn't be too honored, Cap...
'Cause I'm gonna steal everything you said for my Social Studies essay!
ext: X-Men's Kitty Pride!

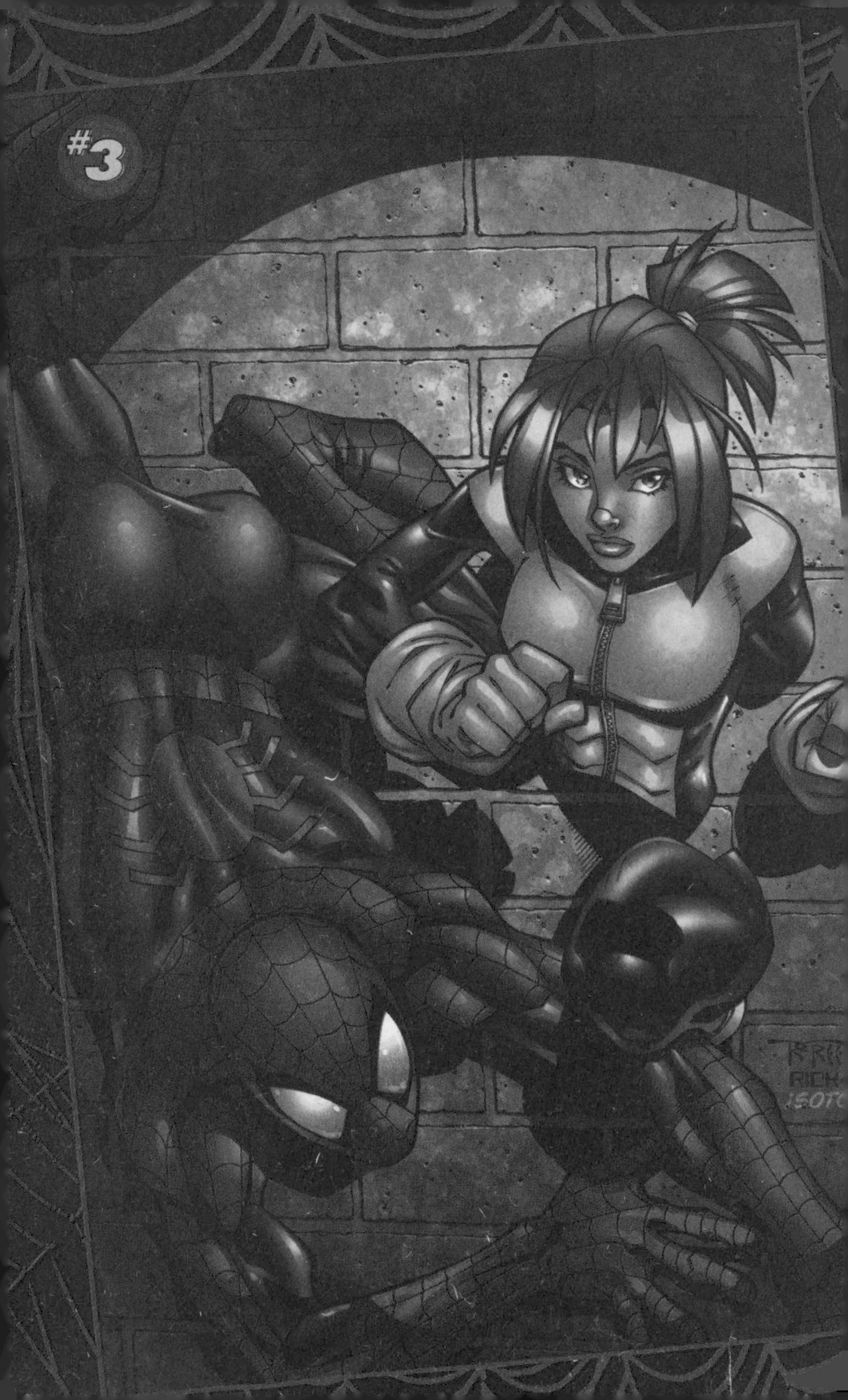
#3

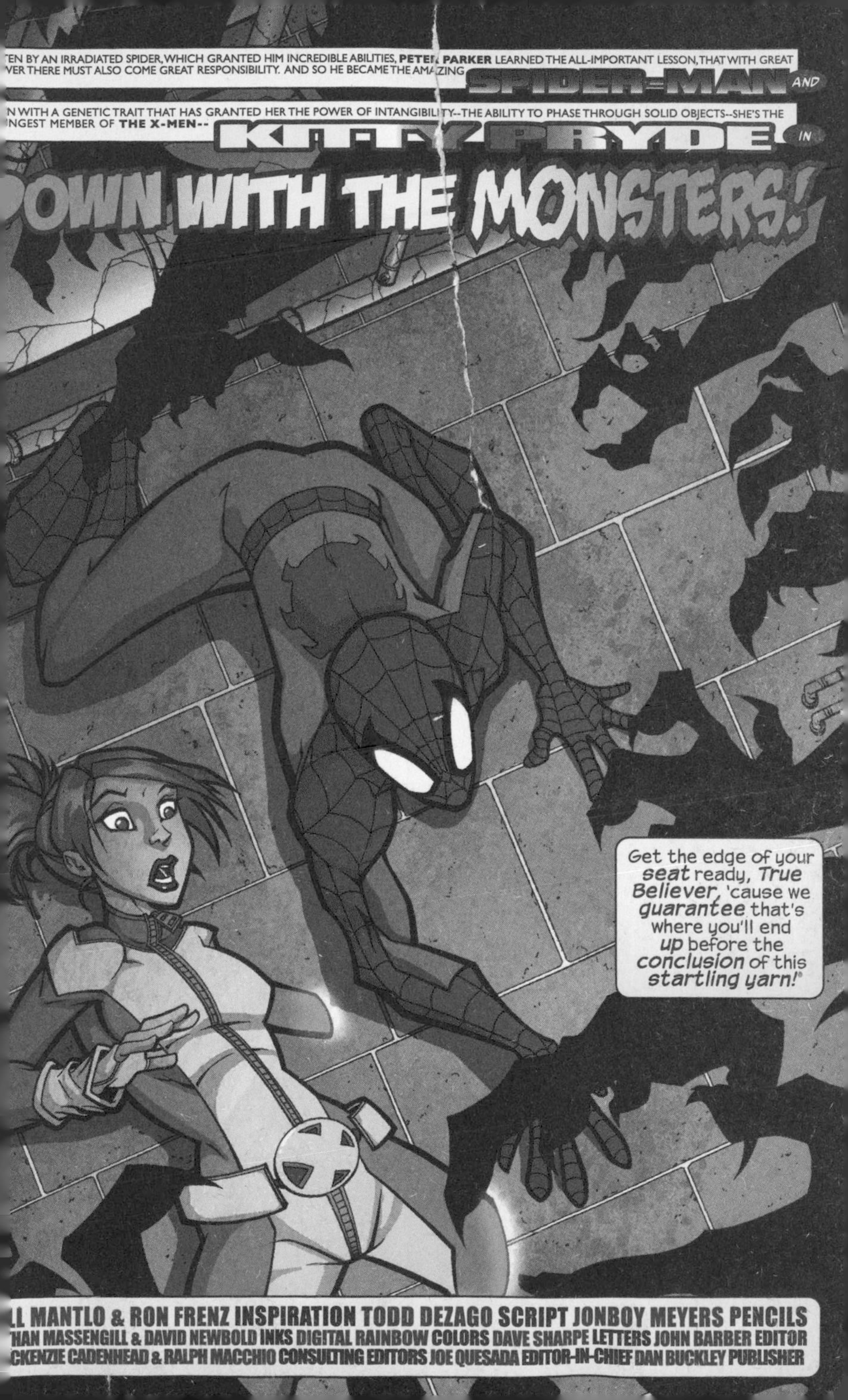
TEN BY AN IRRADIATED SPIDER, WHICH GRANTED HIM INCREDIBLE ABILITIES, PETER PARKER LEARNED THE ALL-IMPORTANT LESSON, THAT WITH GREAT
VER THERE MUST ALSO COME GREAT RESPONSIBILITY. AND SO HE BECAME THE AMAZING
SPIDER-MAN AND
N WITH A GENETIC TRAIT THAT HAS GRANTED HER THE POWER OF INTANGIBILITY--THE ABILITY TO PHASE THROUGH SOLID OBJECTS--SHE'S THE
NGEST MEMBER OF THE X-MEN--
KITTY PRYDE IN
DOWN WITH THE MONSTERS!
Get the edge of your seat ready, True Believer, 'cause we guarantee that's where you'll end up before the conclusion of this startling yarn!
LL MANTLO & RON FRENZ INSPIRATION TODD DEZAGO SCRIPT JONBOY MEYERS PENCILS
HAN MASSENGILL & DAVID NEWBOLD INKS DIGITAL RAINBOW COLORS DAVE SHARPE LETTERS JOHN BARBER EDITOR
CKENZIE CADENHEAD & RALPH MACCHIO CONSULTING EDITORS JOE QUESADA EDITOR-IN-CHIEF DAN BUCKLEY PUBLISHER

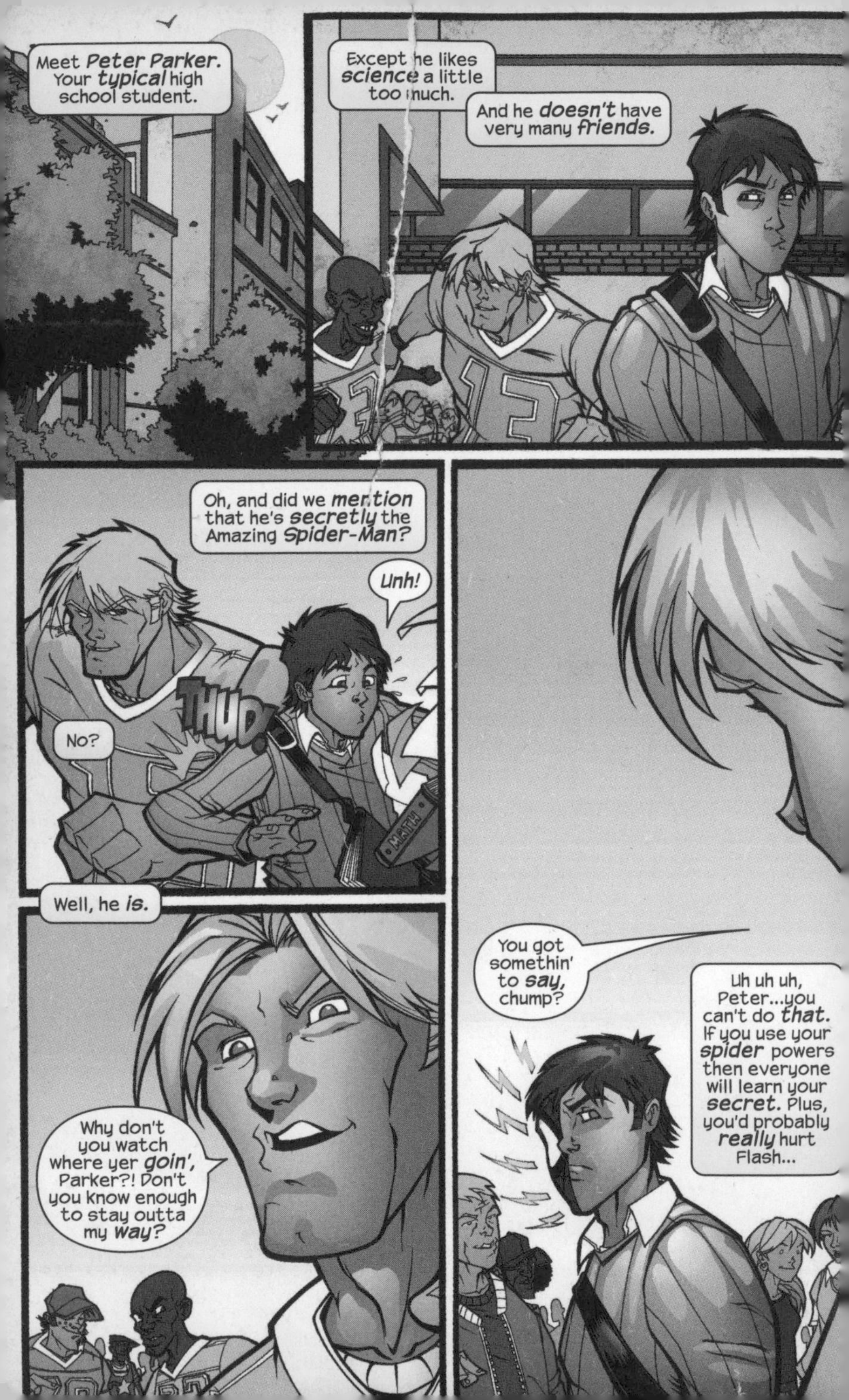
Meet Peter Parker. Your typical high school student.
Except he likes science a little too much.
And he doesn't have very many friends.
Oh, and did we mention that he's secretly the Amazing Spider-Man?
Unh!
THUD!
No?
MATH
Well, he is.
Why don't you watch where yer goin', Parker?! Don't you know enough to stay outta my way?
You got somethin' to say, chump?
Uh uh uh, Peter...you can't do that. If you use your spider powers then everyone will learn your secret. Plus, you'd probably really hurt Flash...

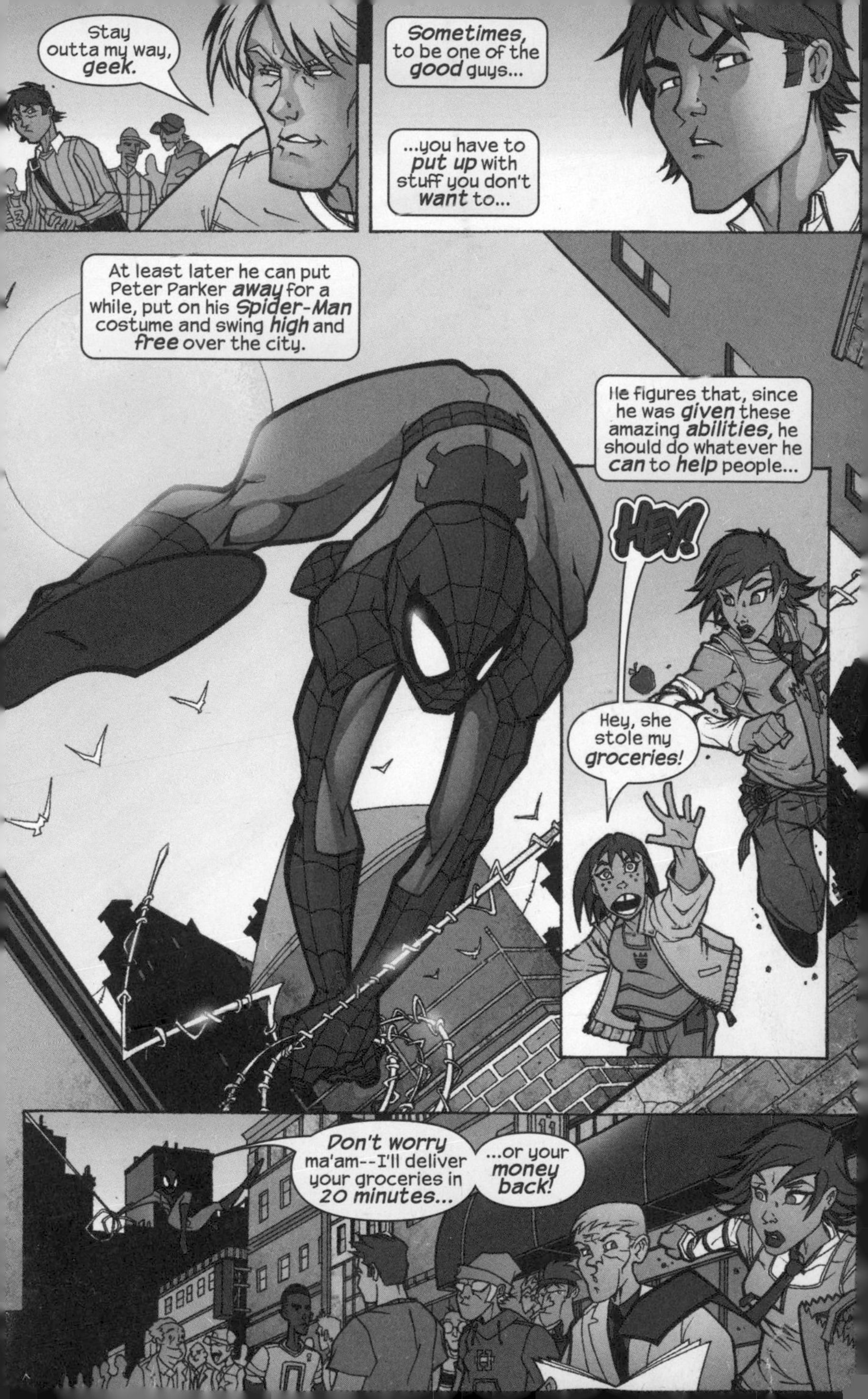
Stay outta my way, geek.
Sometimes, to be one of the good guys...
...you have to put up with stuff you don't want to...
At least later he can put Peter Parker away for a while, put on his Spider-Man costume and swing high and free over the city.
He figures that, since he was given these amazing abilities, he should do whatever he can to help people...
HEY!
Hey, she stole my groceries!
Don't worry ma'am--I'll deliver your groceries in 20 minutes...
...or your money back!

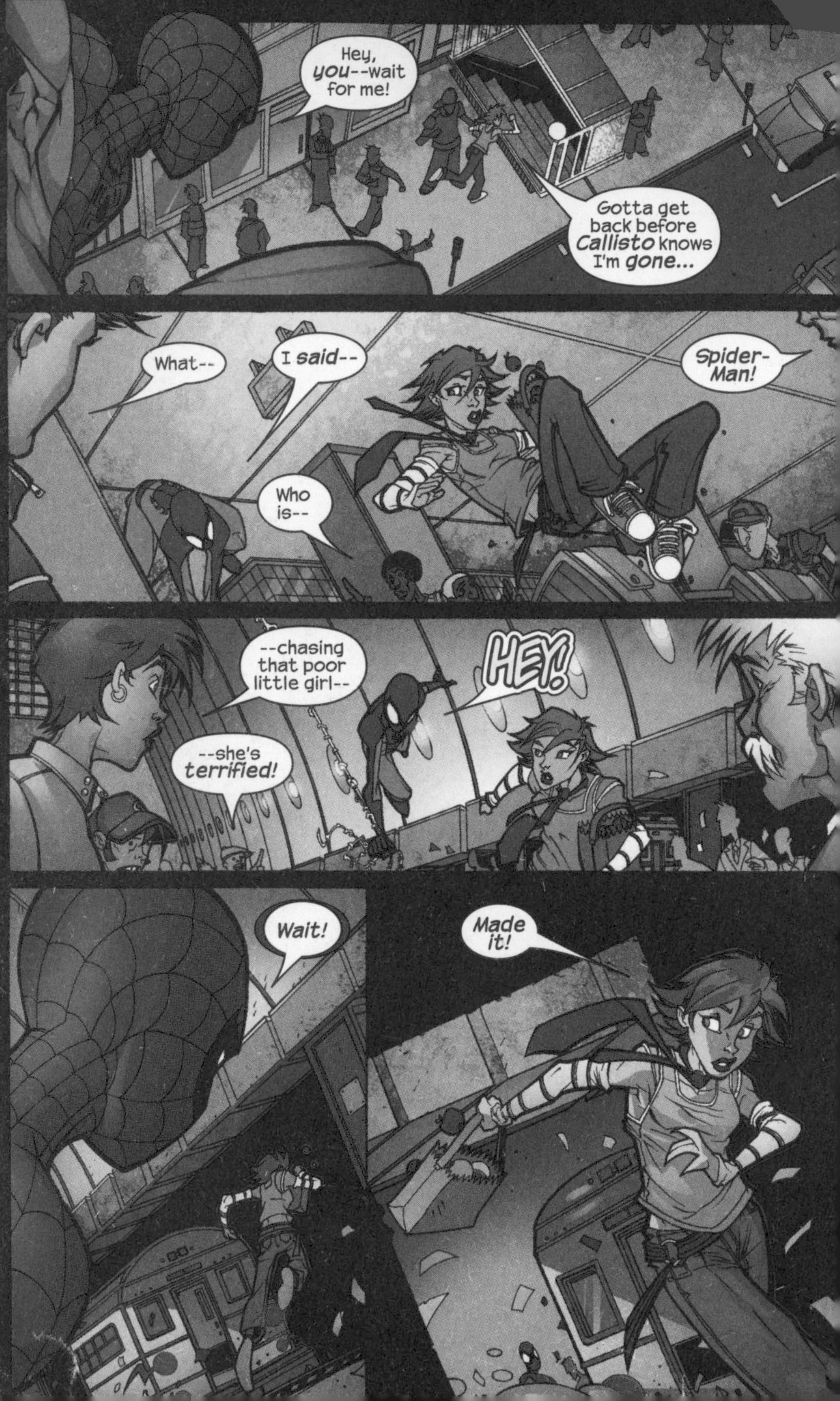
Hey, you--wait for me!
Gotta get back before Callisto knows I'm gone...
What--
I said--
Spider-Man!
Who is--
--chasing that poor little girl--
HEY!
--she's terrified!
Wait!
Made it!

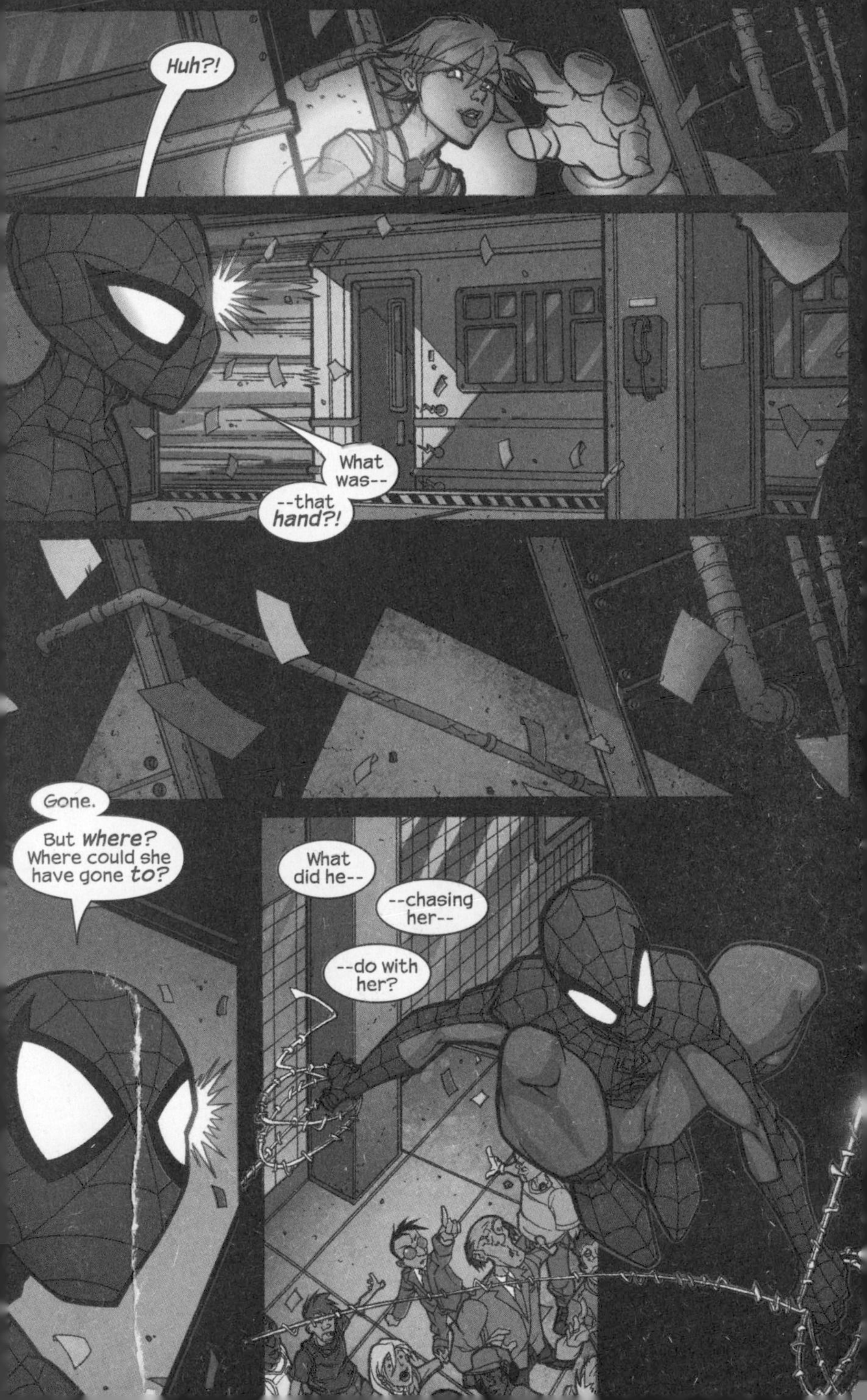
Huh?!
What was--
--that hand?!
Gone.
But where? Where could she have gone to?
What did he--
--chasing her--
--do with her?

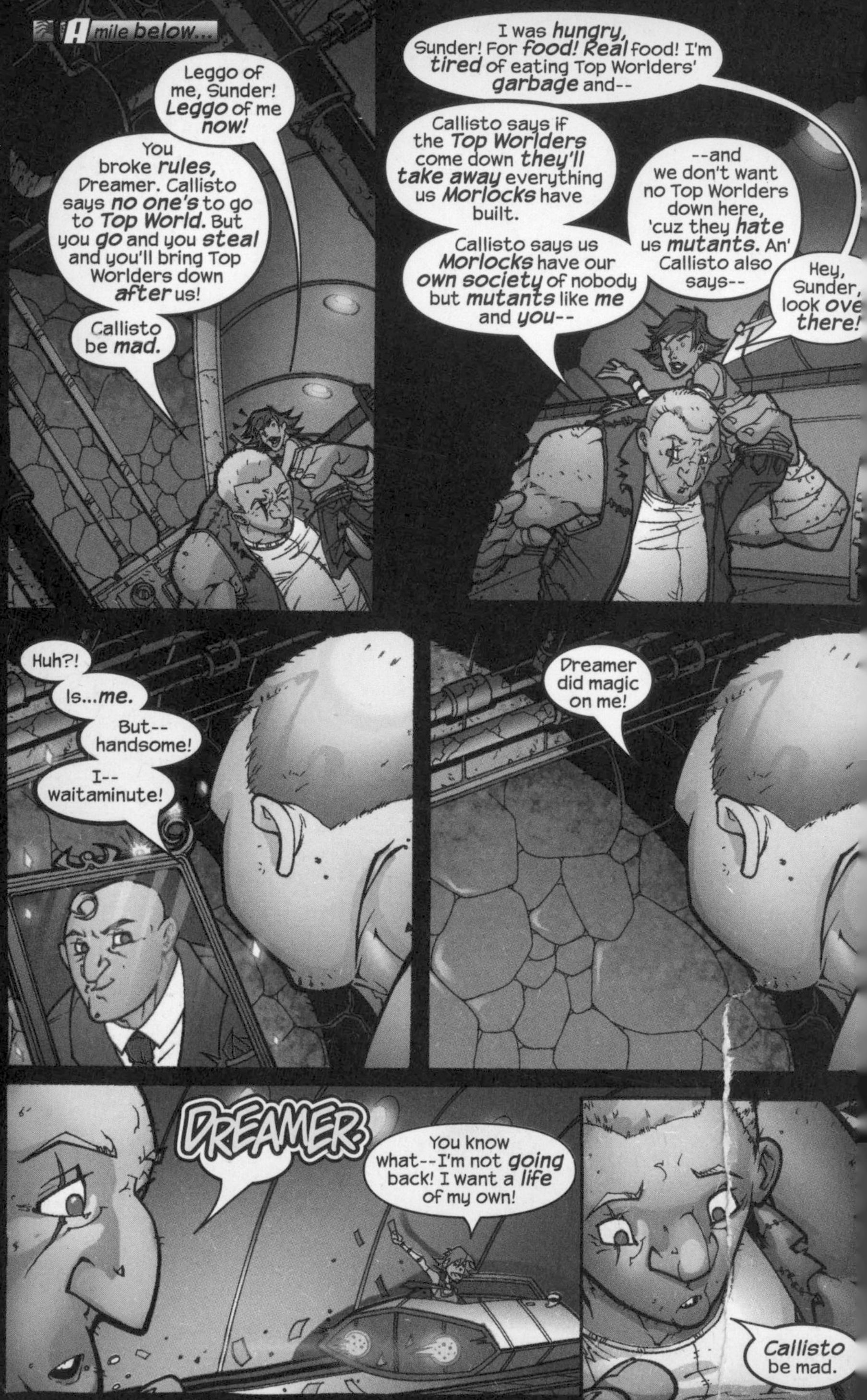
A mile below...
Leggo of me, Sunder! Leggo of me now!
You broke rules, Dreamer. Callisto says no one's to go to Top World. But you go and you steal and you'll bring Top Worlders down after us!
Callisto be mad.
I was hungry, Sunder! For food! Real food! I'm tired of eating Top Worlders' garbage and--
Callisto says if the Top Worlders come down they'll take away everything us Morlocks have built.
Callisto says us Morlocks have our own society of nobody but mutants like me and you--
--and we don't want no Top Worlders down here, 'cuz they hate us mutants. An' Callisto also says--
Hey, Sunder, look ove there!
Huh?!
Is...me.
But-- handsome!
I-- waitaminute!
Dreamer did magic on me!
DREAMER.
You know what--I'm not going back! I want a life of my own!
Callisto be mad.

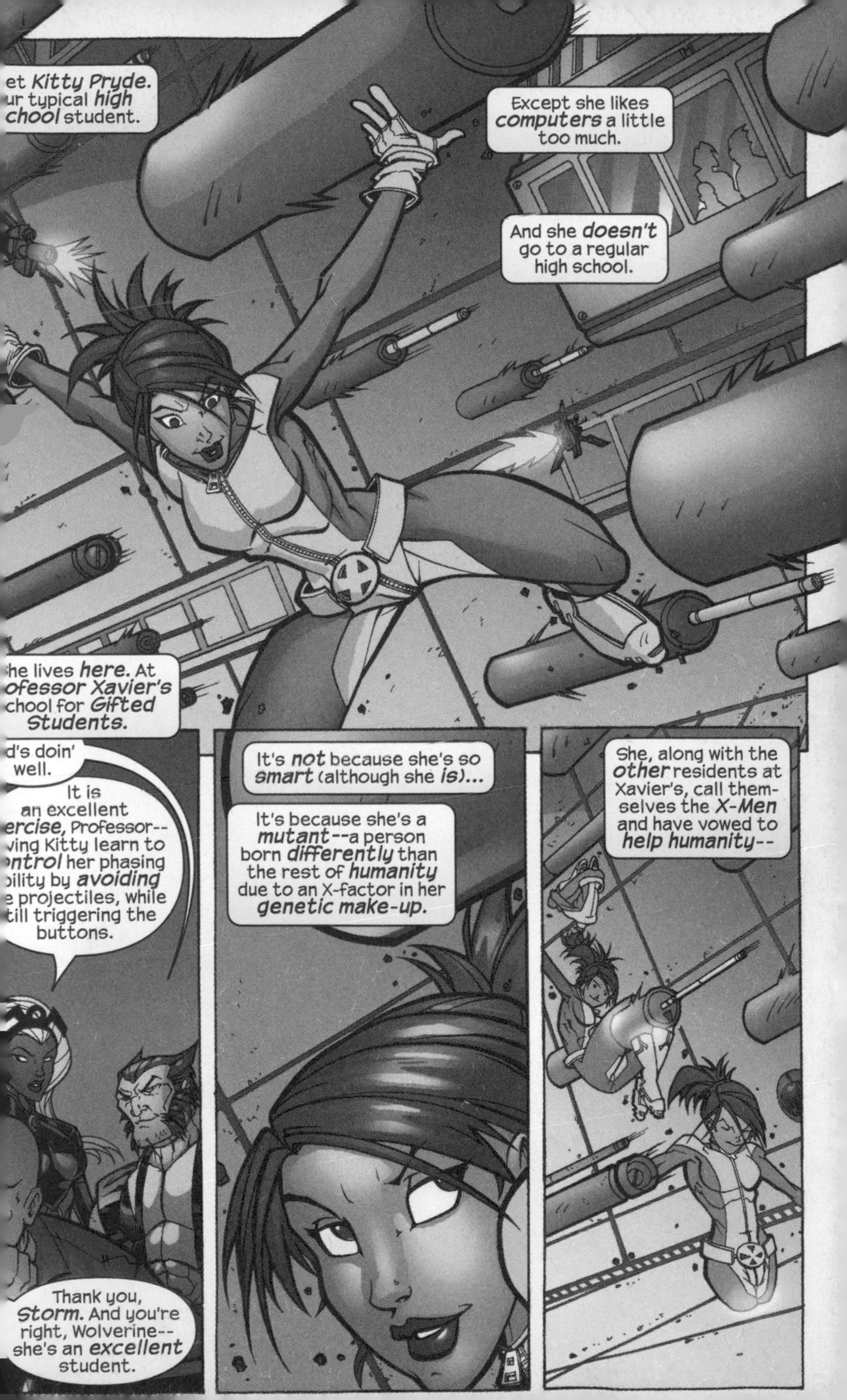
et Kitty Pryde. ur typical high chool student.
Except she likes computers a little too much.
And she doesn't go to a regular high school.
he lives here. At ofessor Xavier's chool for Gifted Students.
d's doin' well.
It is an excellent ercise, Professor-- ving Kitty learn to ntrol her phasing bility by avoiding e projectiles, while till triggering the buttons.
Thank you, Storm. And you're right, Wolverine-- she's an excellent student.
It's not because she's so smart (although she is)...
It's because she's a mutant--a person born differently than the rest of humanity due to an X-factor in her genetic make-up.
She, along with the other residents at Xavier's, call themselves the X-Men and have vowed to help humanity--

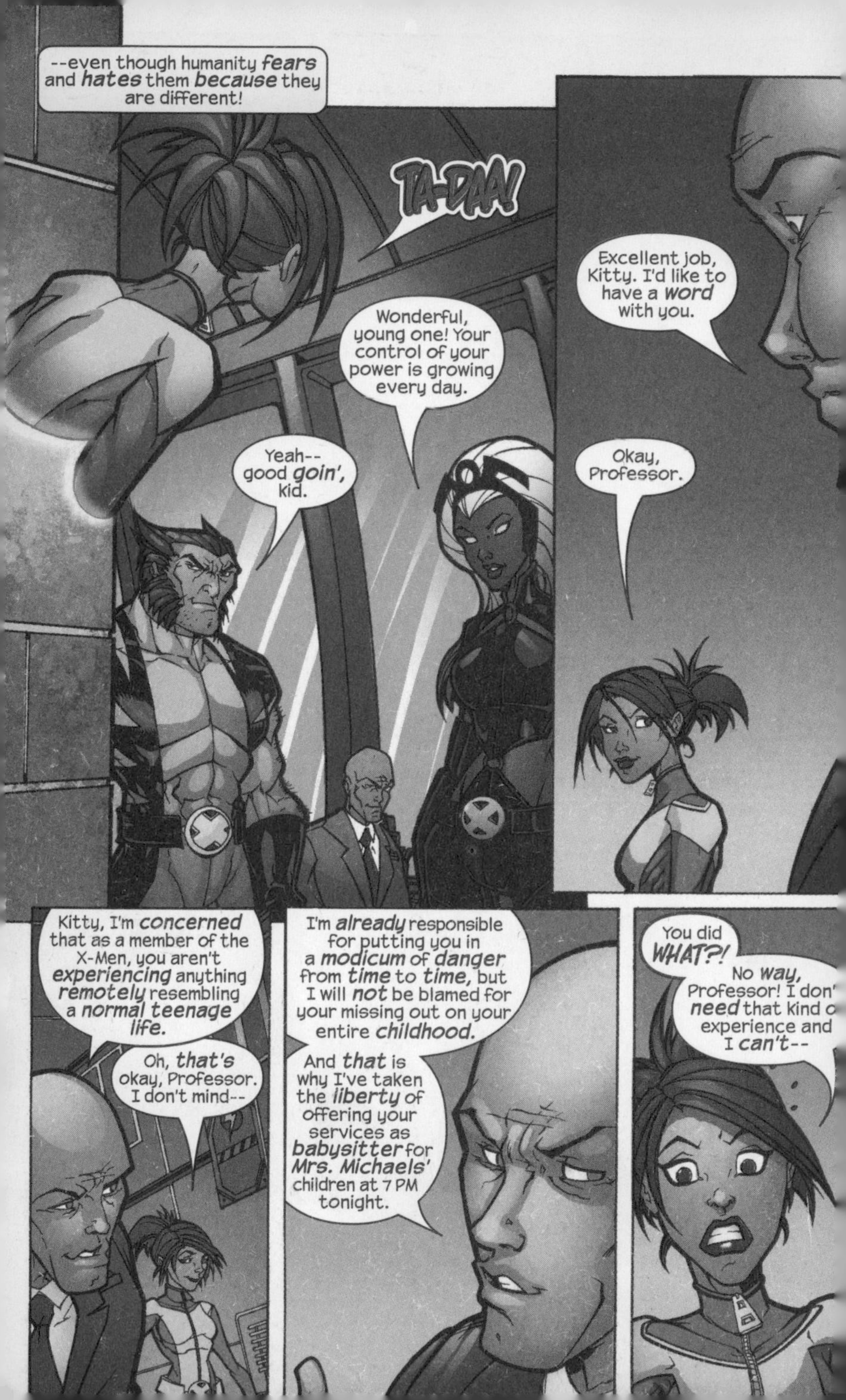
--even though humanity fears and hates them because they are different!
TA-DAA!
Wonderful, young one! Your control of your power is growing every day.
Yeah-- good goin', kid.
Excellent job, Kitty. I'd like to have a word with you.
Okay, Professor.
Kitty, I'm concerned that as a member of the X-Men, you aren't experiencing anything remotely resembling a normal teenage life.
Oh, that's okay, Professor. I don't mind--
I'm already responsible for putting you in a modicum of danger from time to time, but I will not be blamed for your missing out on your entire childhood.
And that is why I've taken the liberty of offering your services as babysitter for Mrs. Michaels' children at 7 PM tonight.
You did WHAT?!
No way, Professor! I don' need that kind o experience and I can't--

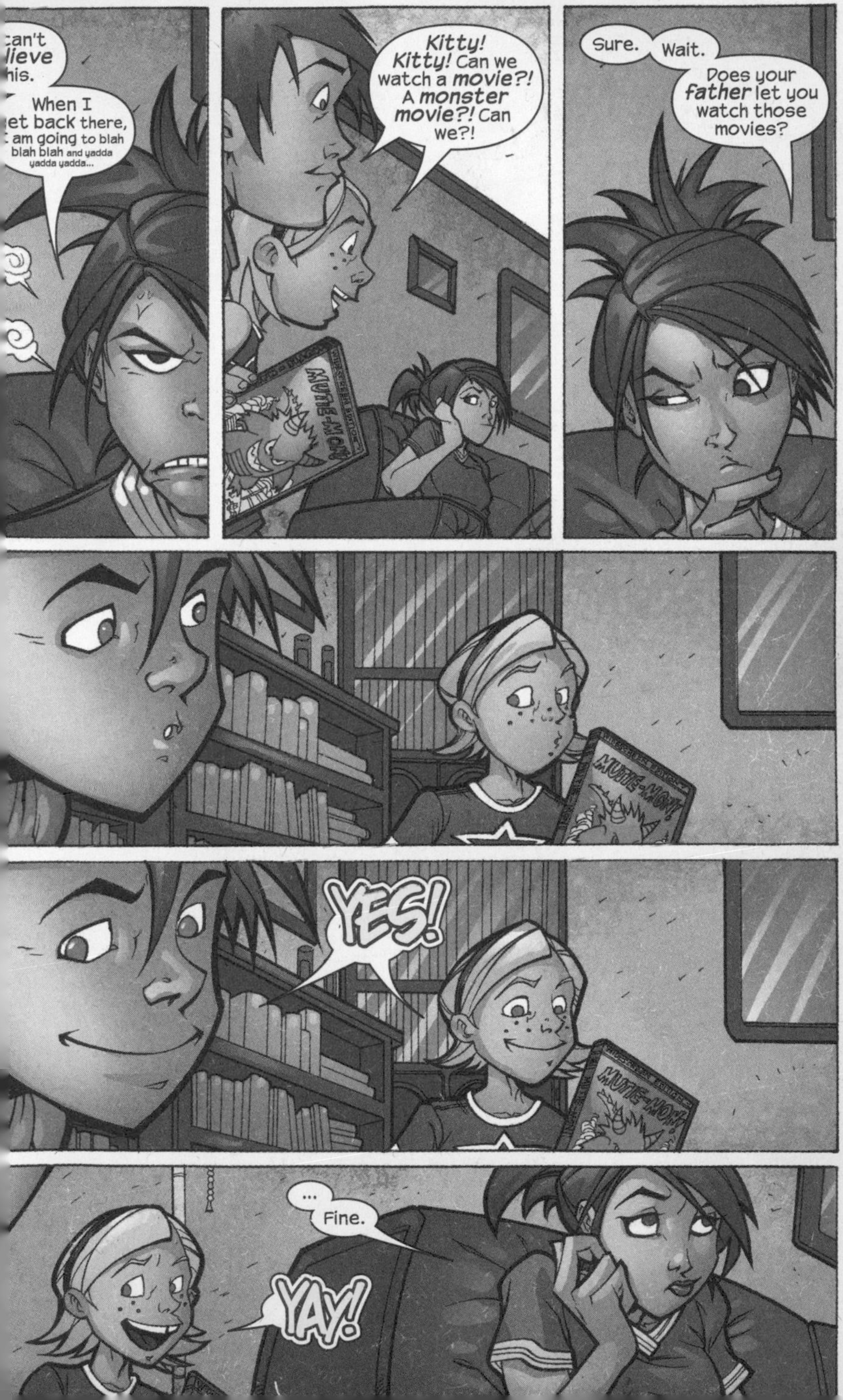
can't
lieve
his.
When I
et back there,
am going to blah
blah blah and yadda
yadda yadda...
Kitty! Kitty! Can we watch a movie?! A monster movie?! Can we?!
MUTIE-MON
Sure.
Wait.
Does your father let you watch those movies?
YES!
...
Fine.
YAY!

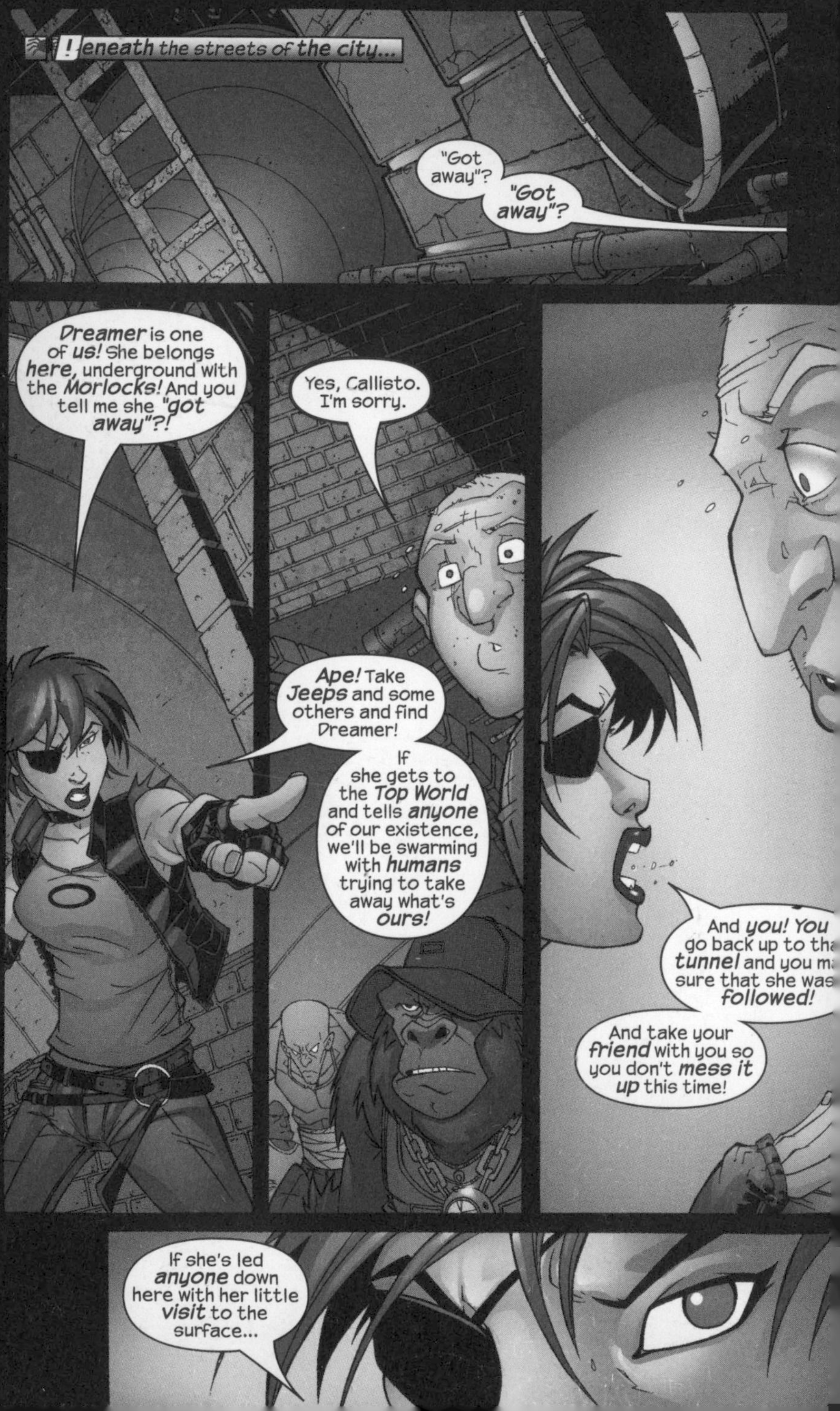
Beneath the streets of the city...
"Got away"?
"Got away"?
Dreamer is one of us! She belongs here, underground with the Morlocks! And you tell me she "got away"?!
Yes, Callisto. I'm sorry.
Ape! Take Jeeps and some others and find Dreamer!
If she gets to the Top World and tells anyone of our existence, we'll be swarming with humans trying to take away what's ours!
And you! You go back up to tha tunnel and you ma sure that she was followed!
And take your friend with you so you don't mess it up this time!
If she's led anyone down here with her little visit to the surface...

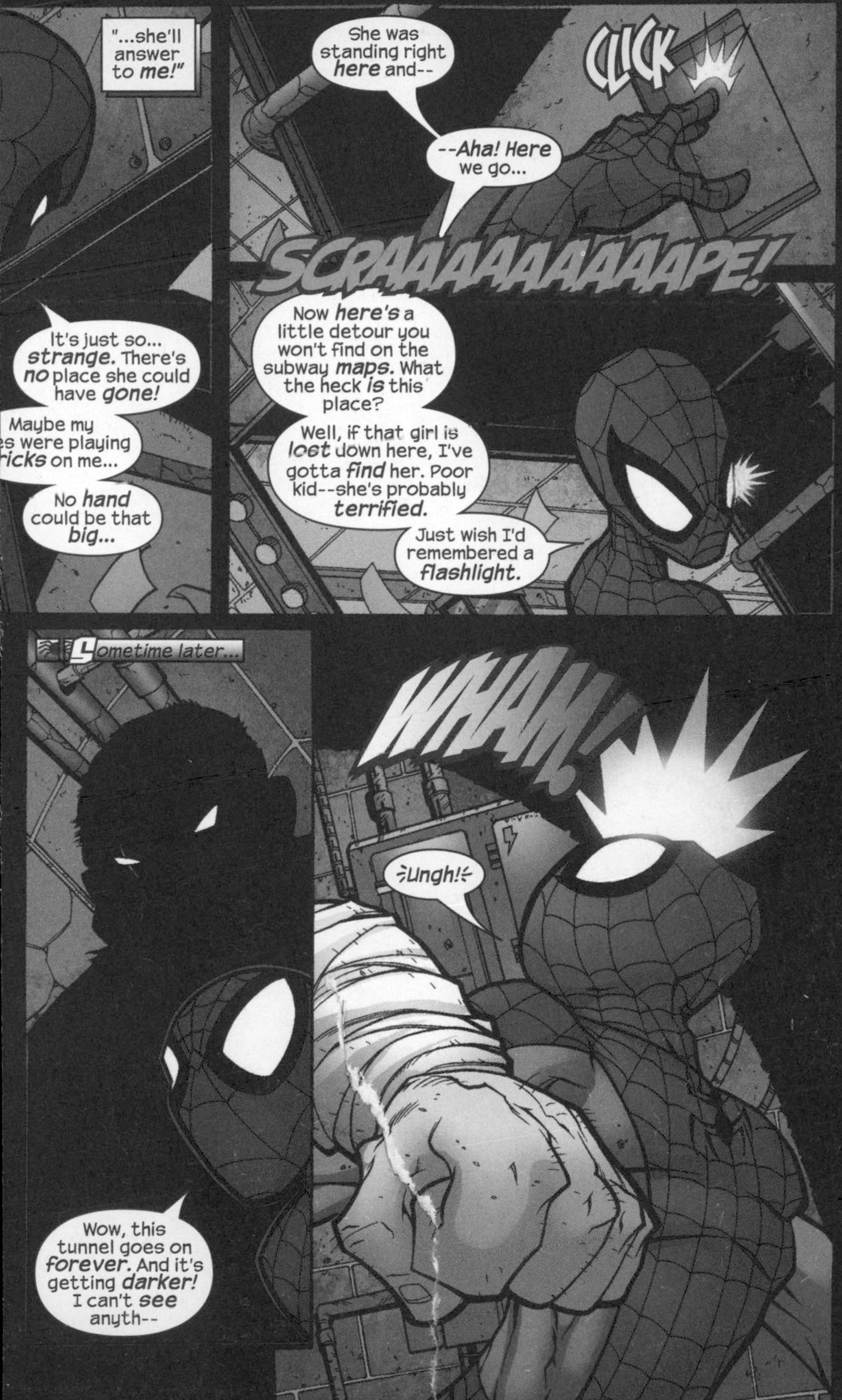
"...she'll answer to me!"
She was standing right here and--
--Aha! Here we go...
CLICK
SCRAAAAAAAAAPE!
It's just so... strange. There's no place she could have gone!
Maybe my
es were playing
ricks on me...
No hand could be that big...
Now here's a little detour you won't find on the subway maps. What the heck is this place?
Well, if that girl is lost down here, I've gotta find her. Poor kid--she's probably terrified.
Just wish I'd remembered a flashlight.
Sometime later...
WHAM!
Ungh!
Wow, this tunnel goes on forever. And it's getting darker! I can't see anyth--

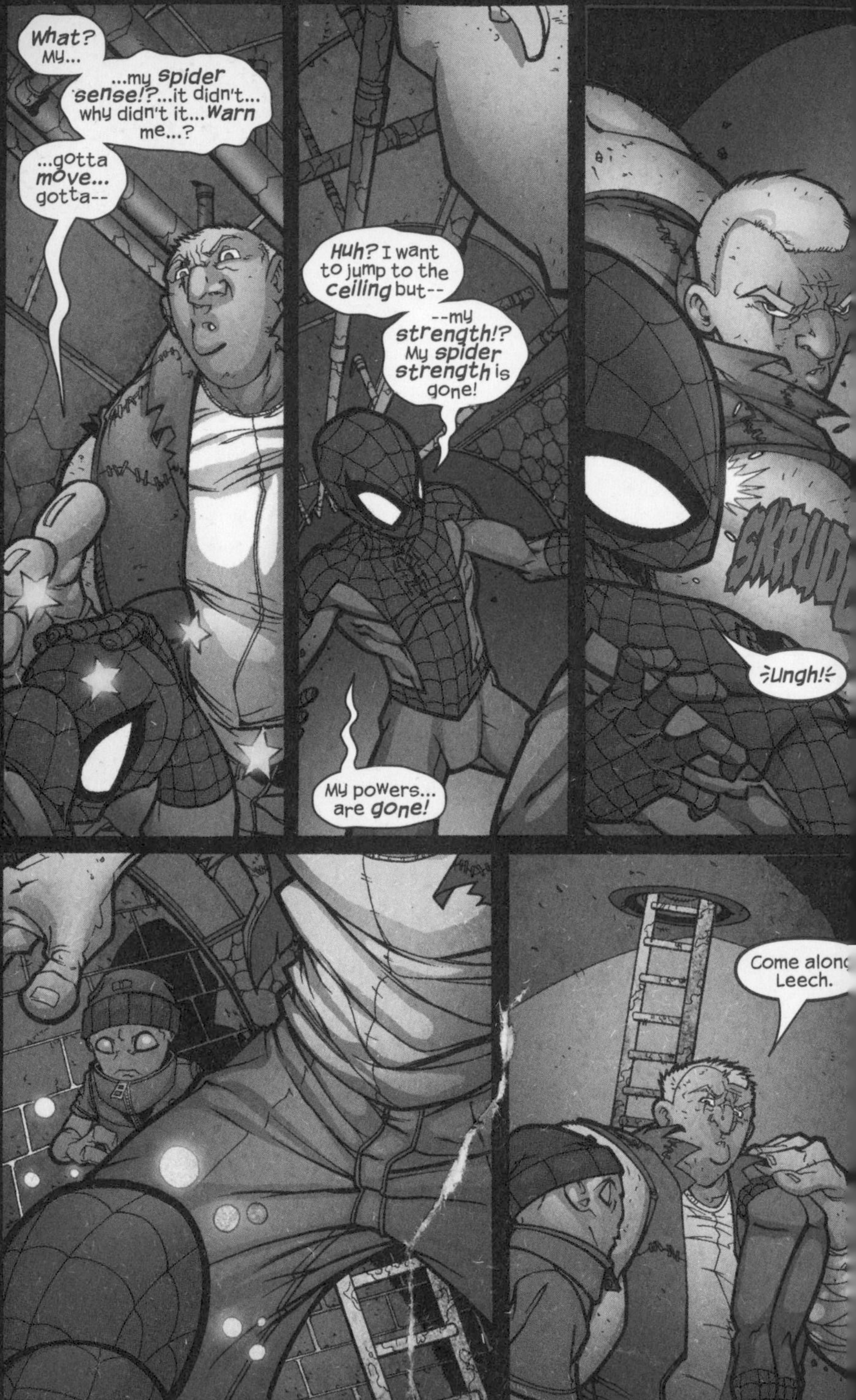
What? My...
...my spider sense!?...it didn't... why didn't it...Warn me...?
...gotta move... gotta--
Huh? I want to jump to the ceiling but--
--my strength!? My spider strength is gone!
My powers... are gone!
SKRUD
Ungh!
Come along Leech.

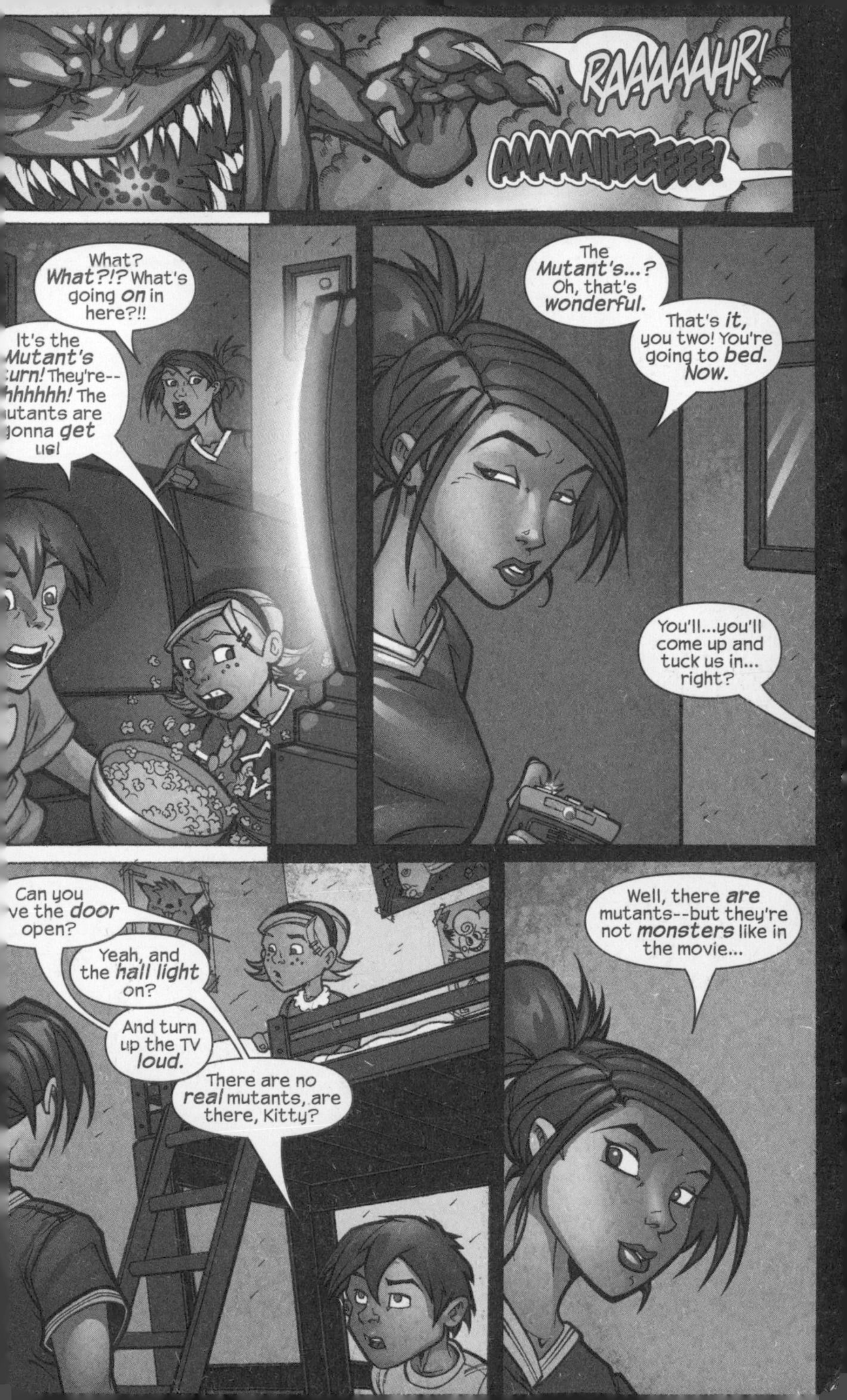
RAAAAAHR!
AAAAAIIIEEEEEEE!
What? What?!? What's going on in here?!!
It's the Mutant's urn! They're-- hhhhhh! The utants are onna get us!
The Mutant's...? Oh, that's wonderful.
That's it, you two! You're going to bed. Now.
You'll...you'll come up and tuck us in... right?
Can you ve the door open?
Yeah, and the hall light on?
And turn up the TV loud.
There are no real mutants, are there, Kitty?
Well, there are mutants--but they're not monsters like in the movie...

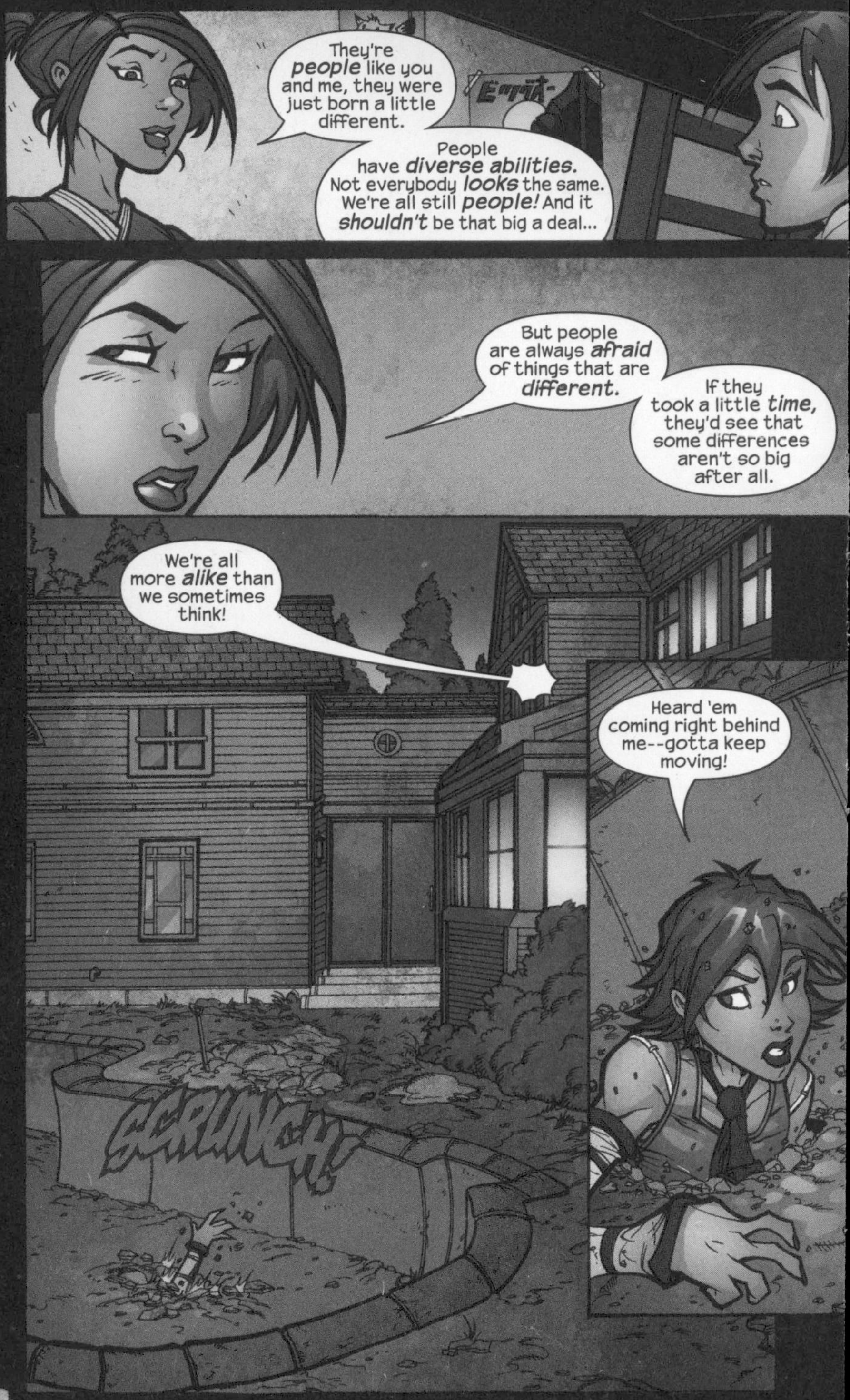
They're *people* like you and me, they were just born a little different.
People have *diverse abilities.* Not everybody *looks* the same. We're all still *people!* And it *shouldn't* be that big a deal...
But people are always *afraid* of things that are *different.*
If they took a little *time,* they'd see that some differences aren't so big after all.
We're all more *alike* than we sometimes think!
Heard 'em coming right behind me--gotta keep moving!
SCRUNCH!

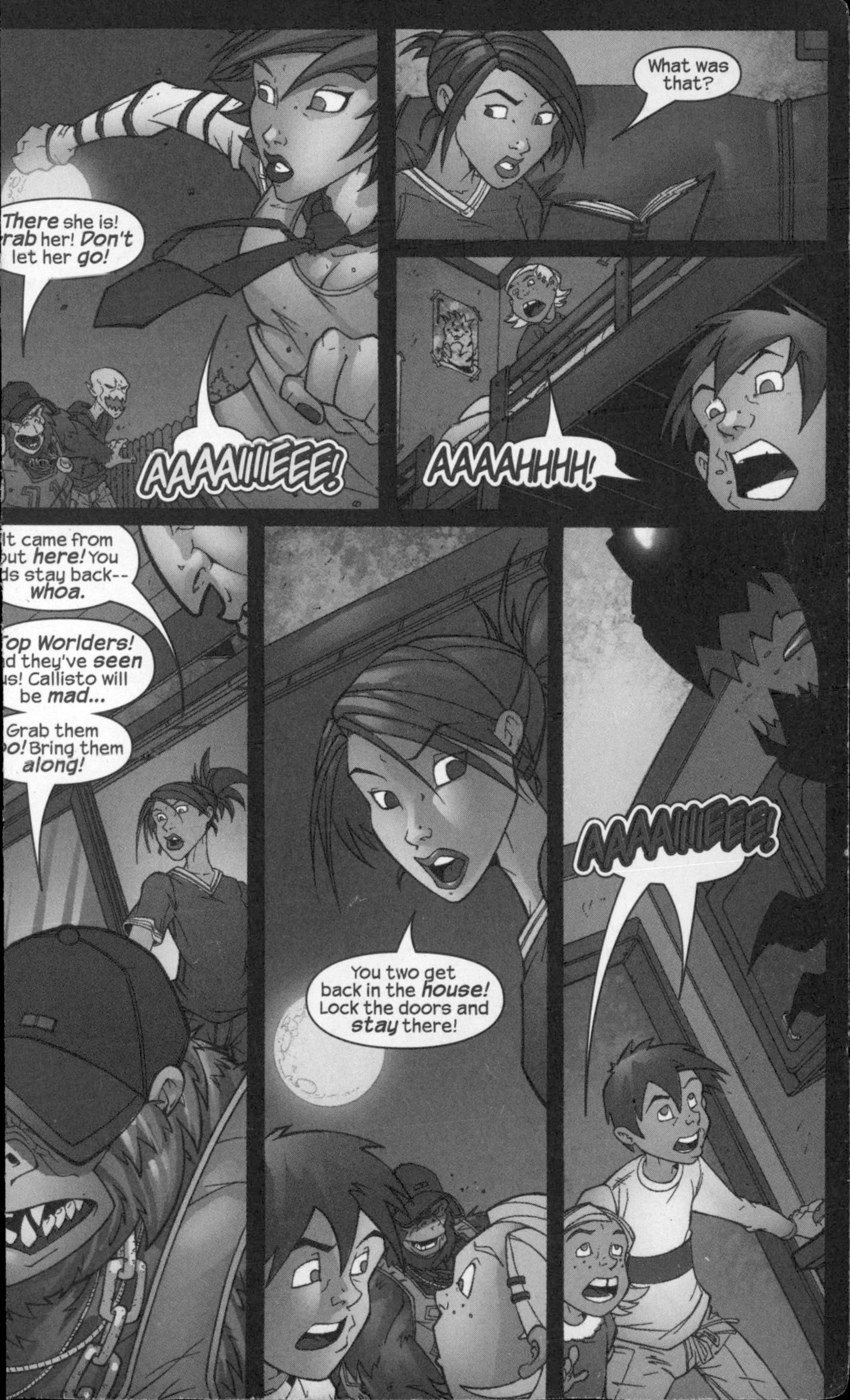
There she is!
rab her! Don't
let her go!
AAAAIIIIEEEE!
What was that?
AAAAHHHH!
It came from
ut here! You
ds stay back--
whoa.
op Worlders!
d they've seen
s! Callisto will
be mad...
Grab them
o! Bring them
along!
You two get back in the house! Lock the doors and stay there!
AAAAIIIIEEEE!

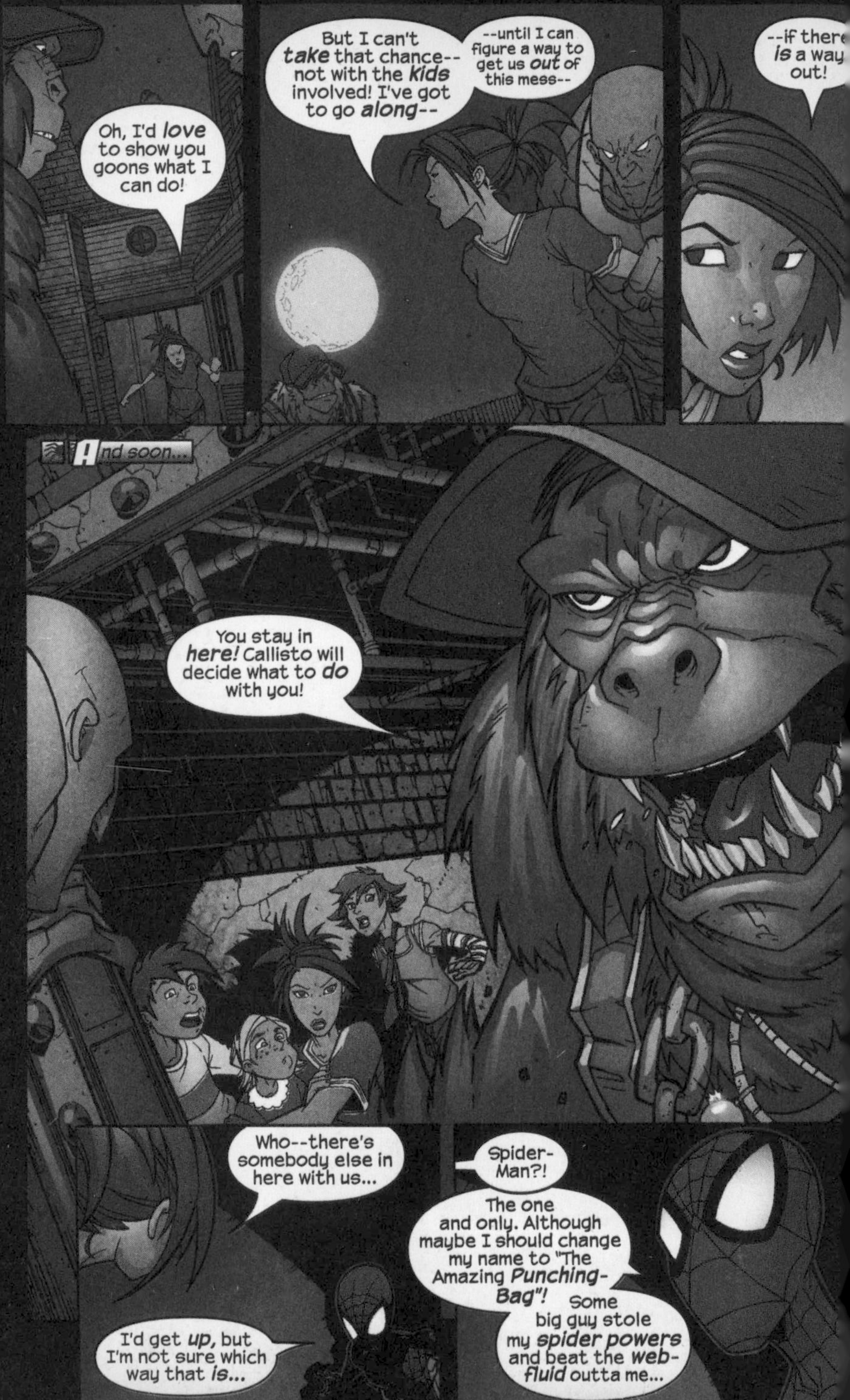
Oh, I'd love to show you goons what I can do!
But I can't take that chance--not with the kids involved! I've got to go along--
--until I can figure a way to get us out of this mess--
--if there is a way out!
And soon...
You stay in here! Callisto will decide what to do with you!
Who--there's somebody else in here with us...
I'd get up, but I'm not sure which way that is...
Spider-Man?!
The one and only. Although maybe I should change my name to "The Amazing Punching-Bag"!
Some big guy stole my spider powers and beat the web-fluid outta me...

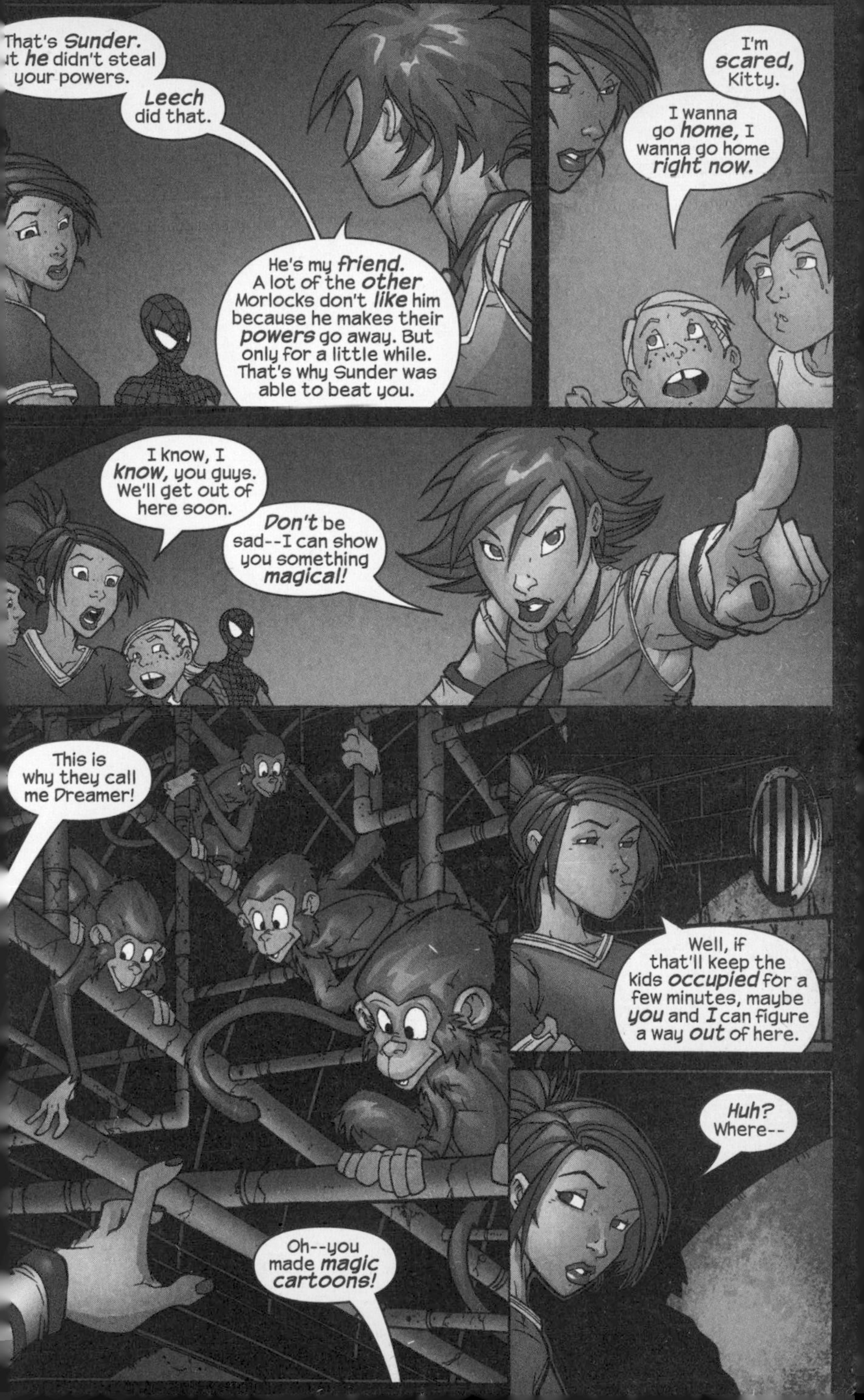
That's Sunder. ...ut he didn't steal your powers.
Leech did that.
He's my friend. A lot of the other Morlocks don't like him because he makes their powers go away. But only for a little while. That's why Sunder was able to beat you.
I'm scared, Kitty.
I wanna go home, I wanna go home right now.
I know, I know, you guys. We'll get out of here soon.
Don't be sad--I can show you something magical!
This is why they call me Dreamer!
Well, if that'll keep the kids occupied for a few minutes, maybe you and I can figure a way out of here.
Huh? Where--
Oh--you made magic cartoons!

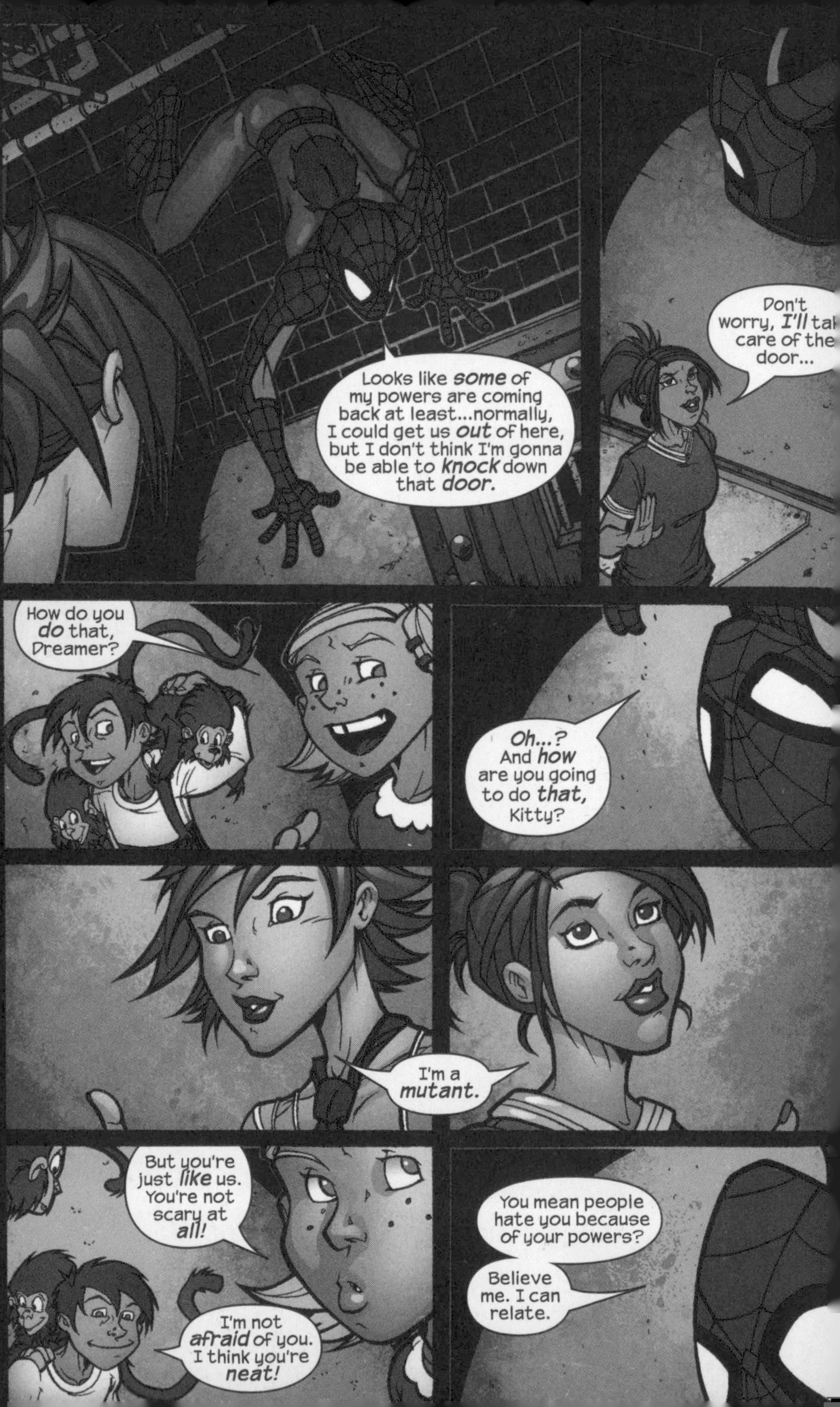
Looks like some of my powers are coming back at least...normally, I could get us out of here, but I don't think I'm gonna be able to knock down that door.
Don't worry, I'll tak care of the door...
How do you do that, Dreamer?
Oh...? And how are you going to do that, Kitty?
I'm a mutant.
But you're just like us. You're not scary at all!
I'm not afraid of you. I think you're neat!
You mean people hate you because of your powers?
Believe me. I can relate.

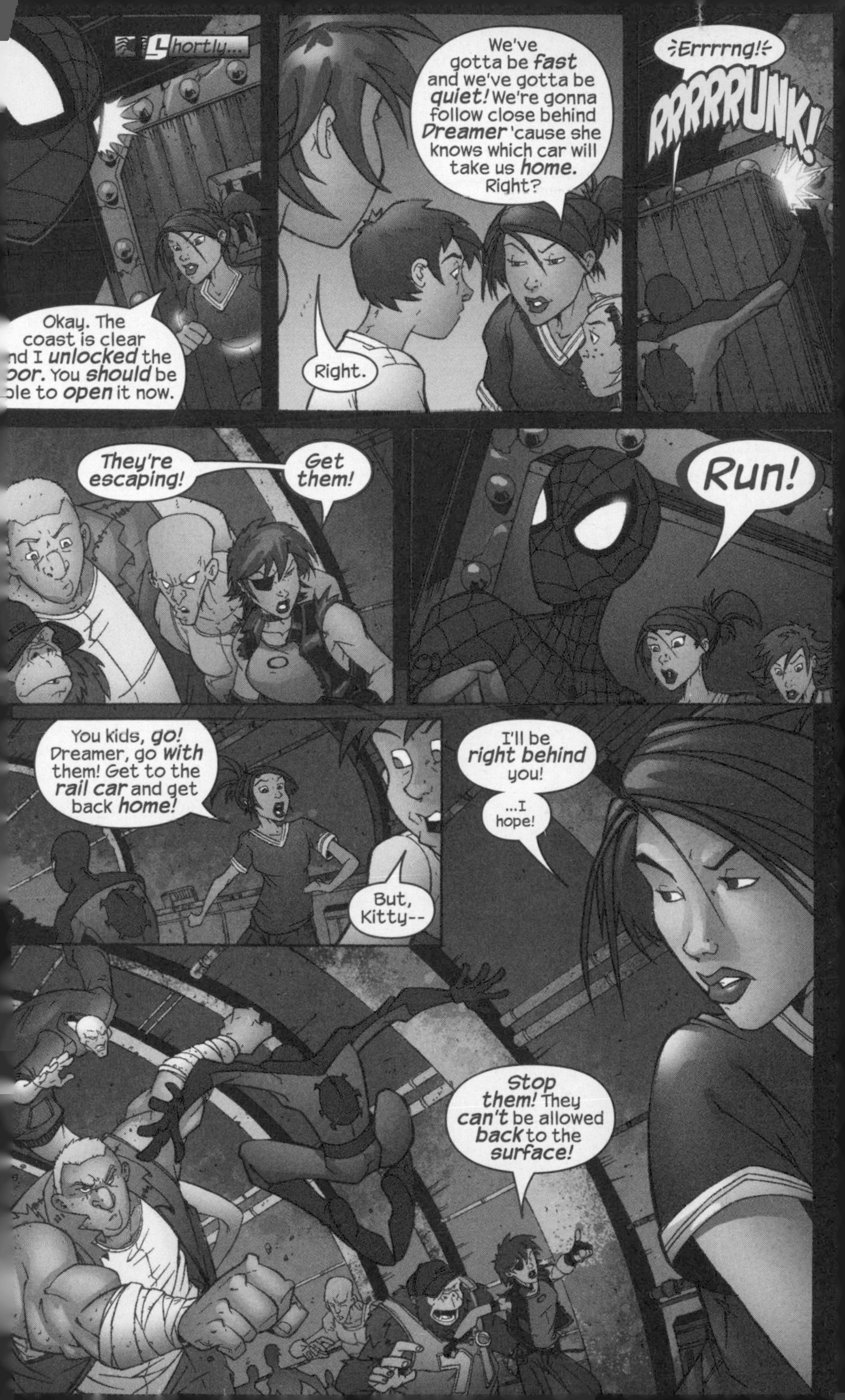
Shortly...
Okay. The coast is clear nd I unlocked the oor. You should be ble to open it now.
We've gotta be fast and we've gotta be quiet! We're gonna follow close behind Dreamer 'cause she knows which car will take us home. Right?
Right.
Errrrng!
RRRRRUNK!
They're escaping!
Get them!
Run!
You kids, go! Dreamer, go with them! Get to the rail car and get back home!
But, Kitty--
I'll be right behind you!
...I hope!
Stop them! They can't be allowed back to the surface!

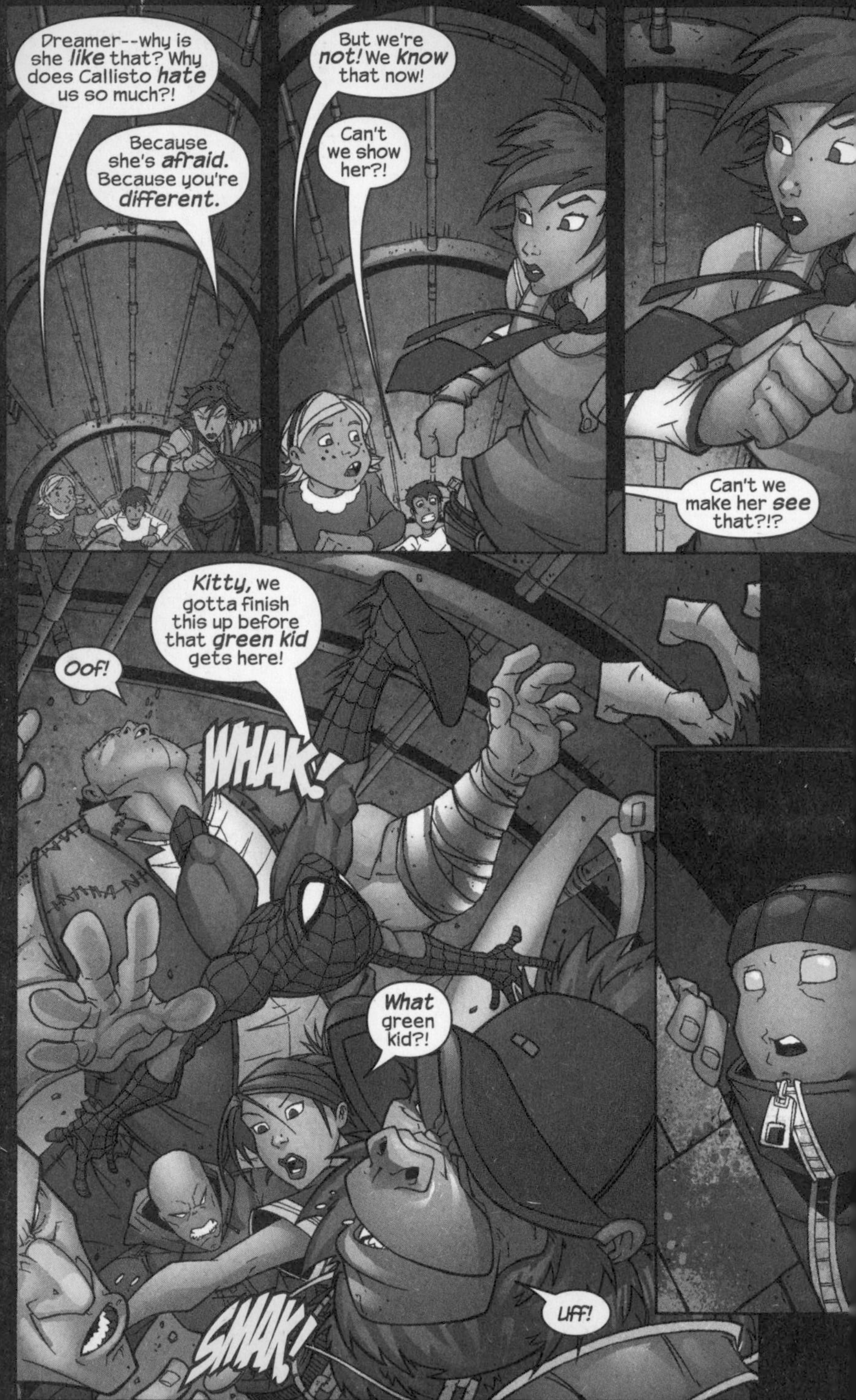

Dreamer--why is she *like* that? Why does Callisto *hate* us so much?!
Because she's *afraid.* Because you're *different.*
But we're *not!* We *know* that now!
Can't we show her?!
Can't we make her *see* that?!?
Kitty, we gotta finish this up before that *green kid* gets here!
Oof!
WHAK!
What green kid?!
SMAK!
UFF!

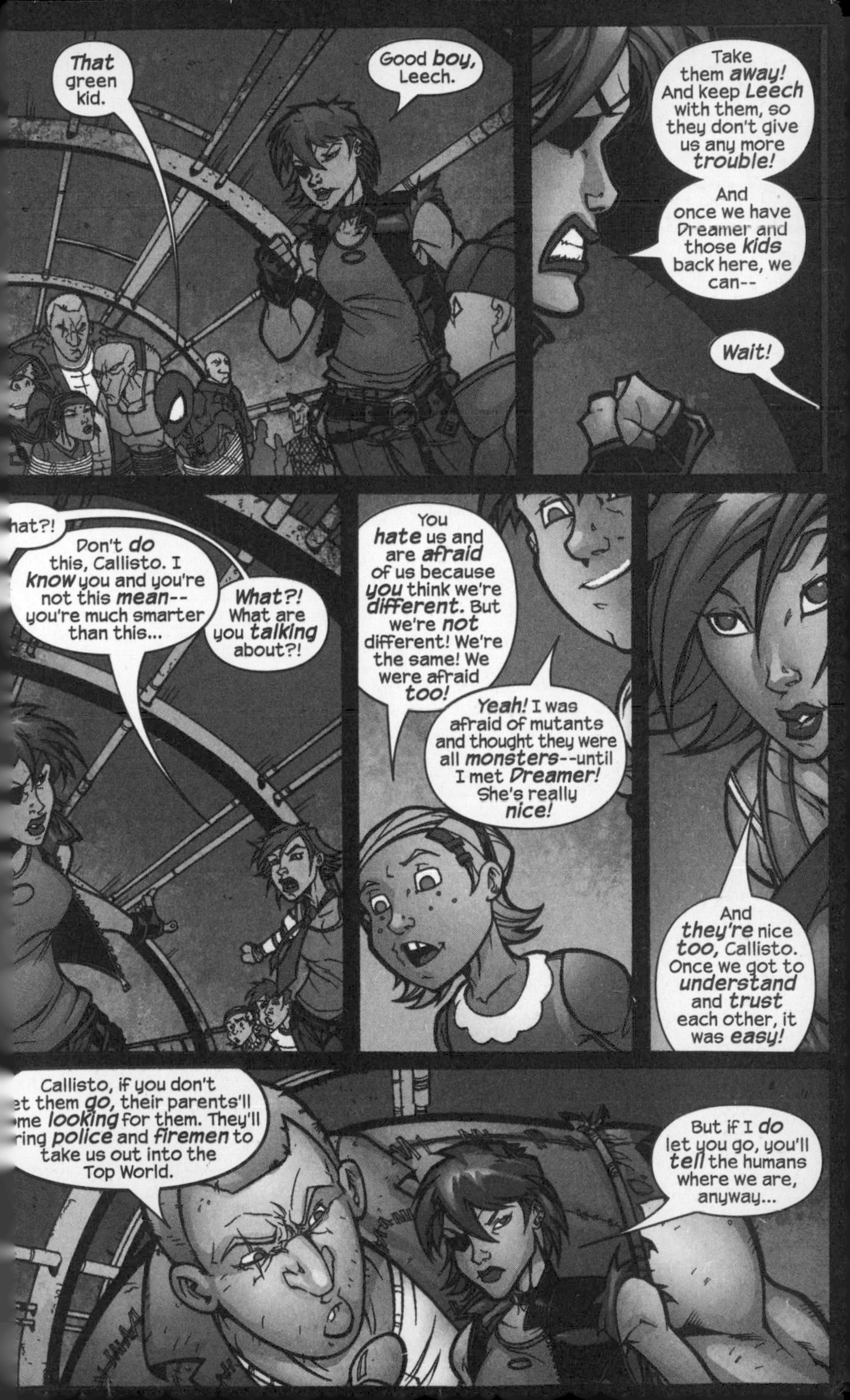
That green kid.
Good boy, Leech.
Take them away! And keep Leech with them, so they don't give us any more trouble!
And once we have Dreamer and those kids back here, we can--
Wait!
hat?!
Don't do this, Callisto. I know you and you're not this mean--you're much smarter than this...
What?! What are you talking about?!
You hate us and are afraid of us because you think we're different. But we're not different! We're the same! We were afraid too!
Yeah! I was afraid of mutants and thought they were all monsters--until I met Dreamer! She's really nice!
And they're nice too, Callisto. Once we got to understand and trust each other, it was easy!
Callisto, if you don't et them go, their parents'll me looking for them. They'll ring police and firemen to take us out into the Top World.
But if I do let you go, you'll tell the humans where we are, anyway...

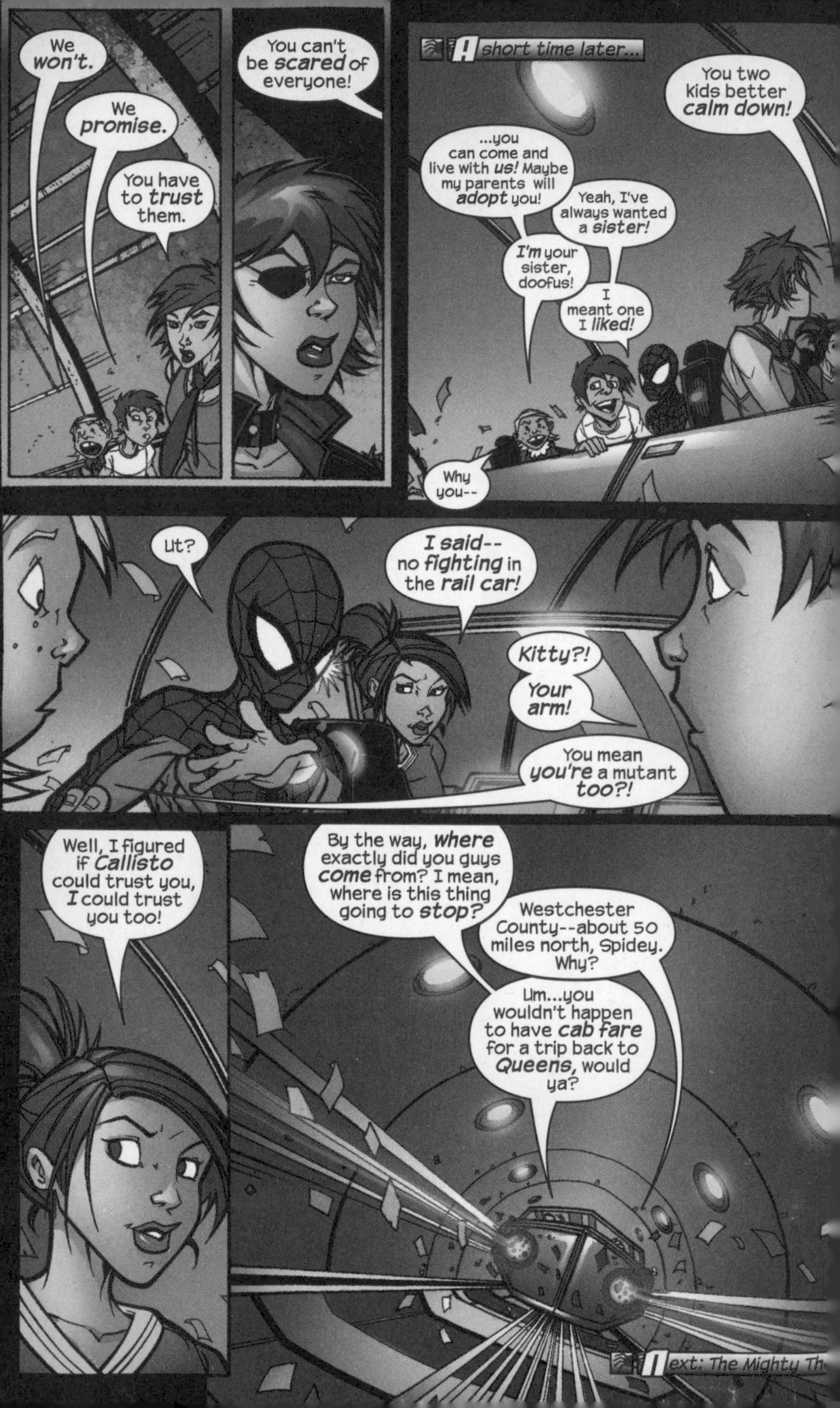
We won't.
We promise.
You have to trust them.
You can't be scared of everyone!
A short time later...
You two kids better calm down!
...you can come and live with us! Maybe my parents will adopt you!
Yeah, I've always wanted a sister!
I'm your sister, doofus!
I meant one I liked!
Why you--
Ut?
I said-- no fighting in the rail car!
Kitty?!
Your arm!
You mean you're a mutant too?!
Well, I figured if Callisto could trust you, I could trust you too!
By the way, where exactly did you guys come from? I mean, where is this thing going to stop?
Westchester County--about 50 miles north, Spidey. Why?
Um...you wouldn't happen to have cab fare for a trip back to Queens, would ya?
Next: The Mighty Th

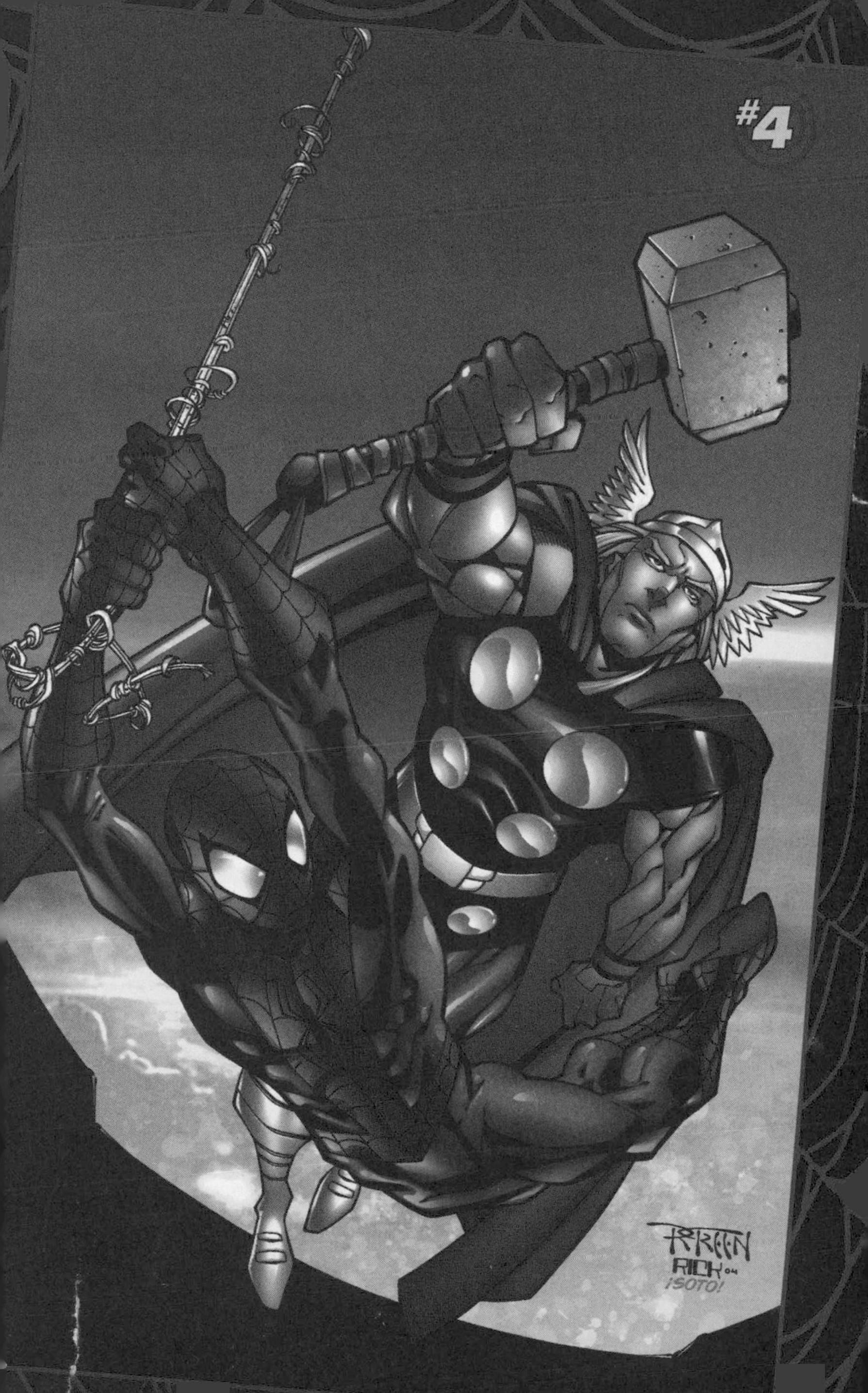
#4
RICK 04
¡SOTO!

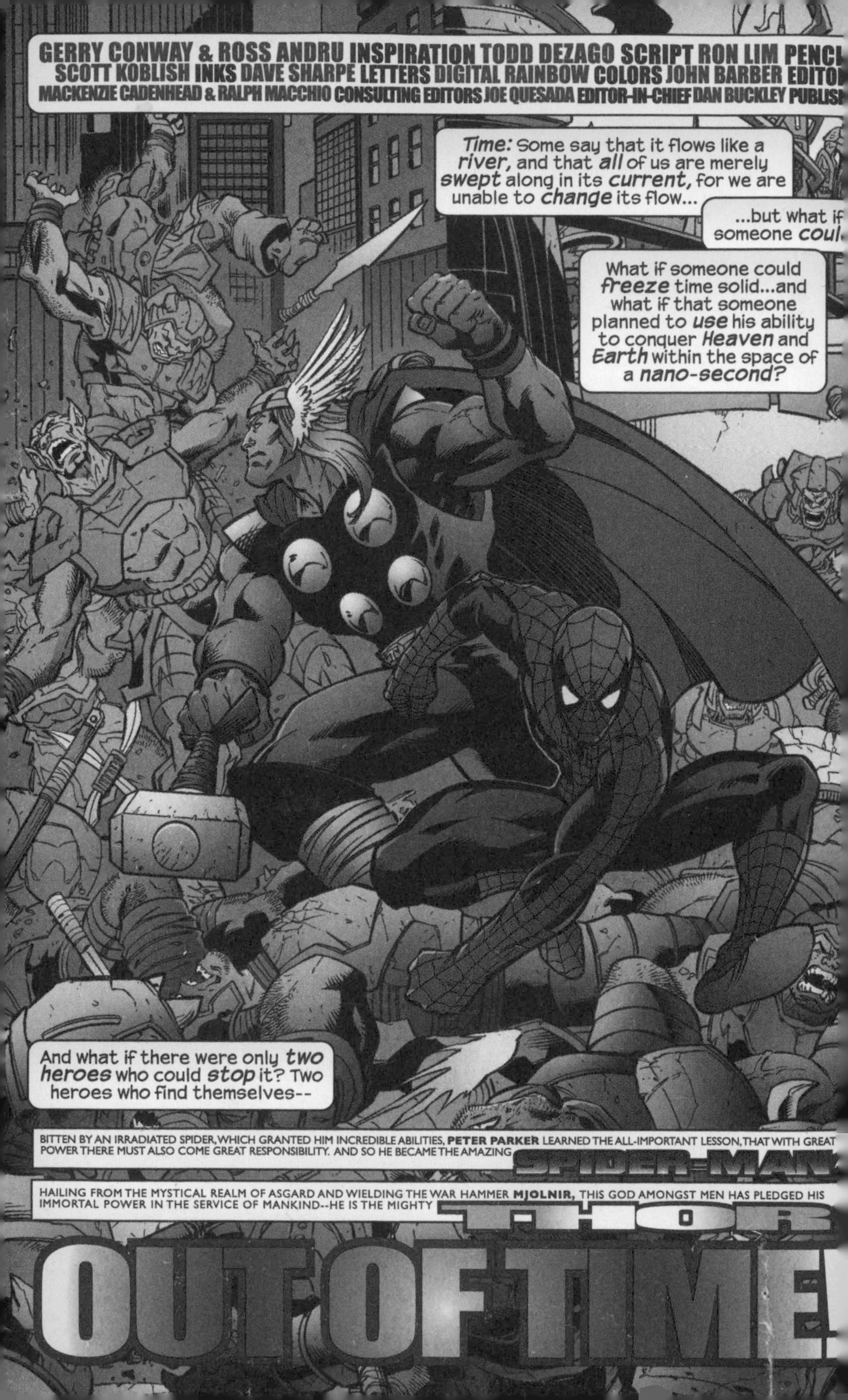
GERRY CONWAY & ROSS ANDRU INSPIRATION TODD DEZAGO SCRIPT RON LIM PENCI
SCOTT KOBLISH INKS DAVE SHARPE LETTERS DIGITAL RAINBOW COLORS JOHN BARBER EDITO
MACKENZIE CADENHEAD & RALPH MACCHIO CONSULTING EDITORS JOE QUESADA EDITOR-IN-CHIEF DAN BUCKLEY PUBLIS
Time: Some say that it flows like a river, and that all of us are merely swept along in its current, for we are unable to change its flow...
...but what if someone coul
What if someone could freeze time solid...and what if that someone planned to use his ability to conquer Heaven and Earth within the space of a nano-second?
And what if there were only two heroes who could stop it? Two heroes who find themselves--
BITTEN BY AN IRRADIATED SPIDER, WHICH GRANTED HIM INCREDIBLE ABILITIES, PETER PARKER LEARNED THE ALL-IMPORTANT LESSON, THAT WITH GREAT POWER THERE MUST ALSO COME GREAT RESPONSIBILITY. AND SO HE BECAME THE AMAZING SPIDER-MAN
HAILING FROM THE MYSTICAL REALM OF ASGARD AND WIELDING THE WAR HAMMER MJOLNIR, THIS GOD AMONGST MEN HAS PLEDGED HIS IMMORTAL POWER IN THE SERVICE OF MANKIND--HE IS THE MIGHTY THOR
OUT OF TIME

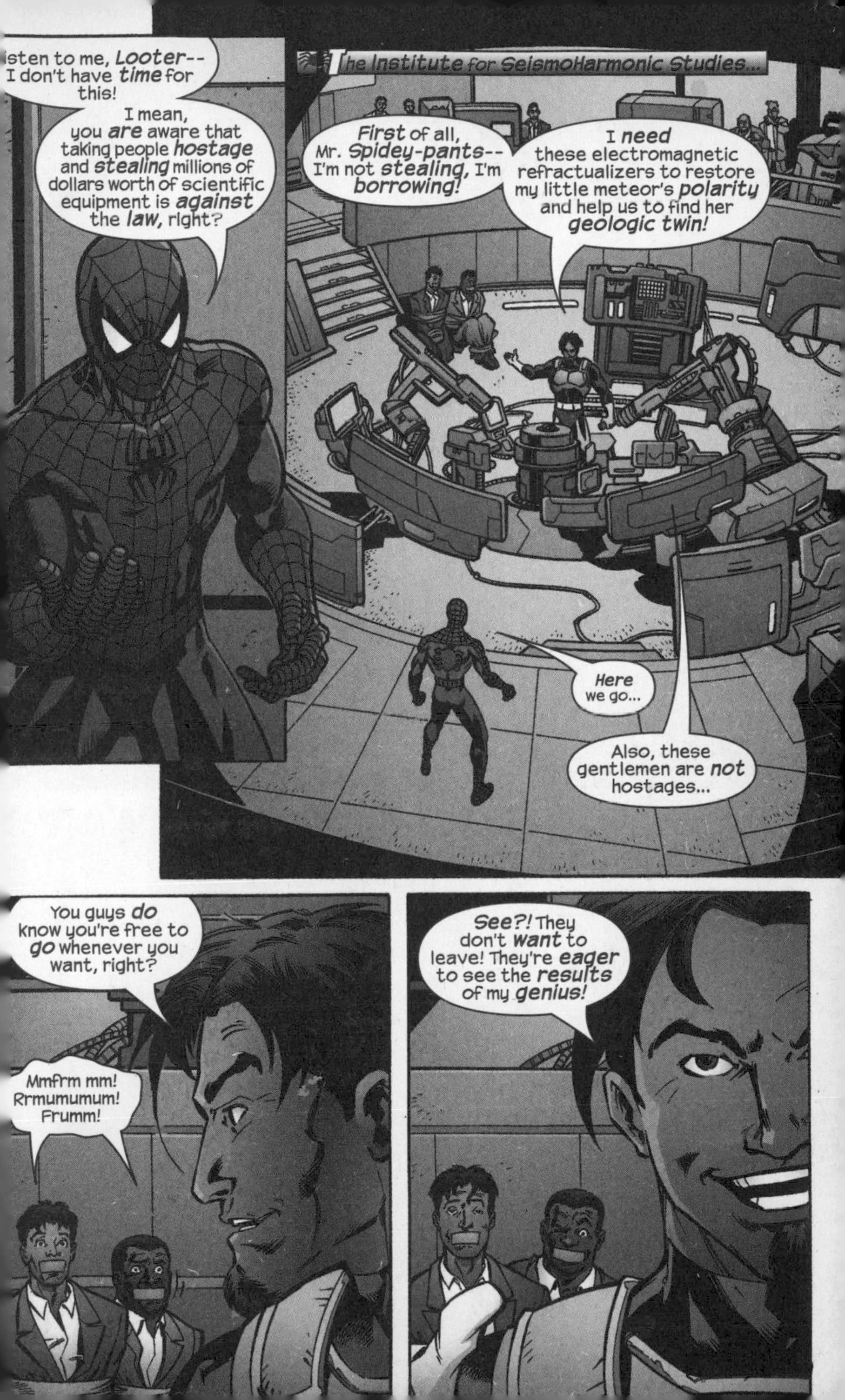
isten to me, Looter--
I don't have time for this!
I mean, you are aware that taking people hostage and stealing millions of dollars worth of scientific equipment is against the law, right?
The Institute for SeismoHarmonic Studies...
First of all, Mr. Spidey-pants-- I'm not stealing, I'm borrowing!
I need these electromagnetic refractualizers to restore my little meteor's polarity and help us to find her geologic twin!
Here we go...
Also, these gentlemen are not hostages...
You guys do know you're free to go whenever you want, right?
Mmfrm mm! Rrmumumum! Frumm!
See?! They don't want to leave! They're eager to see the results of my genius!

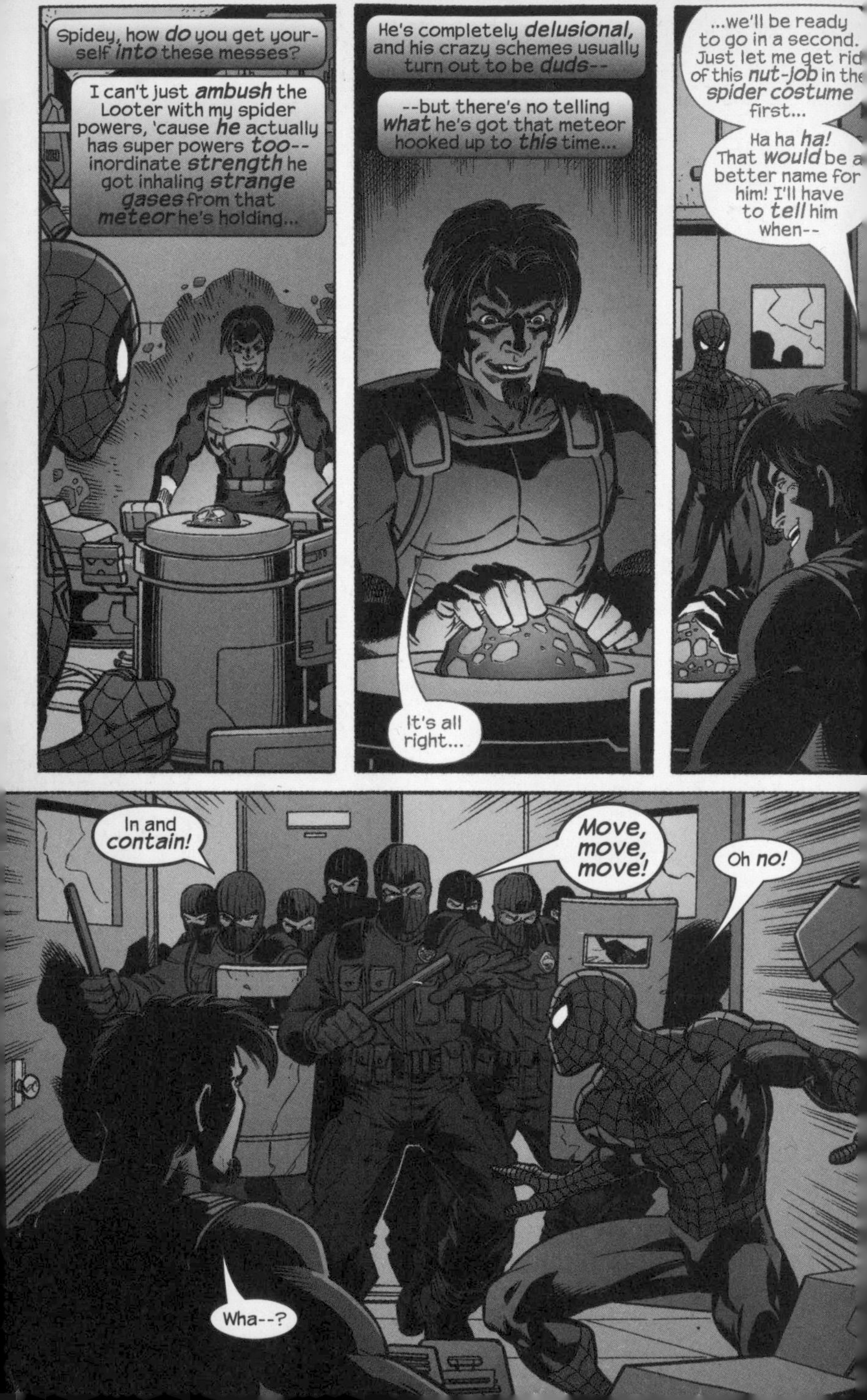
Spidey, how *do* you get yourself *into* these messes?
I can't just *ambush* the Looter with my spider powers, 'cause *he* actually has super powers *too*-- inordinate *strength* he got inhaling *strange gases* from that *meteor* he's holding...
He's completely *delusional*, and his crazy schemes usually turn out to be *duds*--
--but there's no telling *what* he's got that meteor hooked up to *this* time...
It's all right...
...we'll be ready to go in a second. Just let me get rid of this *nut-job* in the *spider costume* first...
Ha ha *ha!* That *would* be a better name for him! I'll have to *tell* him when--
In and *contain!*
Move, move, move!
Oh *no!*
Wha--?

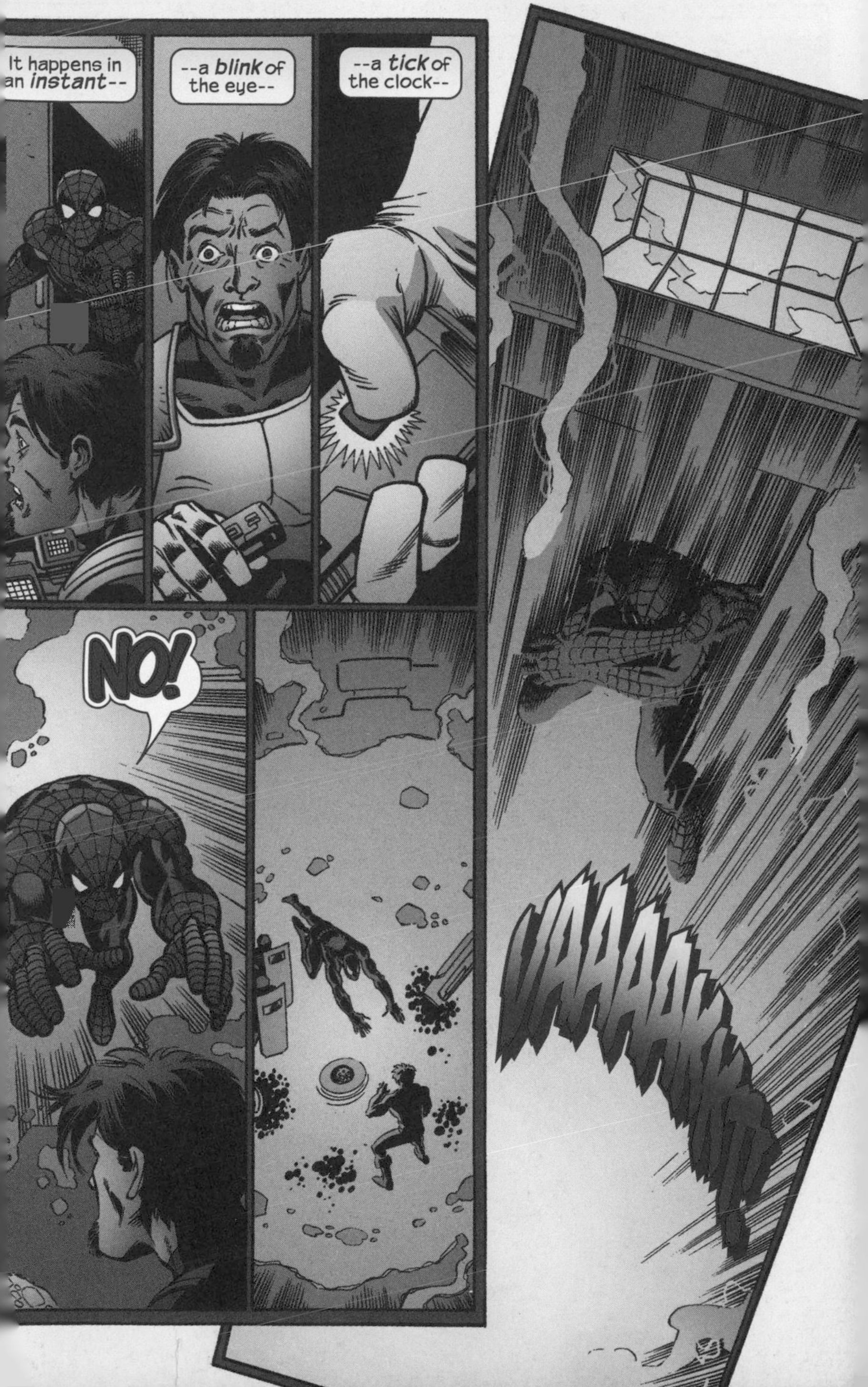
It happens in an instant--
--a blink of the eye--
--a tick of the clock--
NO!

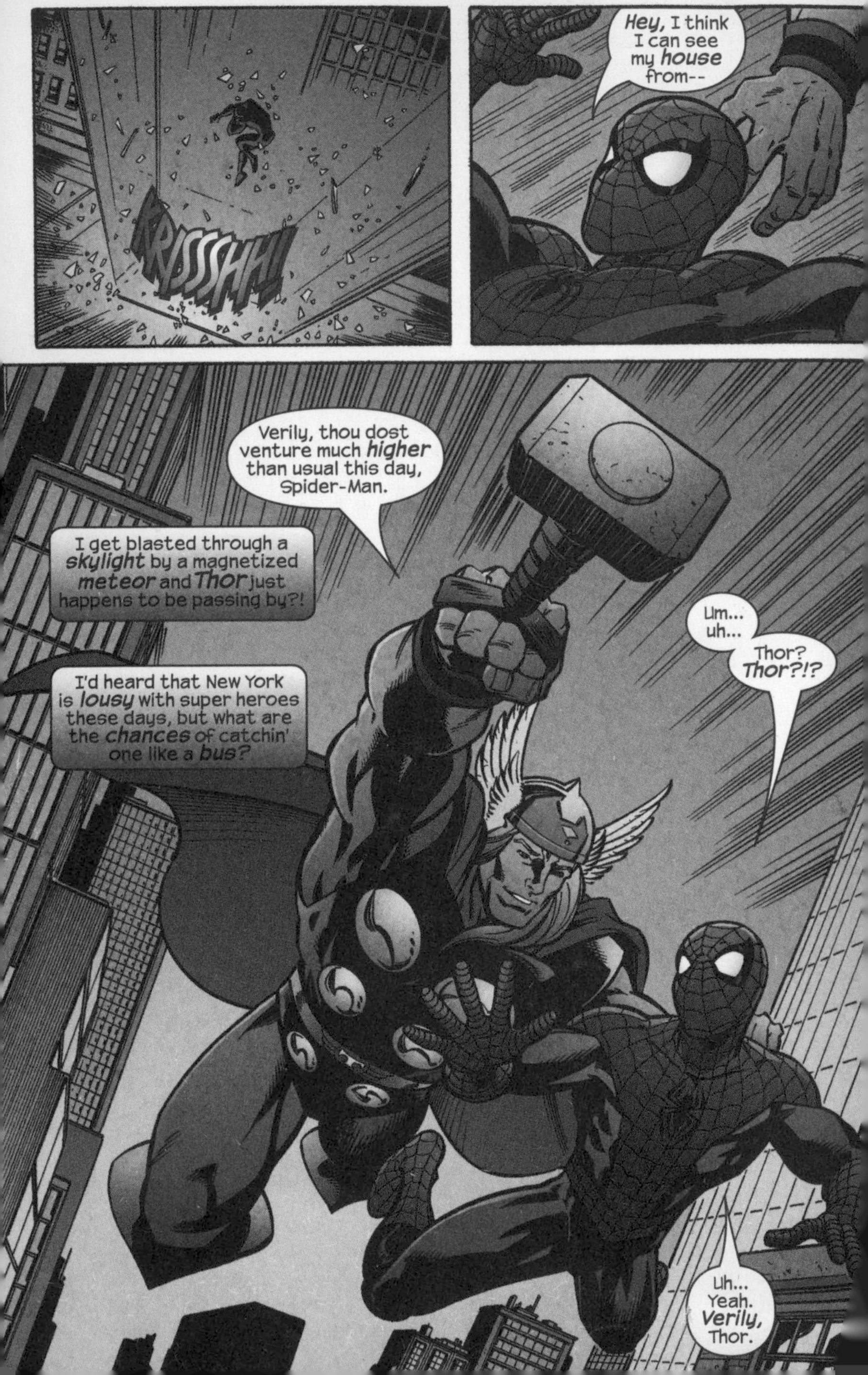
KRISSSHH!
Hey, I think I can see my house from--
Verily, thou dost venture much higher than usual this day, Spider-Man.
I get blasted through a skylight by a magnetized meteor and Thor just happens to be passing by?!
I'd heard that New York is lousy with super heroes these days, but what are the chances of catchin' one like a bus?
Um... uh...
Thor? Thor?!?
Uh... Yeah. Verily, Thor.

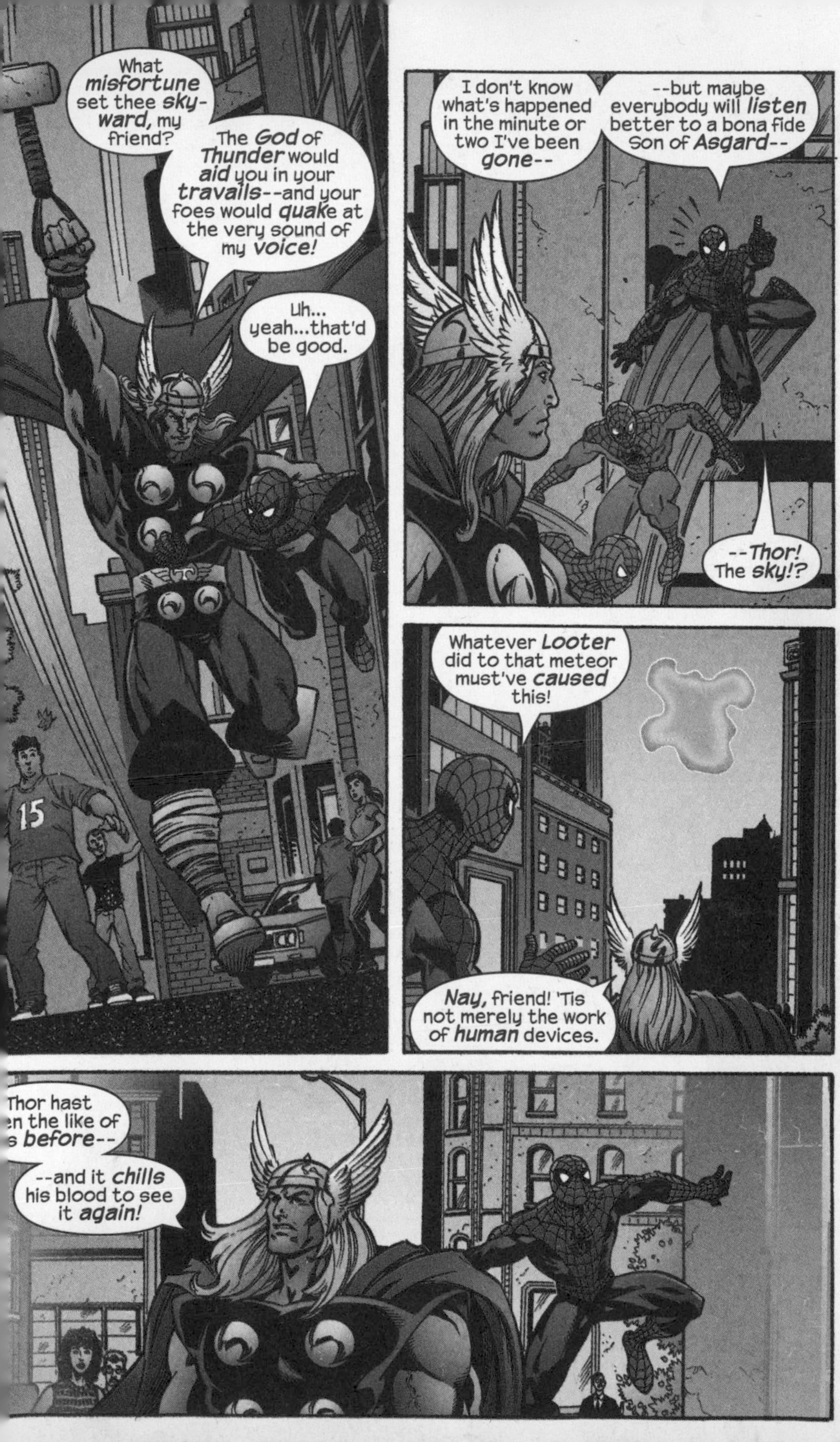
What misfortune set thee skyward, my friend?
The God of Thunder would aid you in your travails--and your foes would quake at the very sound of my voice!
Uh... yeah...that'd be good.
I don't know what's happened in the minute or two I've been gone--
--but maybe everybody will listen better to a bona fide Son of Asgard--
--Thor! The sky!?
Whatever Looter did to that meteor must've caused this!
Nay, friend! 'Tis not merely the work of human devices.
Thor hast
en the like of
s before--
--and it chills his blood to see it again!

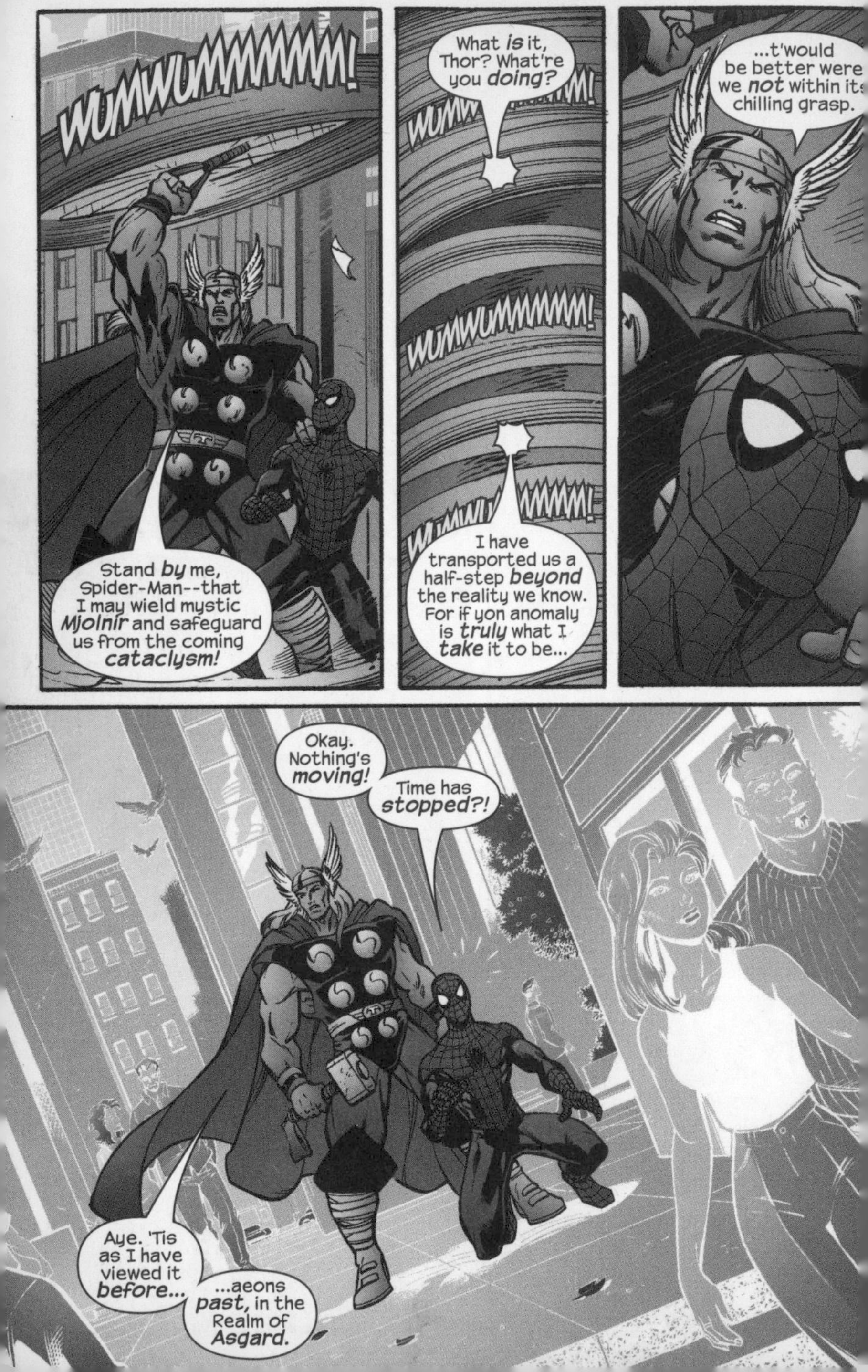

WUMWUMMMMMM!
Stand by me, Spider-Man--that I may wield mystic Mjolnir and safeguard us from the coming cataclysm!
What is it, Thor? What're you doing?
WUMWUMMMMMM!
I have transported us a half-step beyond the reality we know. For if yon anomaly is truly what I take it to be...
...t'would be better were we not within its chilling grasp.
Okay. Nothing's moving!
Time has stopped?!
Aye. 'Tis as I have viewed it before...
...aeons past, in the Realm of Asgard.

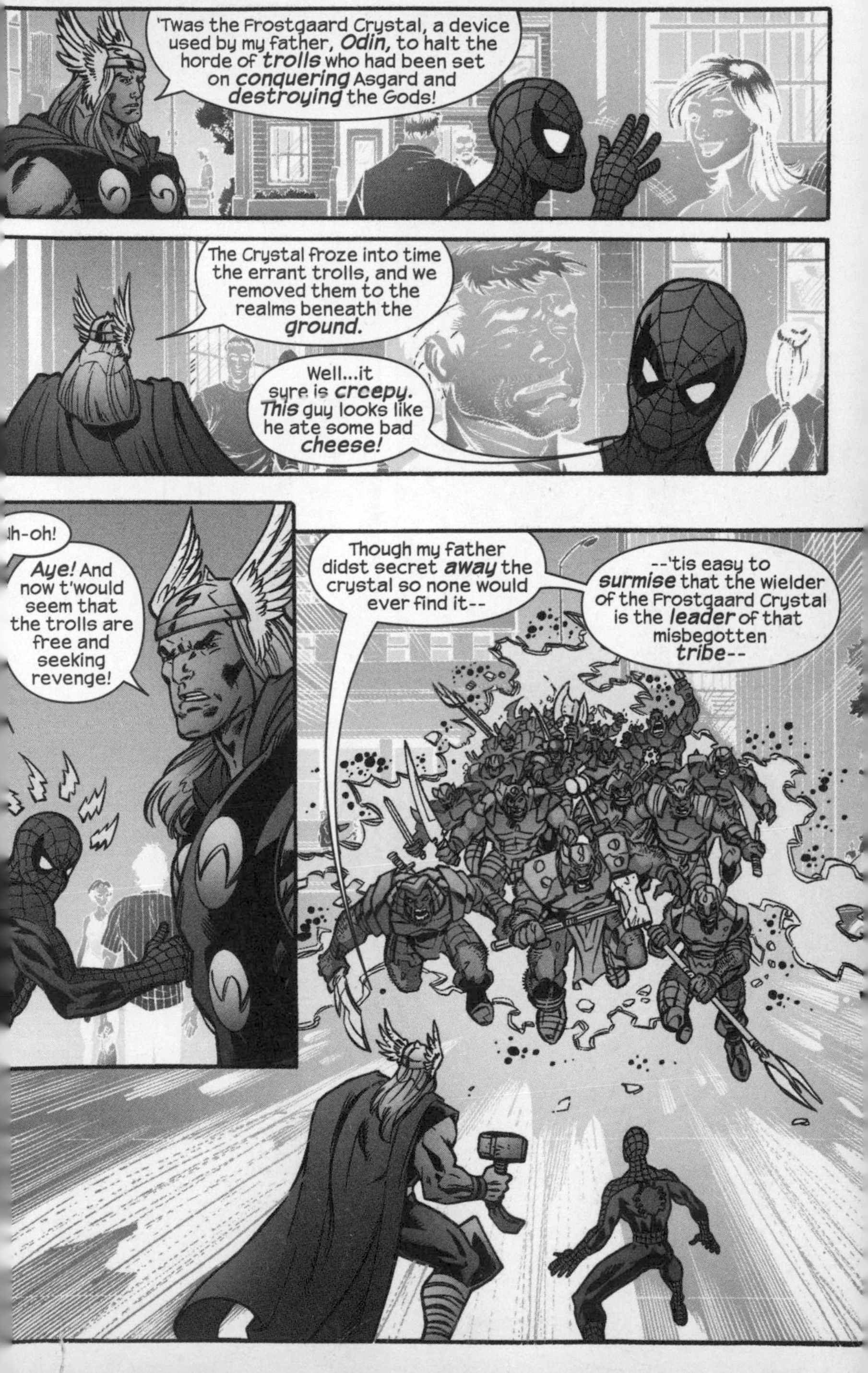

'Twas the Frostgaard Crystal, a device used by my father, Odin, to halt the horde of trolls who had been set on conquering Asgard and destroying the Gods!
The Crystal froze into time the errant trolls, and we removed them to the realms beneath the ground.
Well...it sure is creepy. This guy looks like he ate some bad cheese!
Uh-oh!
Aye! And now t'would seem that the trolls are free and seeking revenge!
Though my father didst secret away the crystal so none would ever find it--
--'tis easy to surmise that the wielder of the Frostgaard Crystal is the leader of that misbegotten tribe--

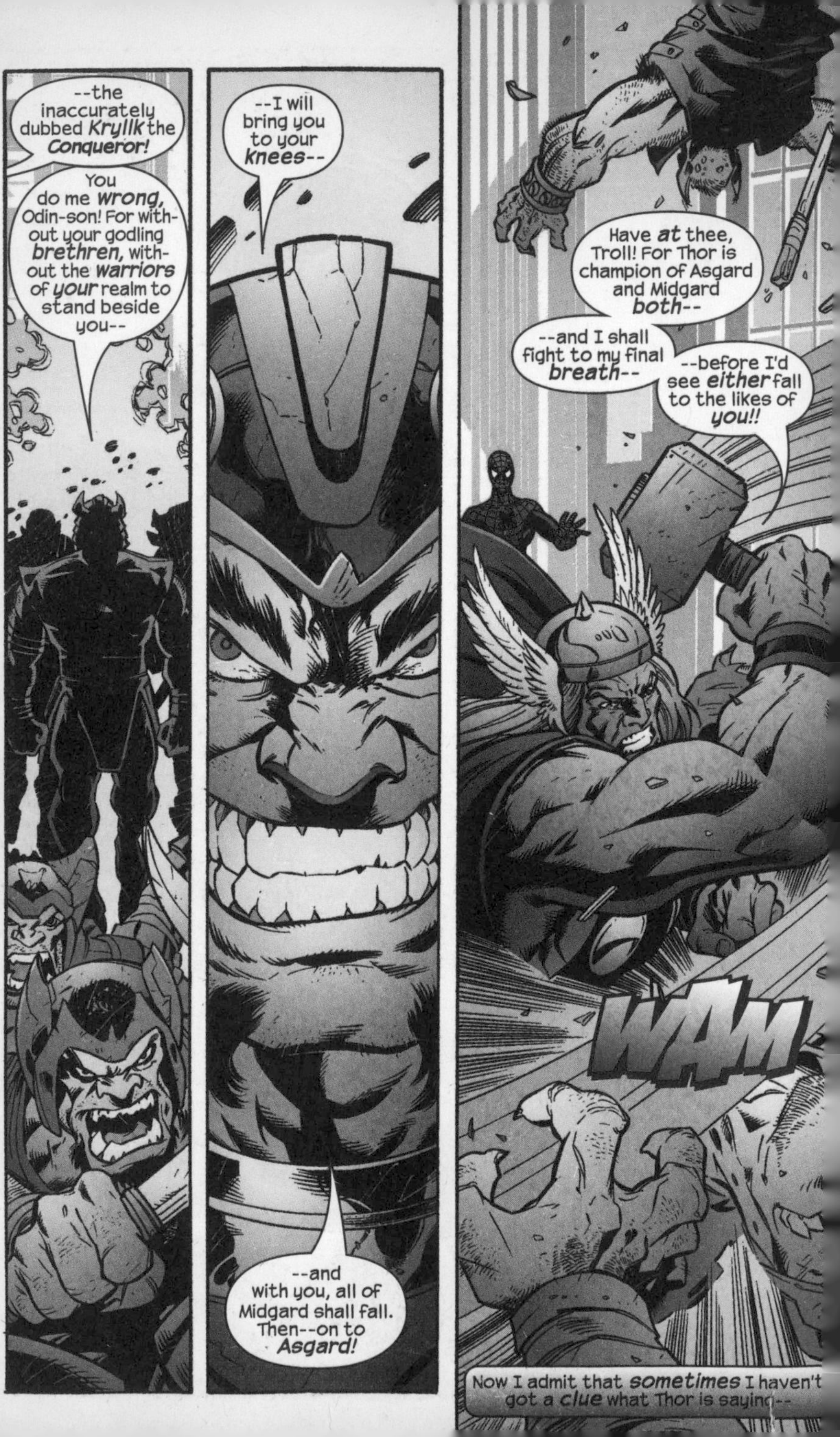
--the inaccurately dubbed Krylik the Conqueror!
You do me wrong, Odin-son! For with-out your godling brethren, with-out the warriors of your realm to stand beside you--
--I will bring you to your knees--
--and with you, all of Midgard shall fall. Then--on to Asgard!
Have at thee, Troll! For Thor is champion of Asgard and Midgard both--
--and I shall fight to my final breath--
--before I'd see either fall to the likes of you!!
WAM
Now I admit that sometimes I haven't got a clue what Thor is saying--

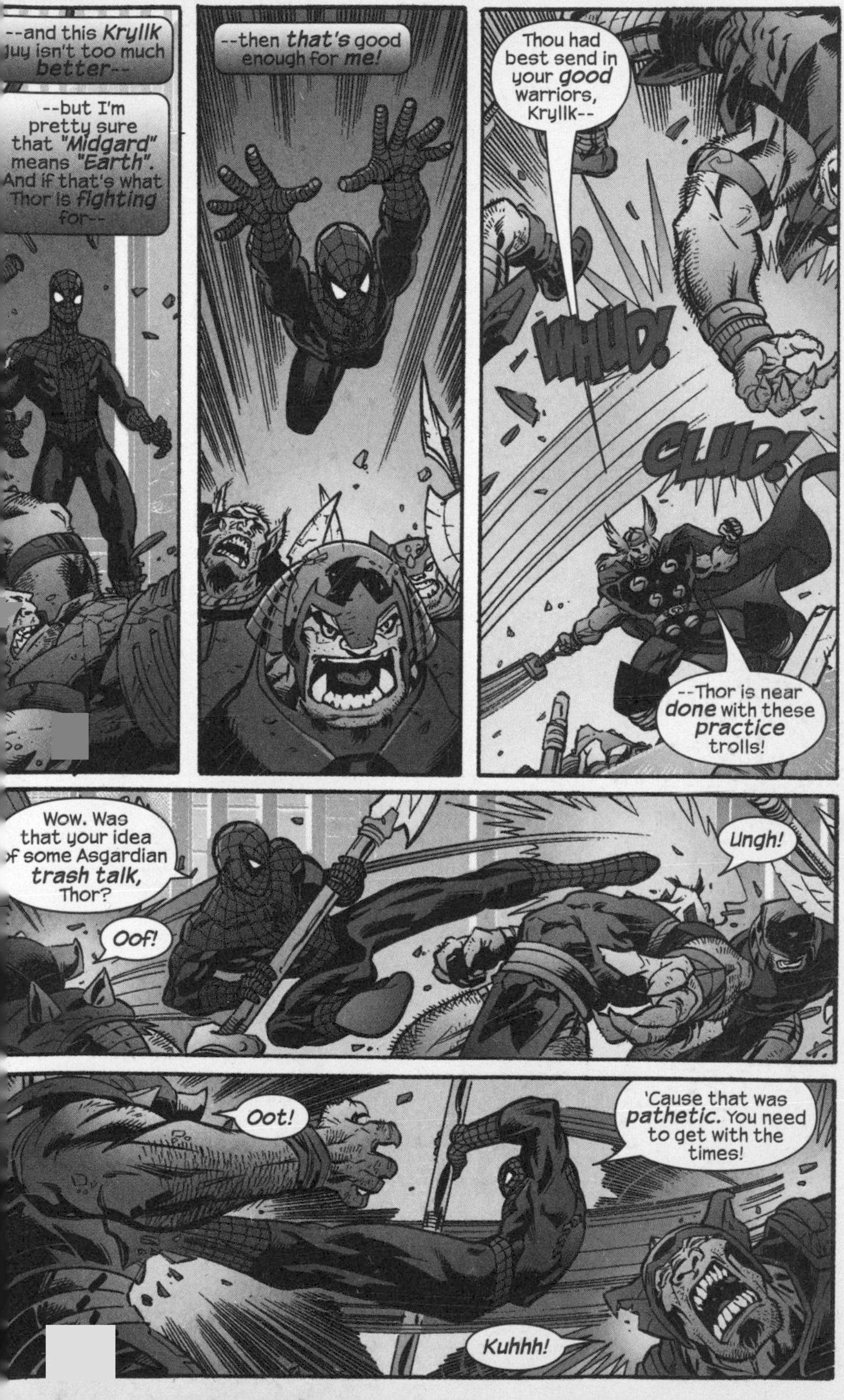
--and this Kryllk
uy isn't too much better--
--but I'm pretty sure that "Midgard" means "Earth". And if that's what Thor is fighting for--
--then that's good enough for me!
Thou had best send in your good warriors, Kryllk--
WHUD!
CLUD!
--Thor is near done with these practice trolls!
Wow. Was that your idea
f some Asgardian trash talk, Thor?
Oof!
Ungh!
Oot!
'Cause that was pathetic. You need to get with the times!
Kuhhh!

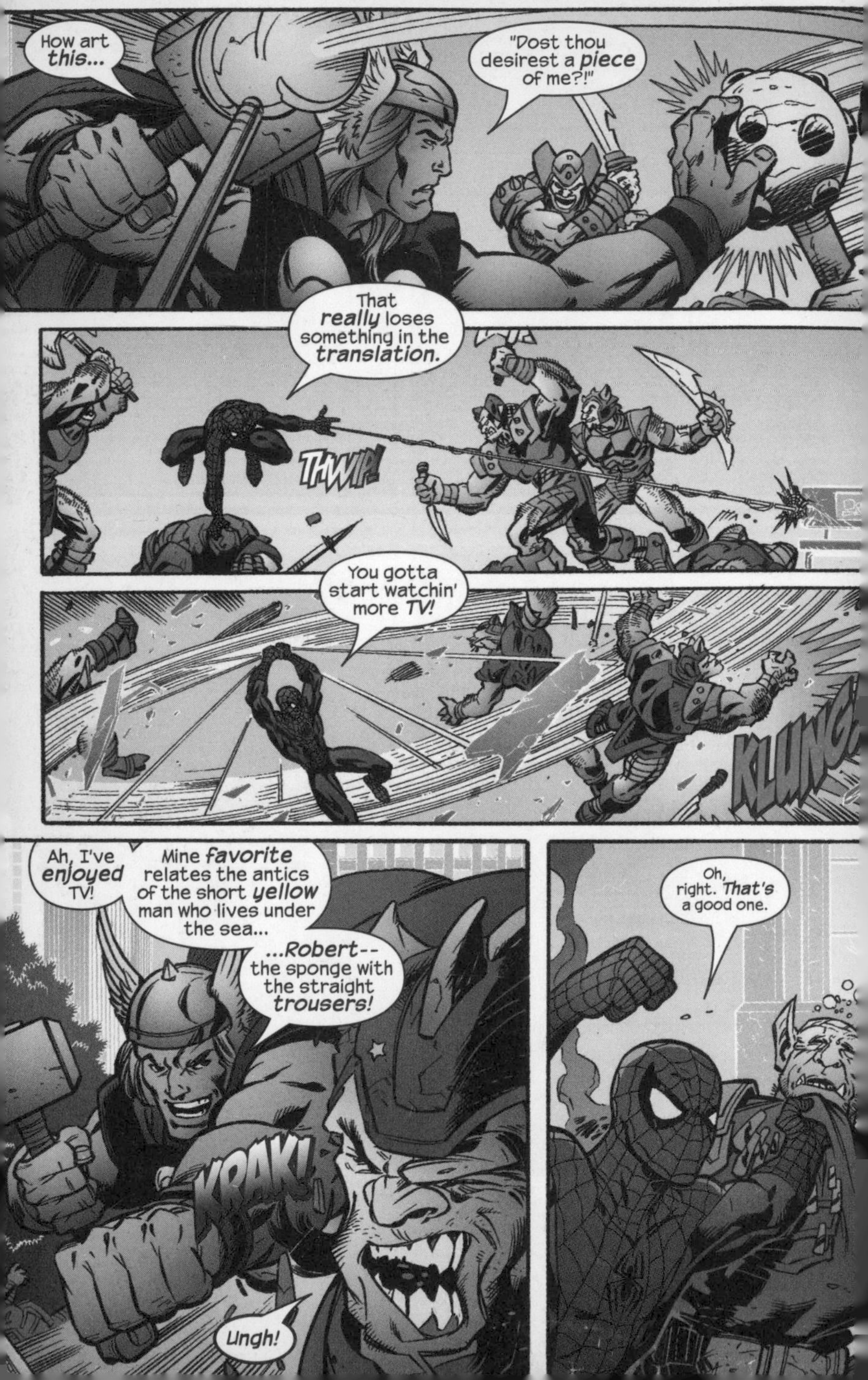
How art this...
"Dost thou desirest a piece of me?!"
That really loses something in the translation.
THWIP!
You gotta start watchin' more TV!
KLUNG!
Ah, I've enjoyed TV!
Mine favorite relates the antics of the short yellow man who lives under the sea...
...Robert-- the sponge with the straight trousers!
KRAK!
Ungh!
Oh, right. That's a good one.

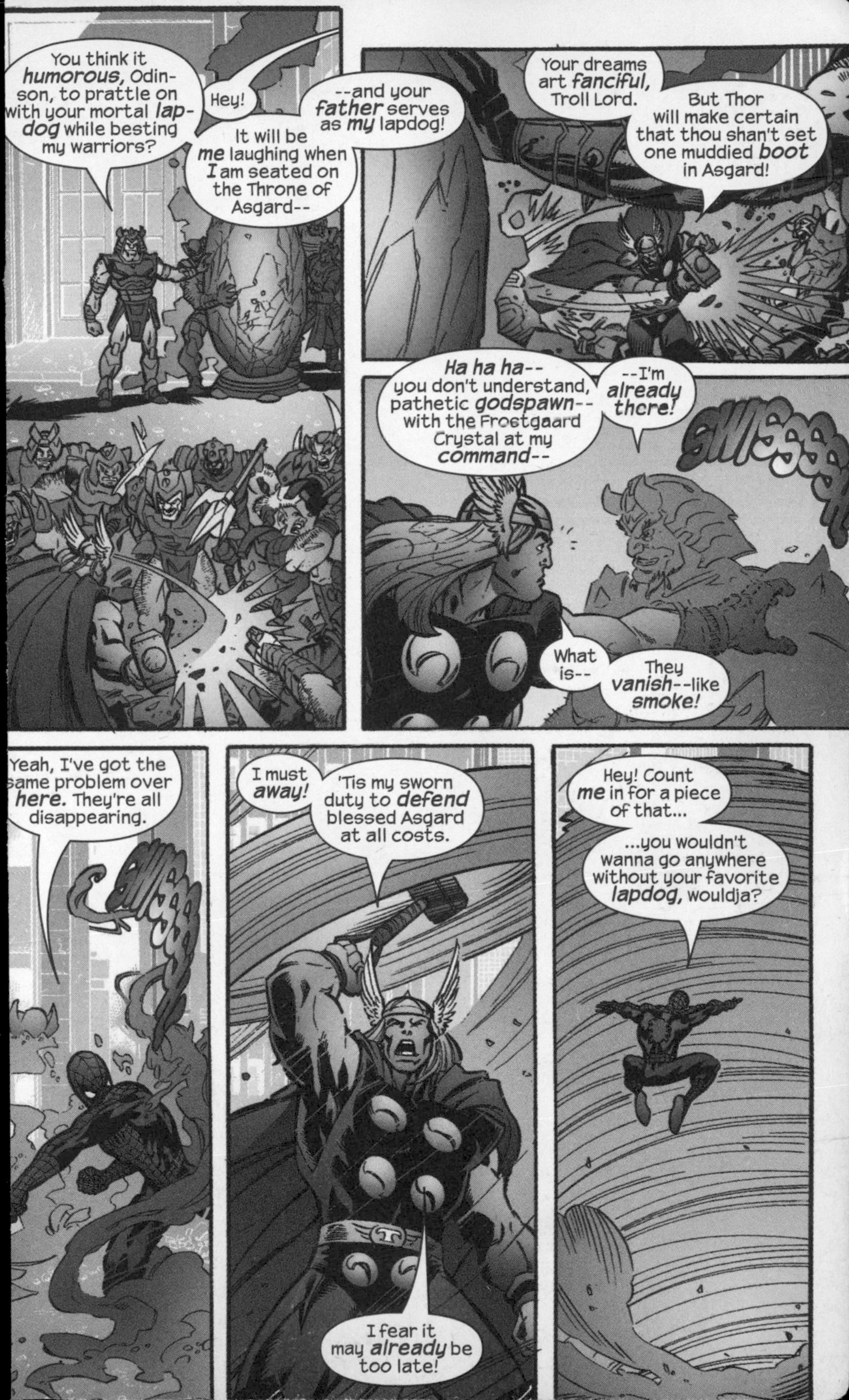
You think it humorous, Odinson, to prattle on with your mortal lapdog while besting my warriors?
Hey!
It will be me laughing when I am seated on the Throne of Asgard--
--and your father serves as my lapdog!
Your dreams art fanciful, Troll Lord.
But Thor will make certain that thou shan't set one muddied boot in Asgard!
Ha ha ha-- you don't understand, pathetic godspawn-- with the Frostgaard Crystal at my command--
--I'm already there!
SWISSSH
What is--
They vanish--like smoke!
Yeah, I've got the same problem over here. They're all disappearing.
I must away!
'Tis my sworn duty to defend blessed Asgard at all costs.
I fear it may already be too late!
Hey! Count me in for a piece of that...
...you wouldn't wanna go anywhere without your favorite lapdog, wouldja?

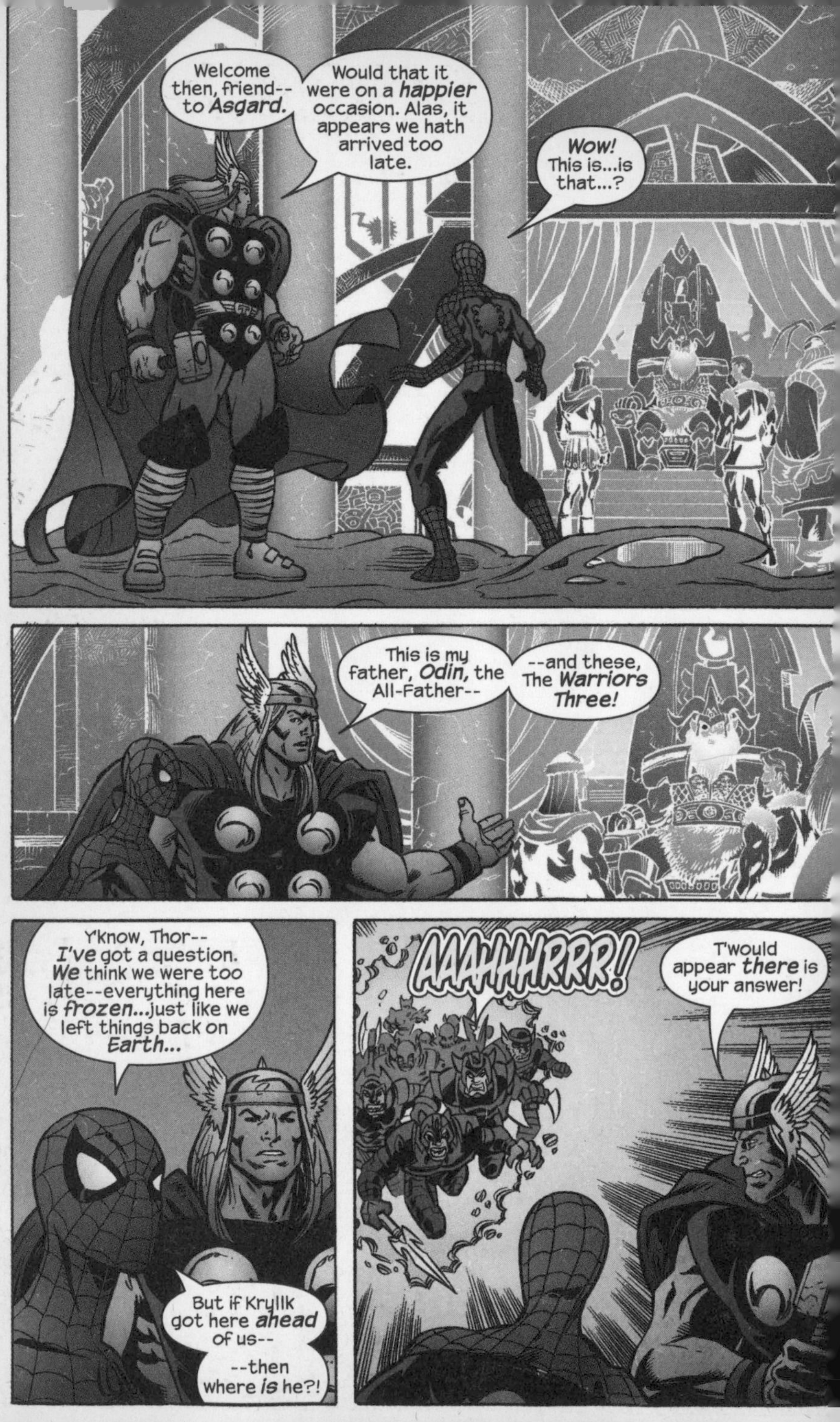
Welcome then, friend-- to Asgard.
Would that it were on a happier occasion. Alas, it appears we hath arrived too late.
Wow! This is...is that...?
This is my father, Odin, the All-Father--
--and these, The Warriors Three!
Y'know, Thor-- I've got a question. We think we were too late--everything here is frozen...just like we left things back on Earth...
But if Krylk got here ahead of us--
--then where is he?!
AAAHHHRRR!
T'would appear there is your answer!

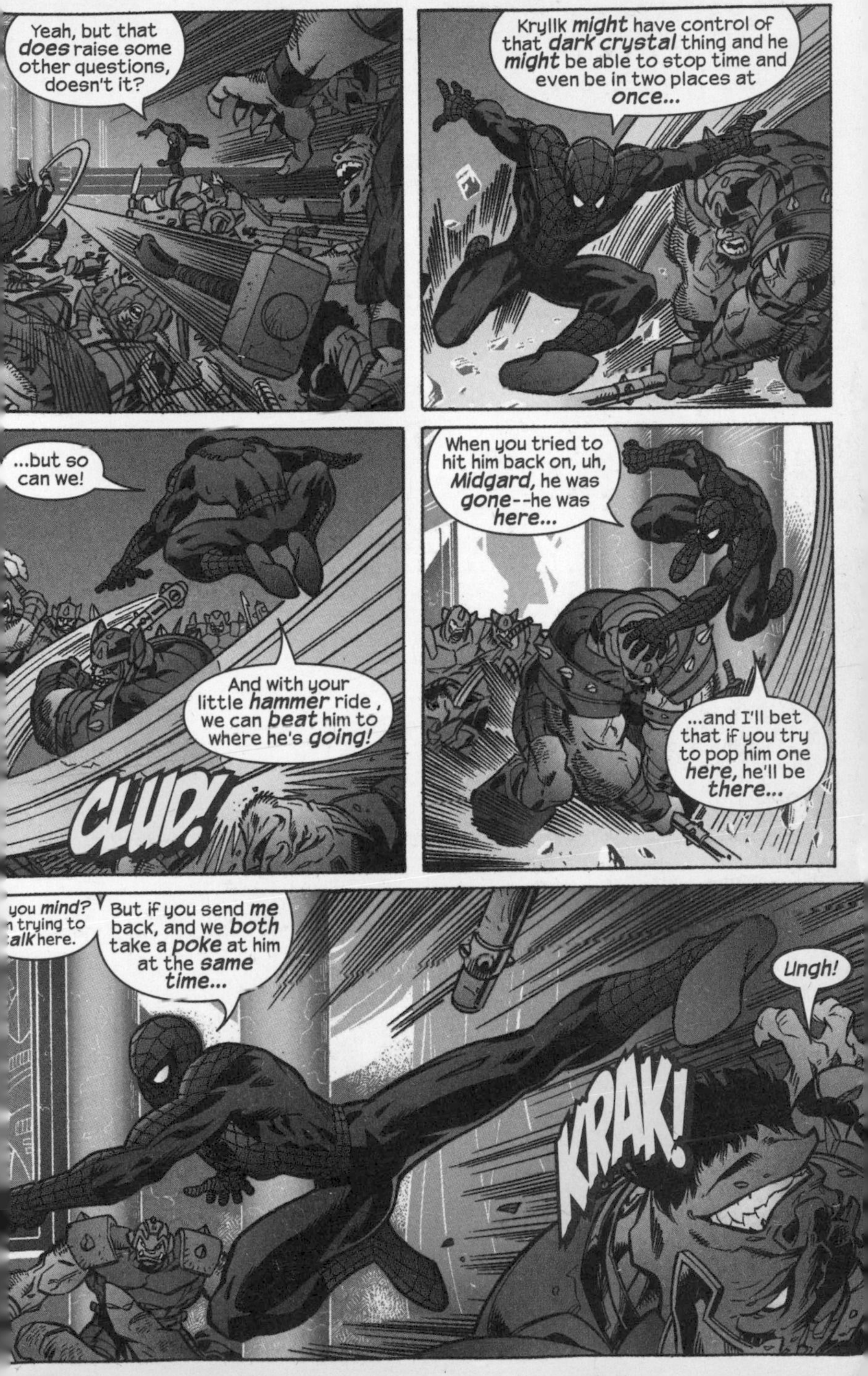
Yeah, but that does raise some other questions, doesn't it?
Kryllk might have control of that dark crystal thing and he might be able to stop time and even be in two places at once...
...but so can we!
And with your little hammer ride , we can beat him to where he's going!
CLUD!
When you tried to hit him back on, uh, Midgard, he was gone--he was here...
...and I'll bet that if you try to pop him one here, he'll be there...
But if you send me back, and we both take a poke at him at the same time...
Ungh!
KRAK!

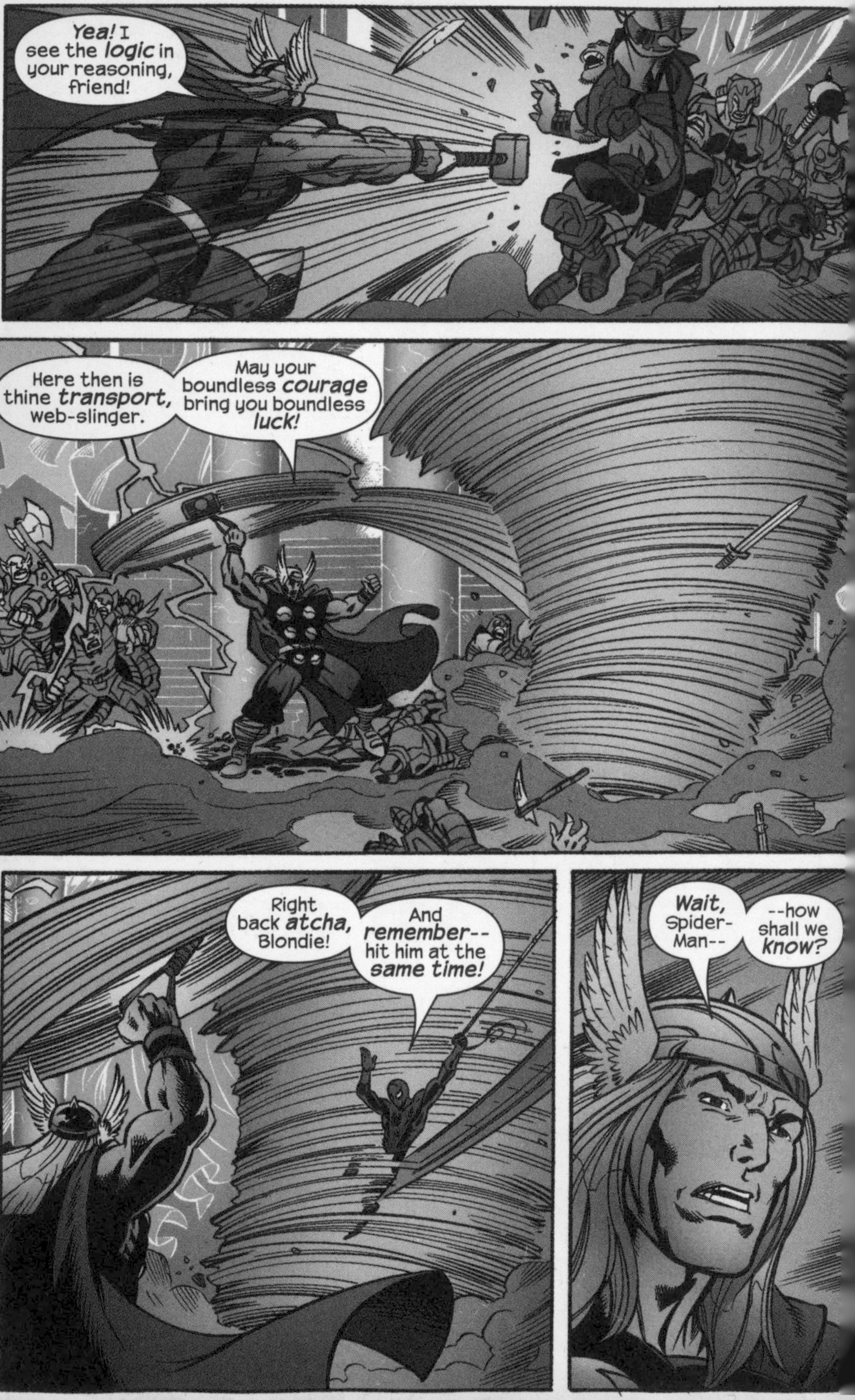
Yea! I see the logic in your reasoning, friend!
Here then is thine transport, web-slinger.
May your boundless courage bring you boundless luck!
Right back atcha, Blondie!
And remember-- hit him at the same time!
Wait, Spider-Man--
--how shall we know?

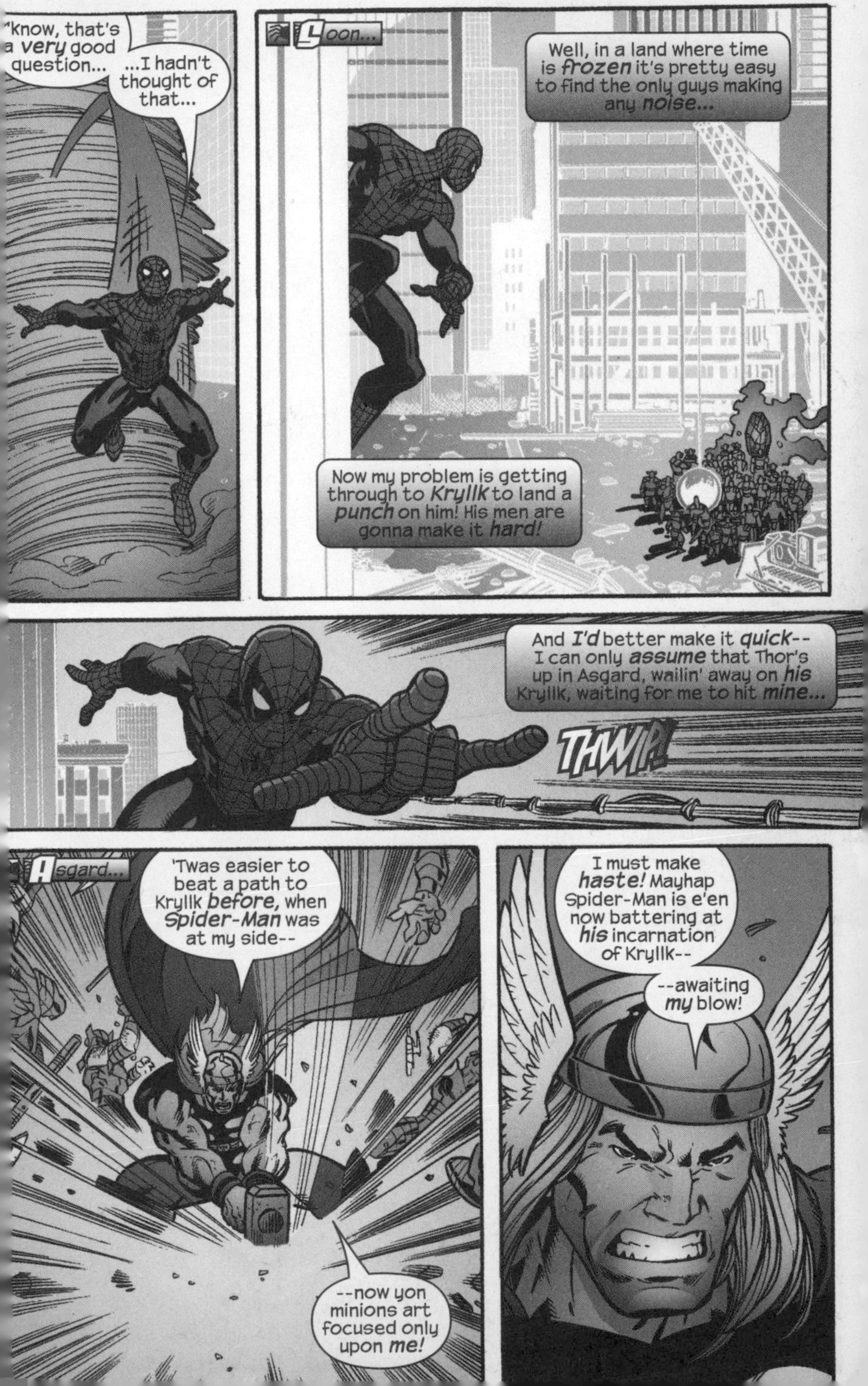
Y'know, that's a very good question...
...I hadn't thought of that...
Soon...
Well, in a land where time is frozen it's pretty easy to find the only guys making any noise...
Now my problem is getting through to Kryllk to land a punch on him! His men are gonna make it hard!
And I'd better make it quick-- I can only assume that Thor's up in Asgard, wailin' away on his Kryllk, waiting for me to hit mine...
THWIP!
Asgard...
'Twas easier to beat a path to Kryllk before, when Spider-Man was at my side--
--now yon minions art focused only upon me!
I must make haste! Mayhap Spider-Man is e'en now battering at his incarnation of Kryllk--
--awaiting my blow!

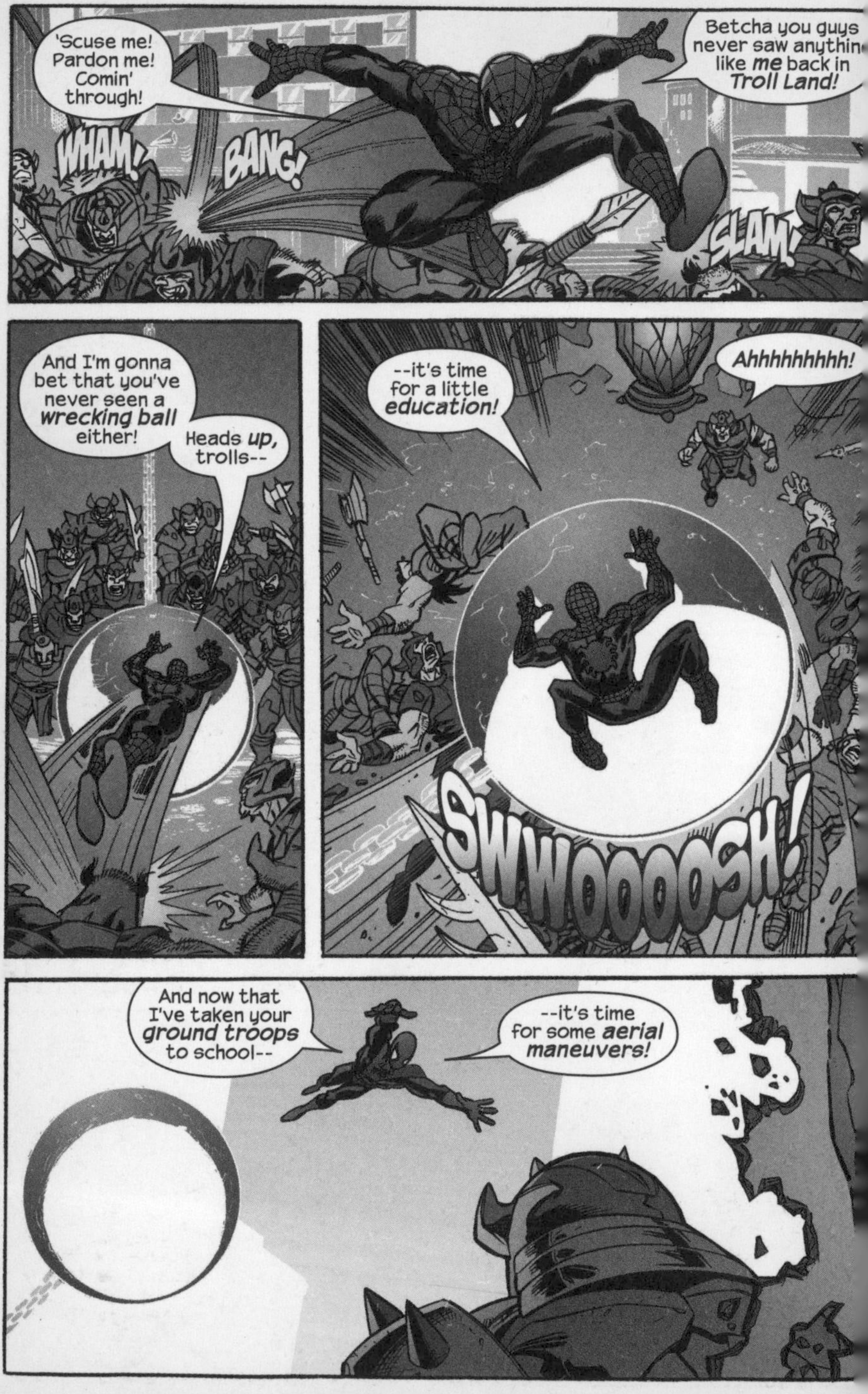
'Scuse me! Pardon me! Comin' through!
Betcha you guys never saw anythin like *me* back in *Troll Land!*
WHAM!
BANG!
SLAM!
And I'm gonna bet that you've never seen a *wrecking ball* either!
Heads *up,* trolls--
--it's time for a little *education!*
Ahhhhhhhhh!
SWWOOOOSH!
And now that I've taken your *ground troops* to school--
--it's time for some *aerial maneuvers!*

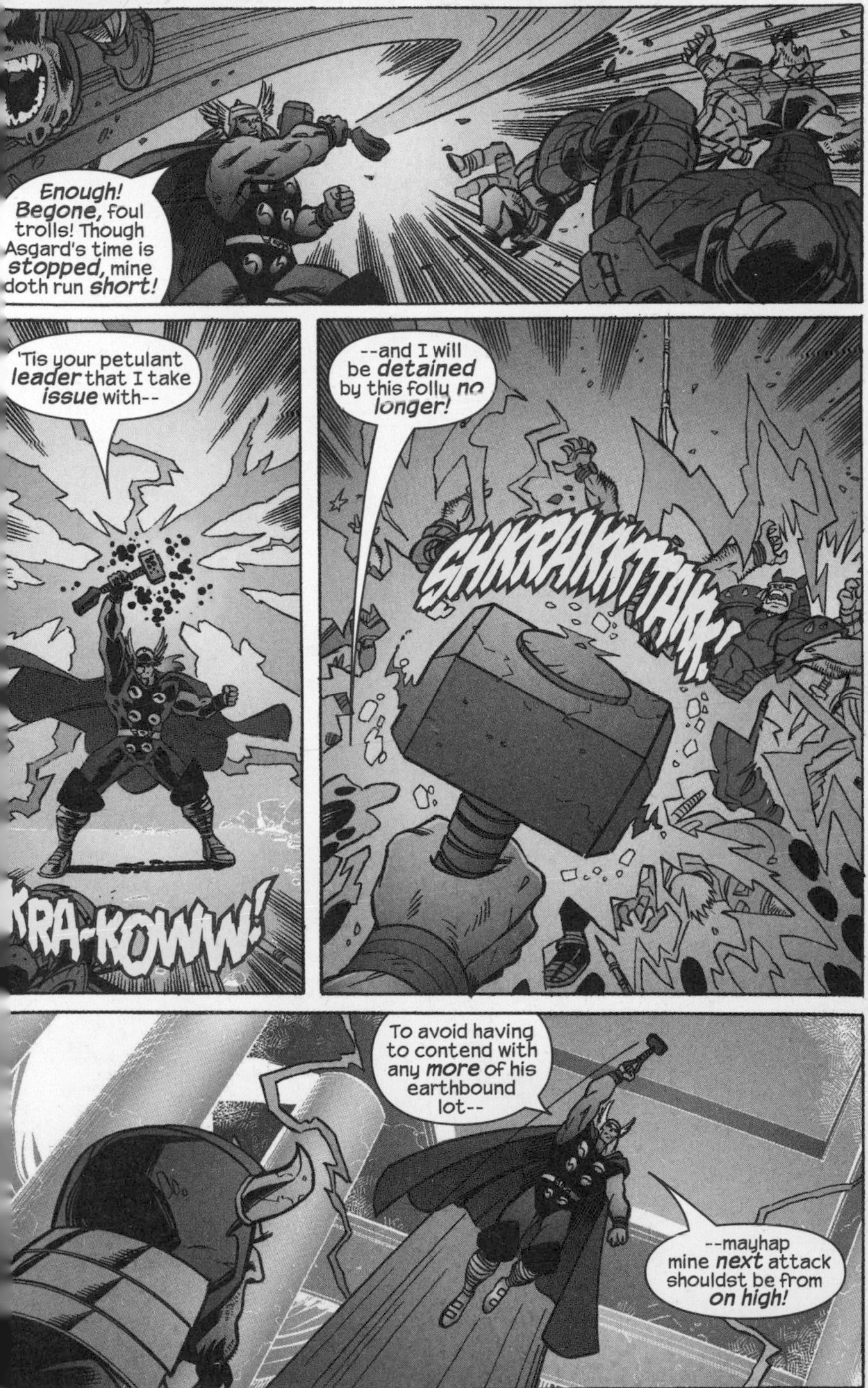
Enough! Begone, foul trolls! Though Asgard's time is stopped, mine doth run short!
'Tis your petulant leader that I take issue with--
KRA-KOWW!
--and I will be detained by this folly no longer!
SHKRAKKTAKK!
To avoid having to contend with any more of his earthbound lot--
--mayhap mine next attack shouldst be from on high!

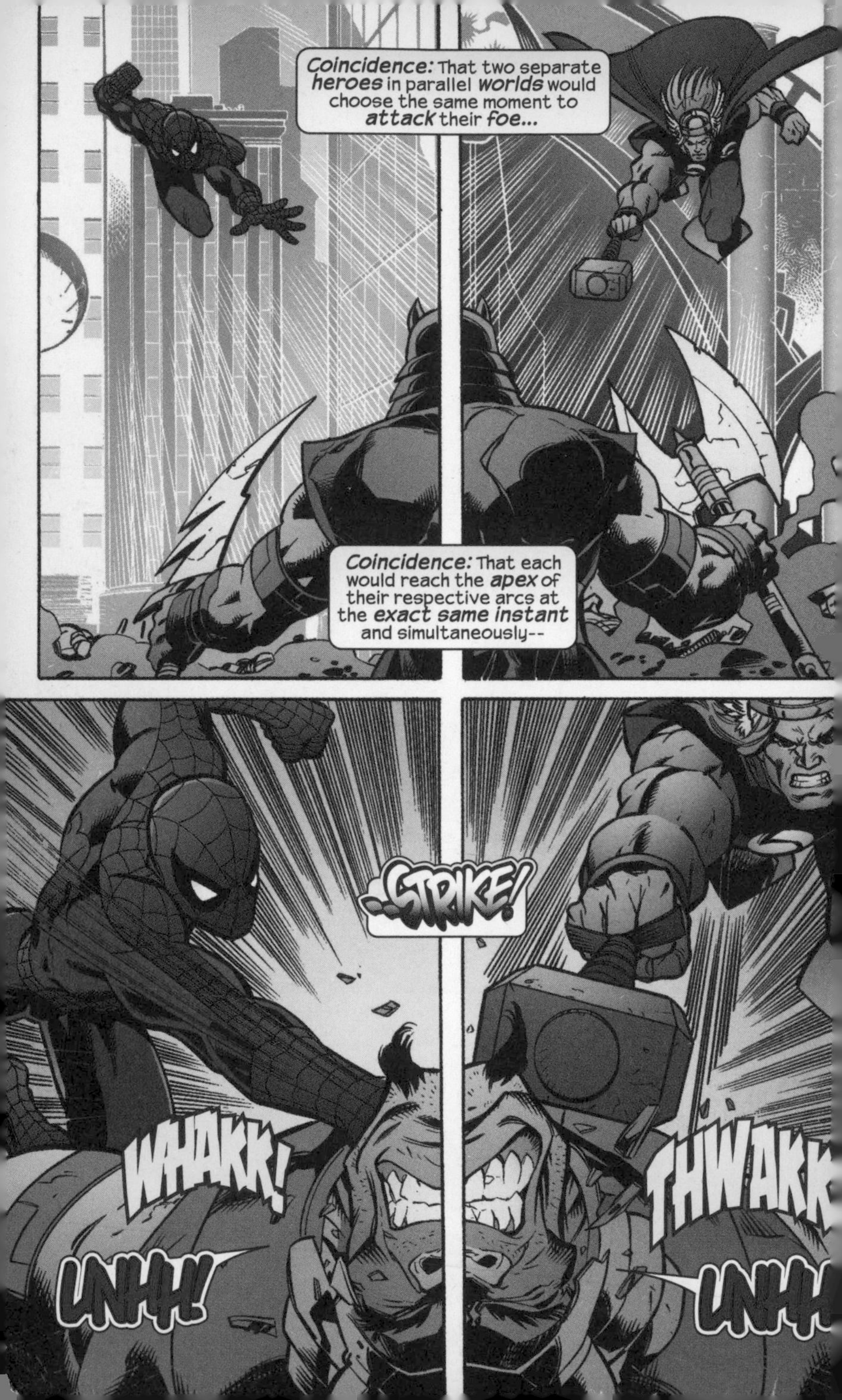

Coincidence: That two separate heroes in parallel worlds would choose the same moment to attack their foe...
Coincidence: That each would reach the apex of their respective arcs at the exact same instant and simultaneously--
STRIKE!
WHAKK!
THWAKK
UNHH!
UNHH

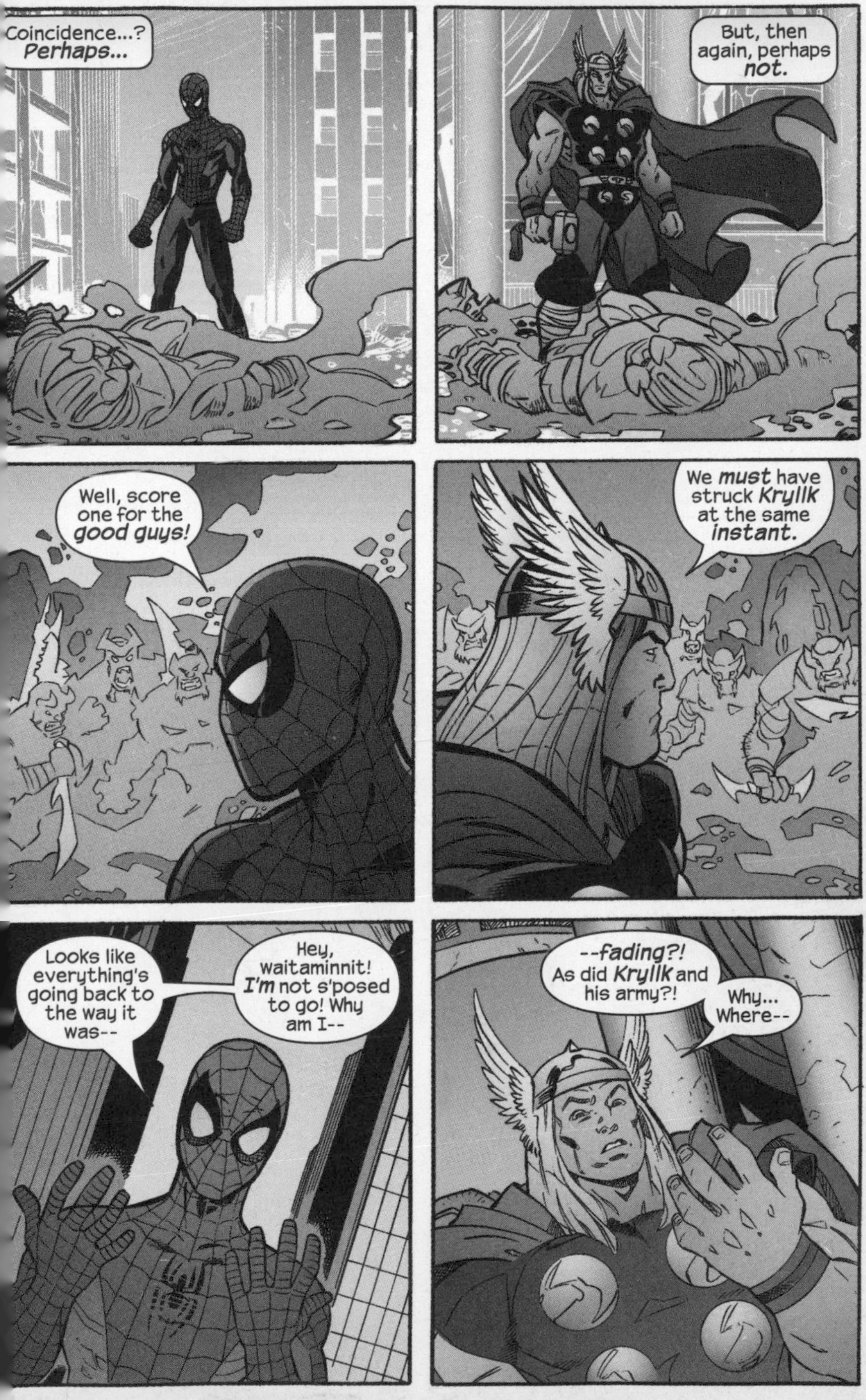
Coincidence...? Perhaps...
But, then again, perhaps not.
Well, score one for the good guys!
We must have struck Kryllk at the same instant.
Looks like everything's going back to the way it was--
Hey, waitaminnit! I'm not s'posed to go! Why am I--
--fading?! As did Kryllk and his army?!
Why... Where--

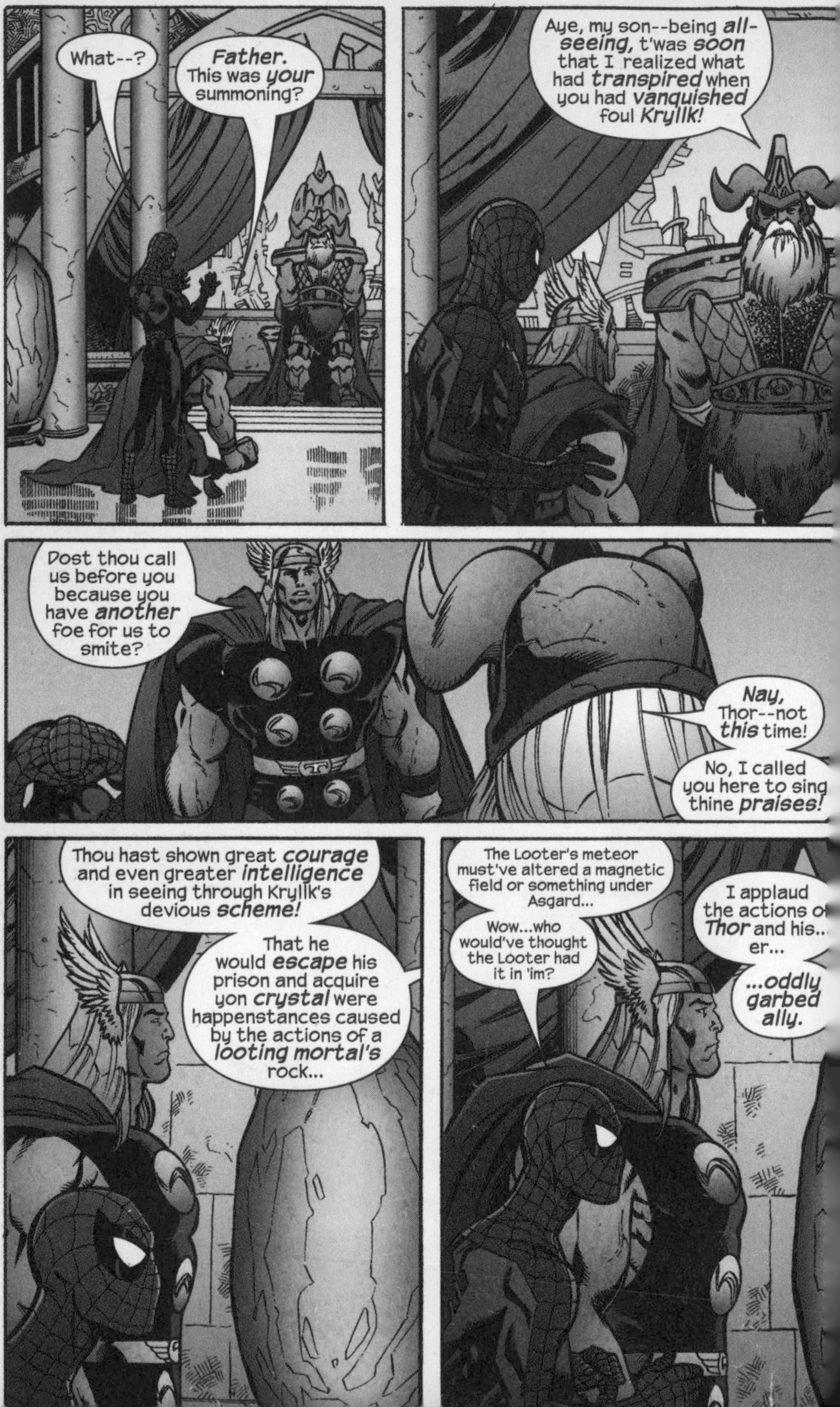
What--?
Father. This was your summoning?
Aye, my son--being all-seeing, t'was soon that I realized what had transpired when you had vanquished foul Kryllk!
Dost thou call us before you because you have another foe for us to smite?
Nay, Thor--not this time!
No, I called you here to sing thine praises!
Thou hast shown great courage and even greater intelligence in seeing through Kryllk's devious scheme!
That he would escape his prison and acquire yon crystal were happenstances caused by the actions of a looting mortal's rock...
The Looter's meteor must've altered a magnetic field or something under Asgard...
Wow...who would've thought the Looter had it in 'im?
I applaud the actions of Thor and his... er...
...oddly garbed ally.

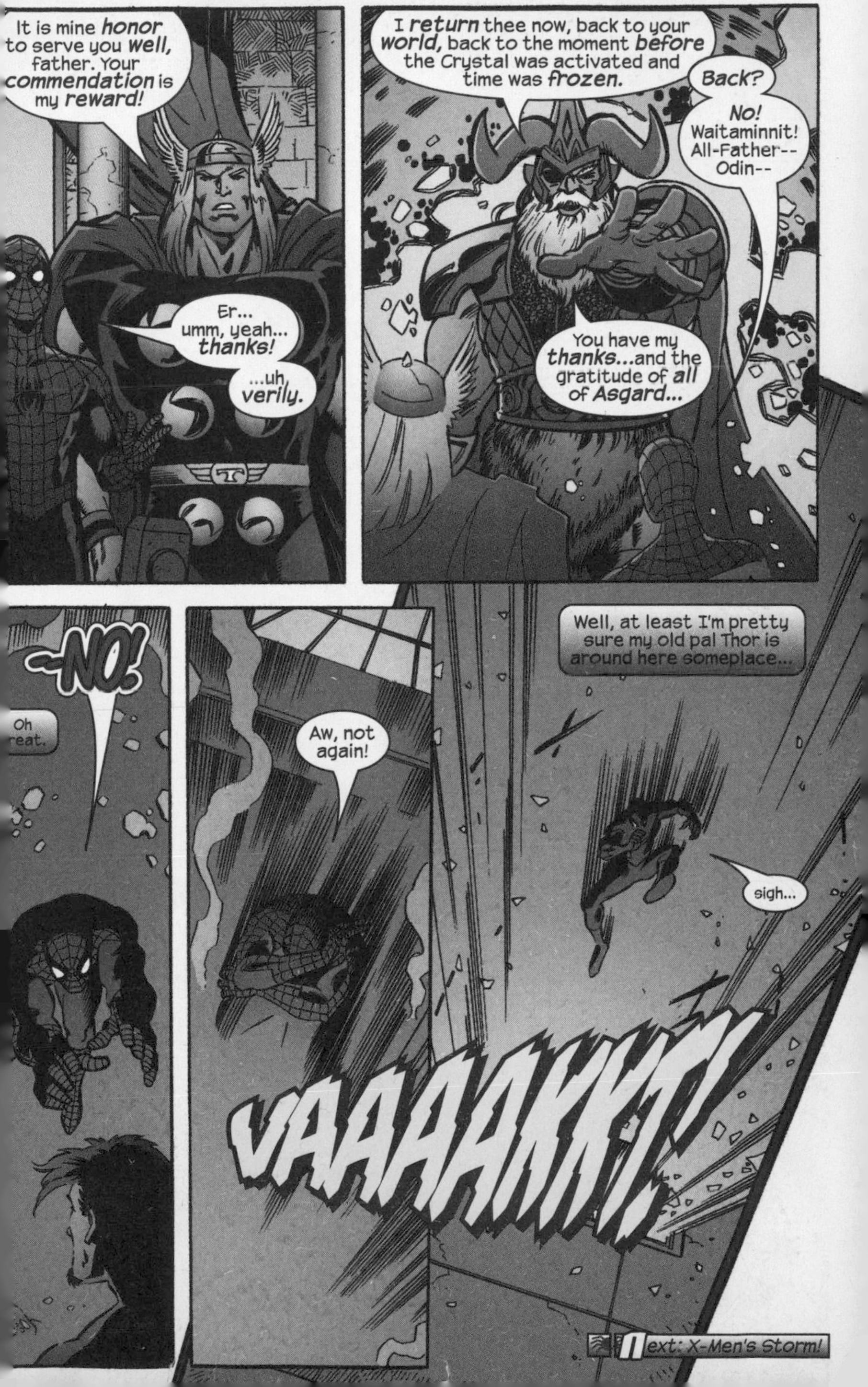

It is mine honor to serve you well, father. Your commendation is my reward!
Er... umm, yeah... thanks!
...uh verily.
I return thee now, back to your world, back to the moment before the Crystal was activated and time was frozen.
Back?
No! Waitaminnit! All-Father-- Odin--
You have my thanks...and the gratitude of all of Asgard...
--NO!
Oh reat.
Aw, not again!
Well, at least I'm pretty sure my old pal Thor is around here someplace...
sigh...
VAAAAKKT!
ext: X-Men's Storm!

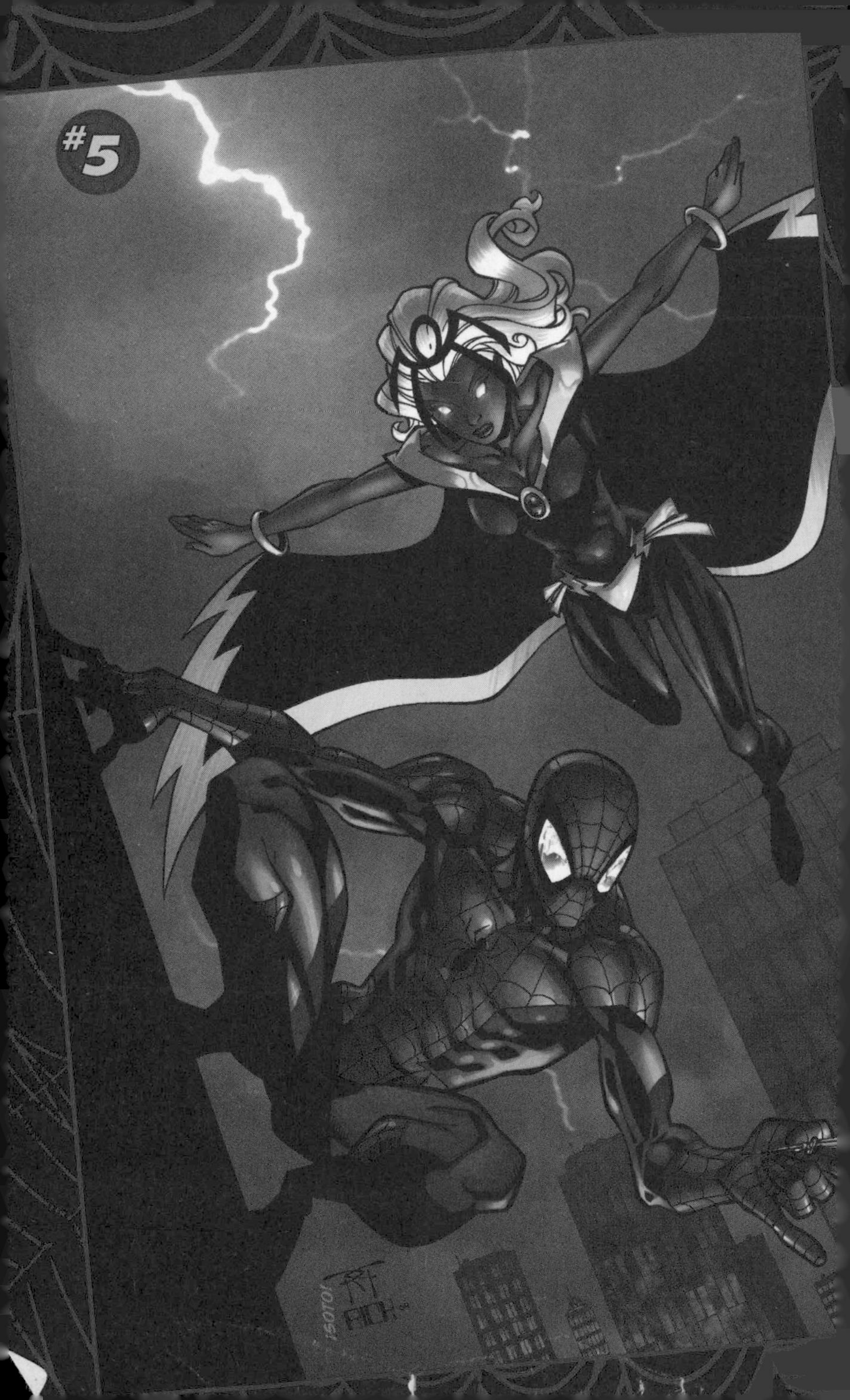
#5

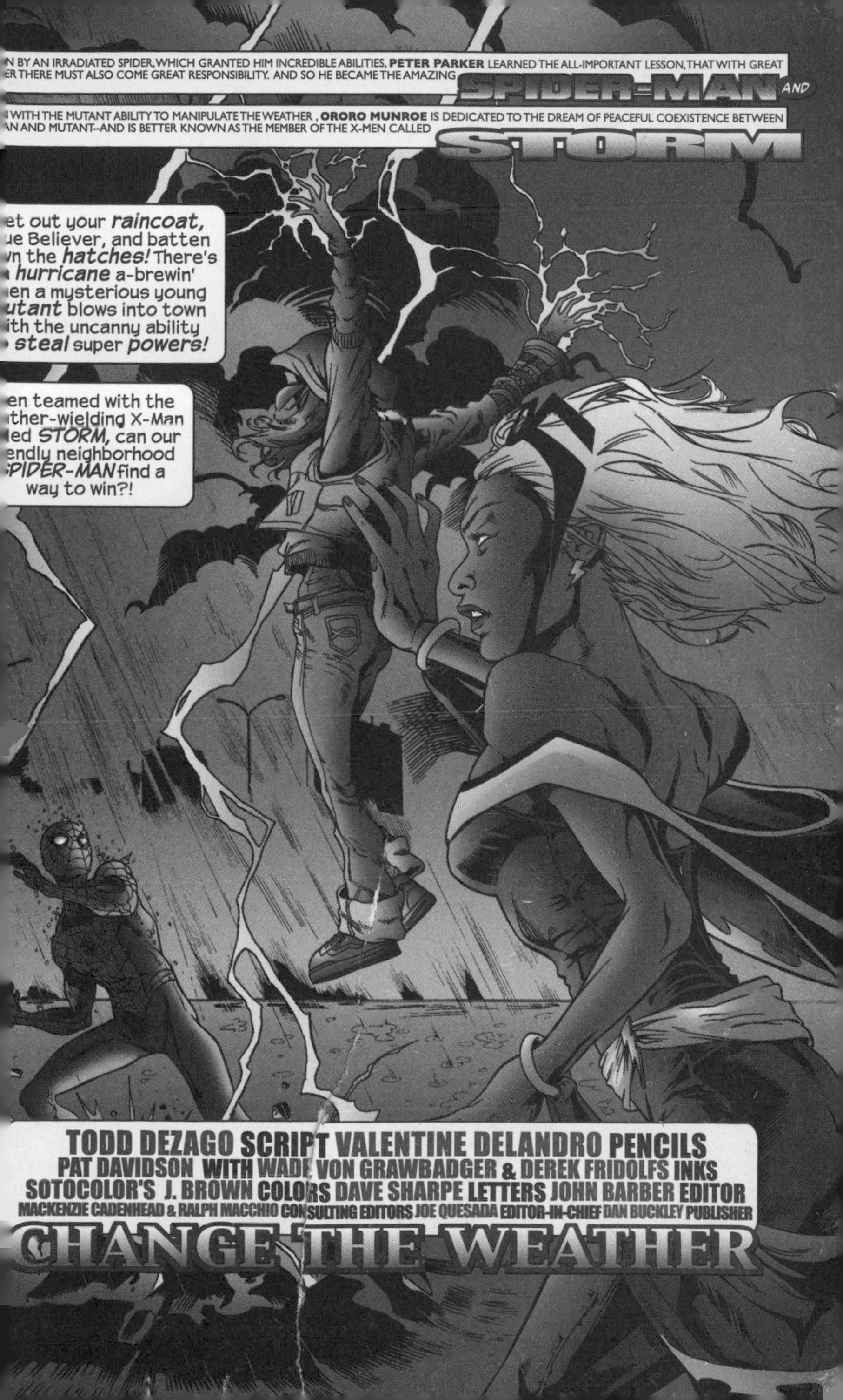
N BY AN IRRADIATED SPIDER, WHICH GRANTED HIM INCREDIBLE ABILITIES, PETER PARKER LEARNED THE ALL-IMPORTANT LESSON, THAT WITH GREAT
ER THERE MUST ALSO COME GREAT RESPONSIBILITY. AND SO HE BECAME THE AMAZING
SPIDER-MAN AND
N WITH THE MUTANT ABILITY TO MANIPULATE THE WEATHER, ORORO MUNROE IS DEDICATED TO THE DREAM OF PEACEFUL COEXISTENCE BETWEEN
AN AND MUTANT--AND IS BETTER KNOWN AS THE MEMBER OF THE X-MEN CALLED
STORM
et out your raincoat, ue Believer, and batten wn the hatches! There's hurricane a-brewin' en a mysterious young utant blows into town ith the uncanny ability steal super powers!
en teamed with the ther-wielding X-Man led STORM, can our endly neighborhood SPIDER-MAN find a way to win?!
TODD DEZAGO SCRIPT VALENTINE DELANDRO PENCILS
PAT DAVIDSON WITH WADE VON GRAWBADGER & DEREK FRIDOLFS INKS
SOTOCOLOR'S J. BROWN COLORS DAVE SHARPE LETTERS JOHN BARBER EDITOR
MACKENZIE CADENHEAD & RALPH MACCHIO CONSULTING EDITORS JOE QUESADA EDITOR-IN-CHIEF DAN BUCKLEY PUBLISHER
CHANGE THE WEATHER

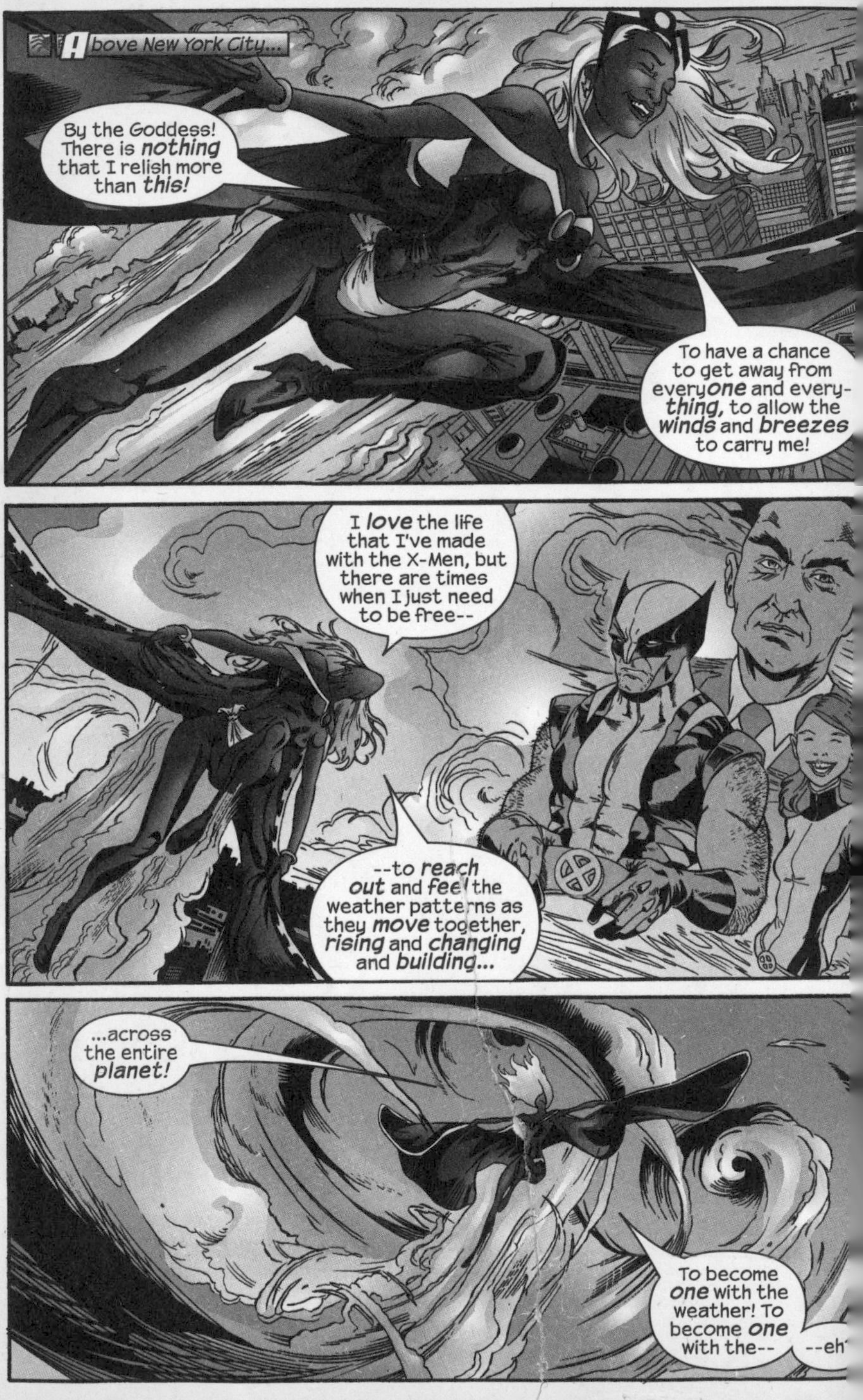
Above New York City...
By the Goddess! There is nothing that I relish more than this!
To have a chance to get away from everyone and everything, to allow the winds and breezes to carry me!
I love the life that I've made with the X-Men, but there are times when I just need to be free--
--to reach out and feel the weather patterns as they move together, rising and changing and building...
...across the entire planet!
To become one with the weather! To become one with the--
--eh

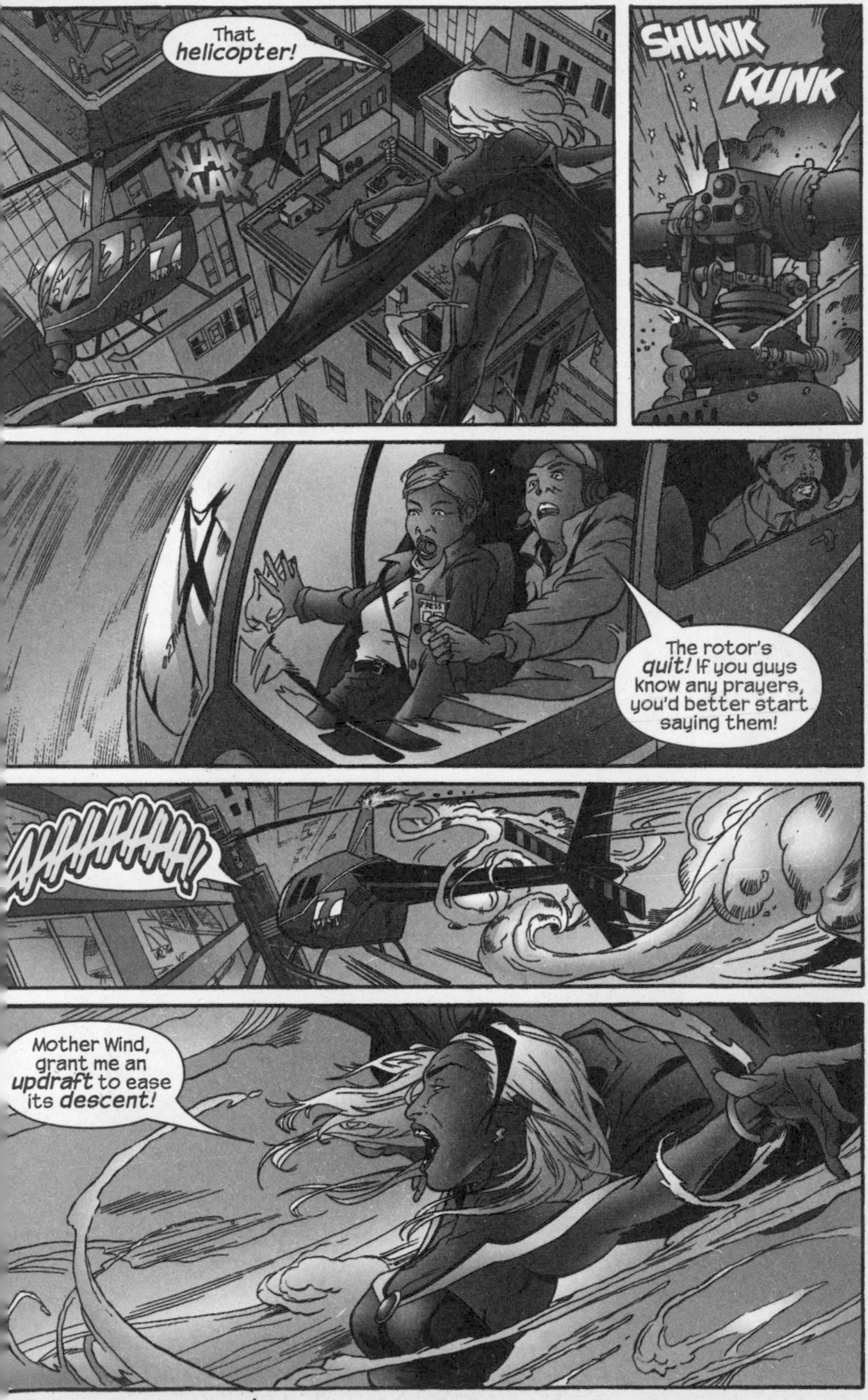
That helicopter!
KLAK-KLAK
SHUNK
KUNK
The rotor's quit! If you guys know any prayers, you'd better start saying them!
AAAAAAAAH!
Mother Wind, grant me an updraft to ease its descent!

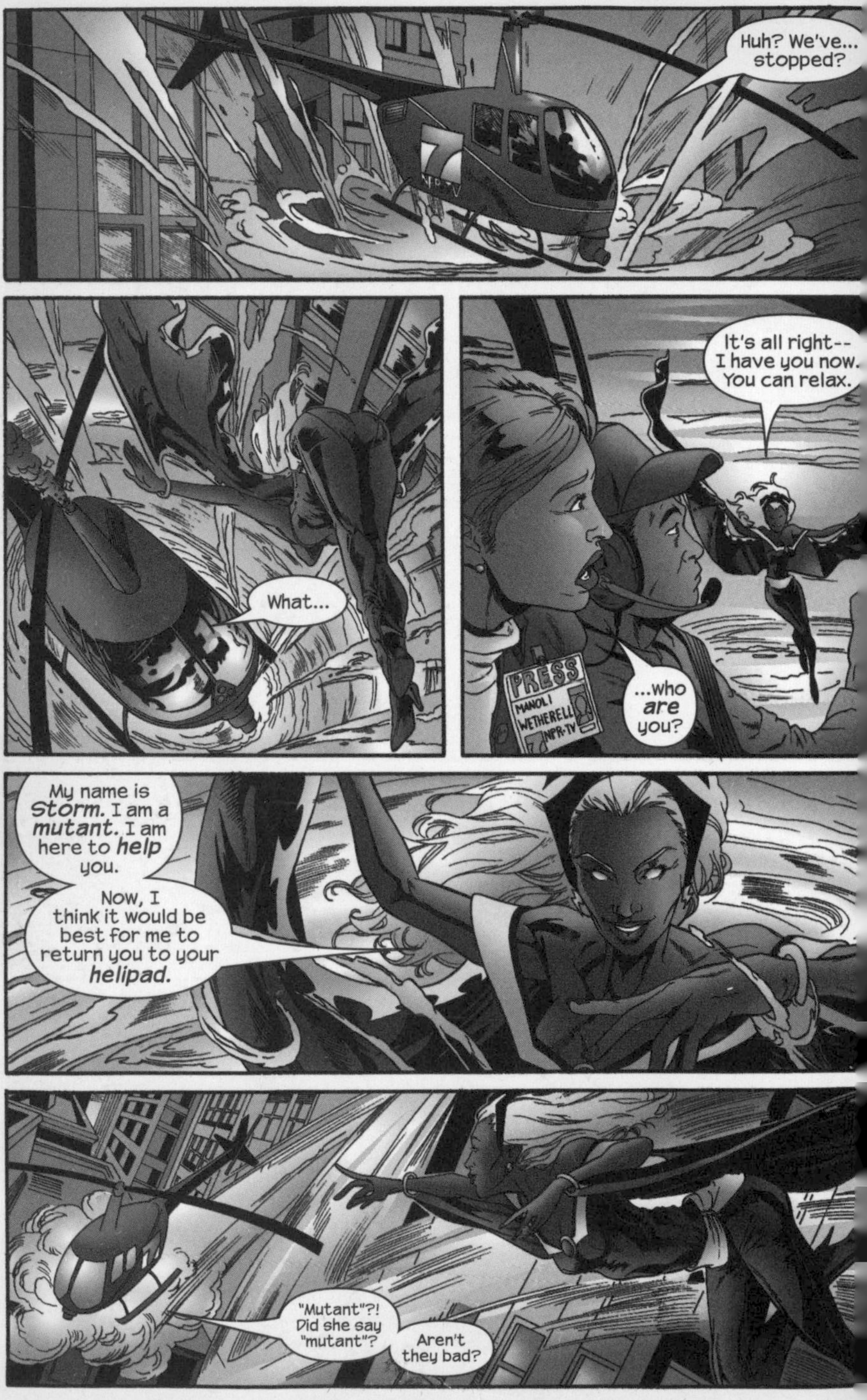
Huh? We've... stopped?
What...
It's all right-- I have you now. You can relax.
PRESS MANOLI WETHERELL NPR-TV
...who are you?
My name is Storm. I am a mutant. I am here to help you.
Now, I think it would be best for me to return you to your helipad.
"Mutant"?! Did she say "mutant"?
Aren't they bad?

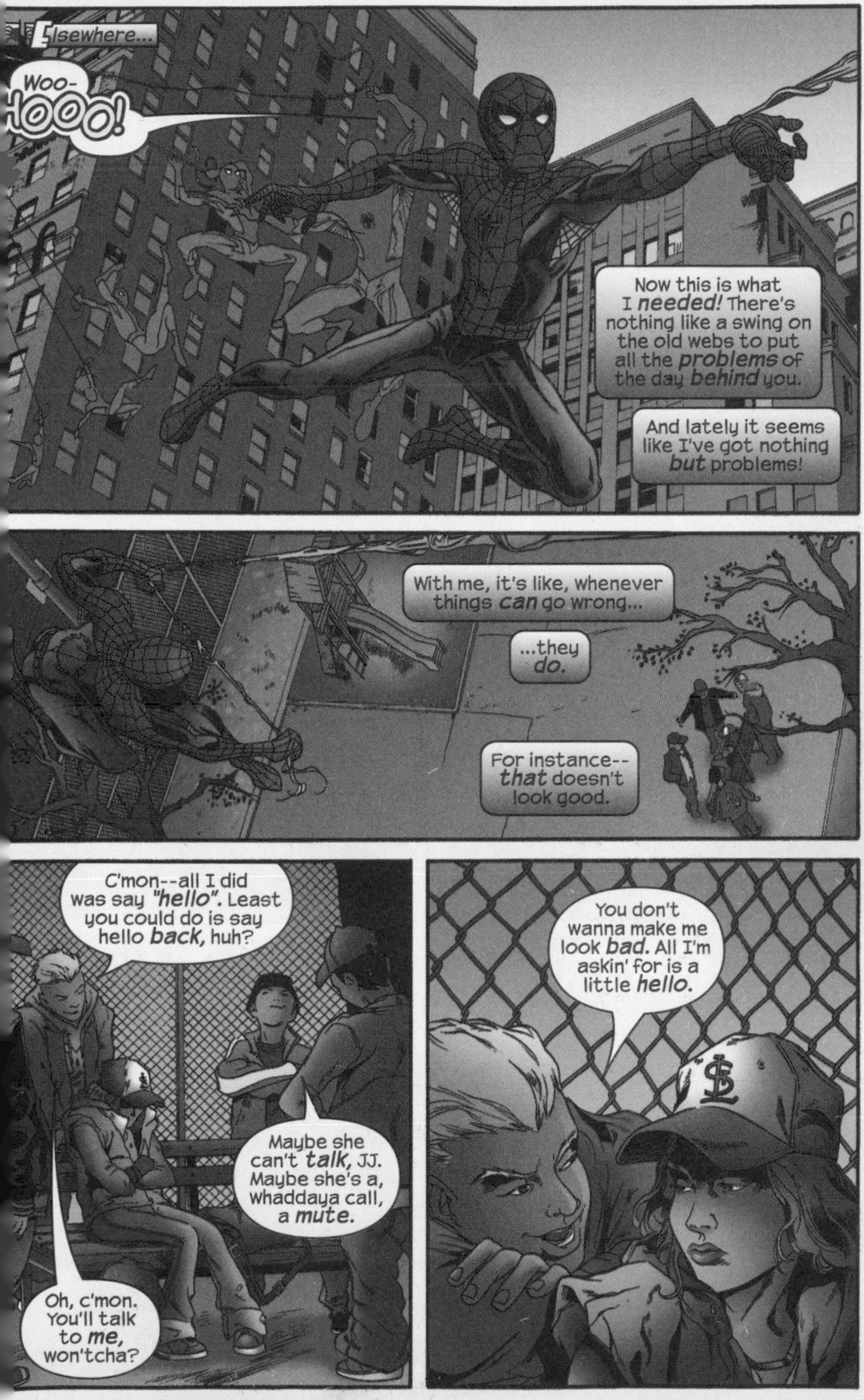
Elsewhere...
Woo-HOOO!
Now this is what I needed! There's nothing like a swing on the old webs to put all the problems of the day behind you.
And lately it seems like I've got nothing but problems!
With me, it's like, whenever things can go wrong...
...they do.
For instance--that doesn't look good.
C'mon--all I did was say "hello". Least you could do is say hello back, huh?
Maybe she can't talk, JJ. Maybe she's a, whaddaya call, a mute.
Oh, c'mon. You'll talk to me, won'tcha?
You don't wanna make me look bad. All I'm askin' for is a little hello.

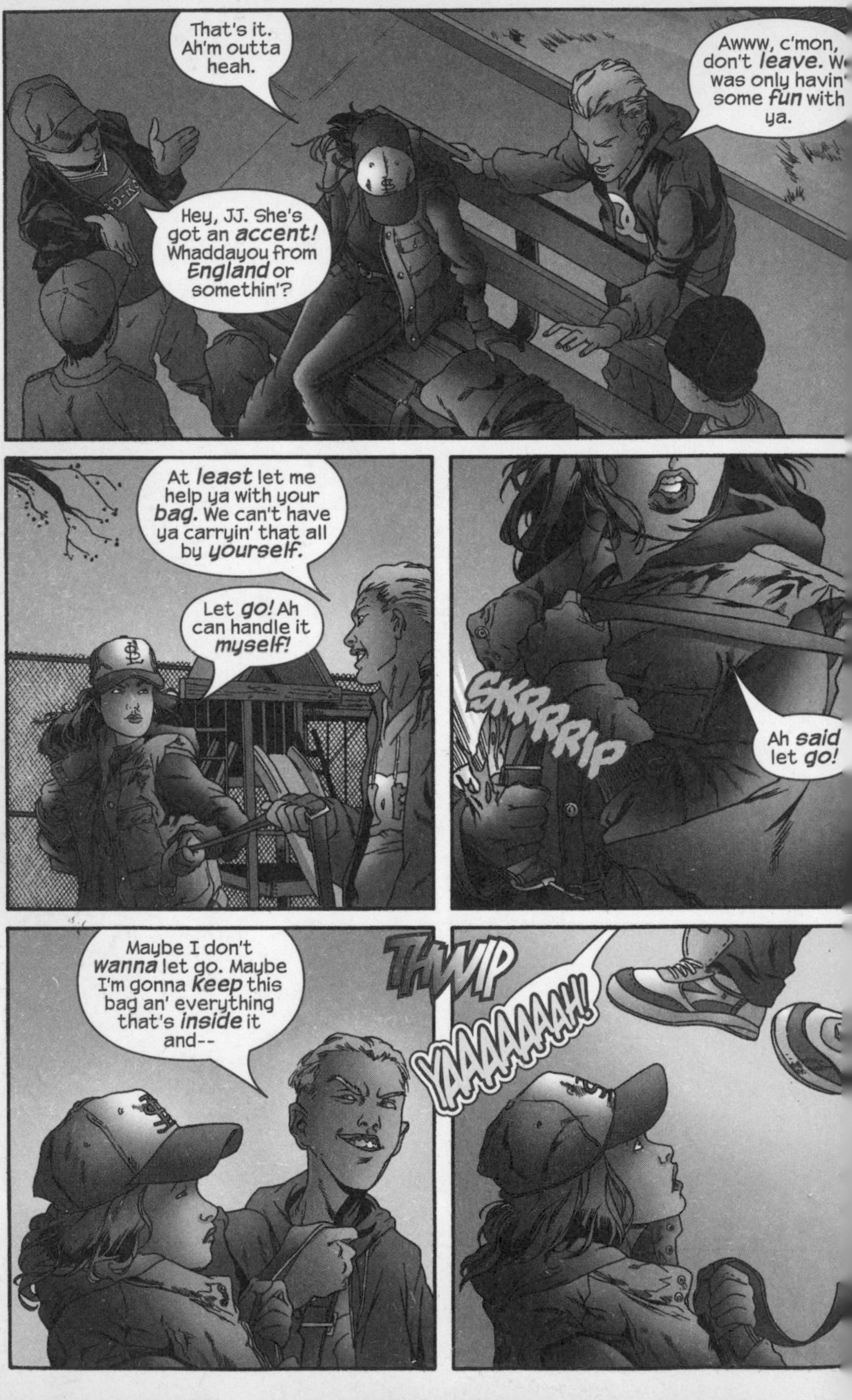
That's it. Ah'm outta heah.
Awww, c'mon, don't leave. We was only havin' some fun with ya.
Hey, JJ. She's got an accent! Whaddayou from England or somethin'?
At least let me help ya with your bag. We can't have ya carryin' that all by yourself.
Let go! Ah can handle it myself!
SKRRRIP
Ah said let go!
Maybe I don't wanna let go. Maybe I'm gonna keep this bag an' everything that's inside it and--
THWIP
YAAAAAAH!

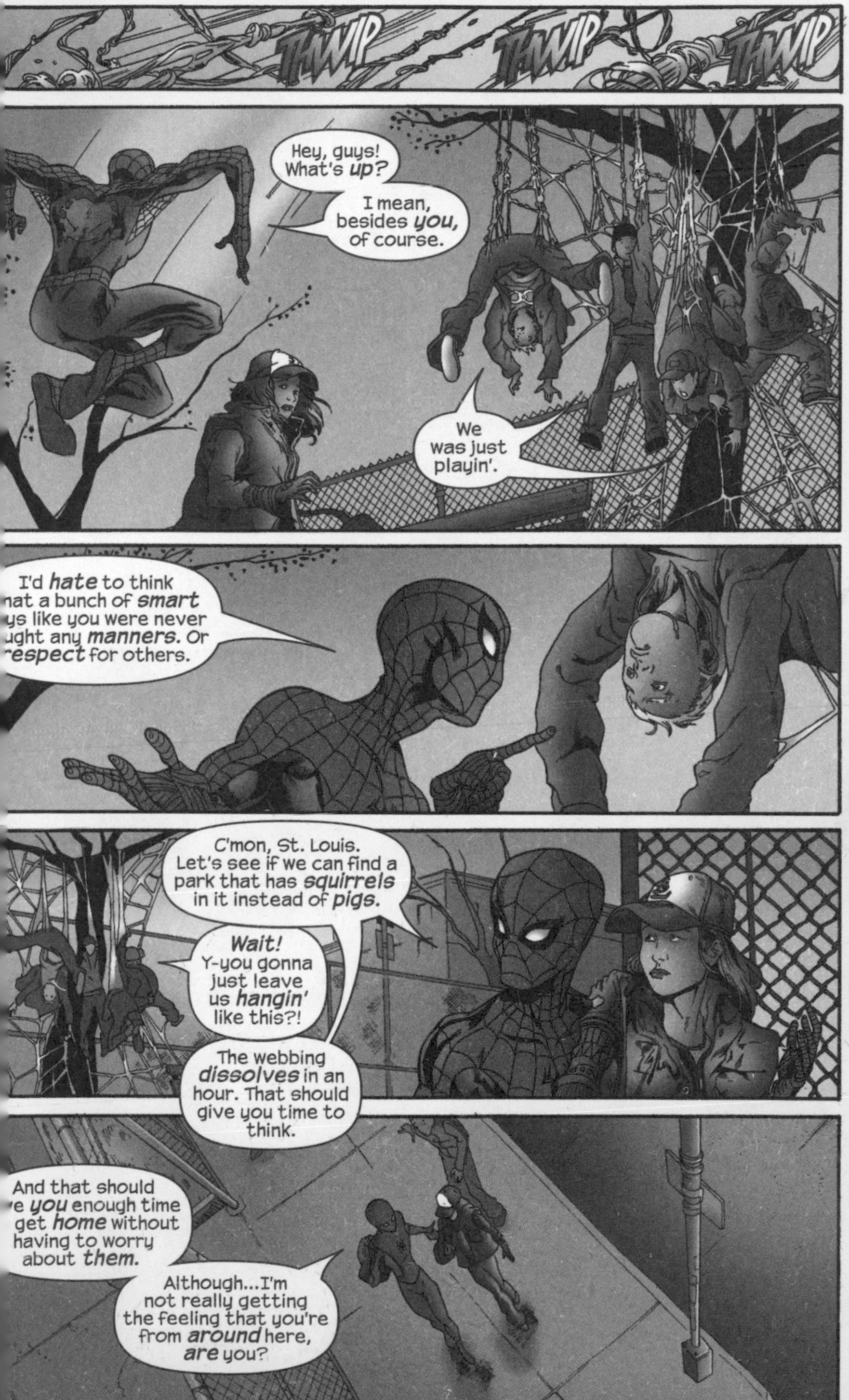

THWIP THWIP THWIP
Hey, guys! What's *up?*
I mean, besides *you,* of course.
We was just playin'.
I'd *hate* to think
hat a bunch of *smart*
ys like you were never
ught any *manners.* Or
respect for others.
C'mon, St. Louis. Let's see if we can find a park that has *squirrels* in it instead of *pigs.*
Wait! Y-you gonna just leave us *hangin'* like this?!
The webbing *dissolves* in an hour. That should give you time to think.
And that should
e *you* enough time
get *home* without
having to worry
about *them.*
Although...I'm not really getting the feeling that you're from *around* here, *are* you?

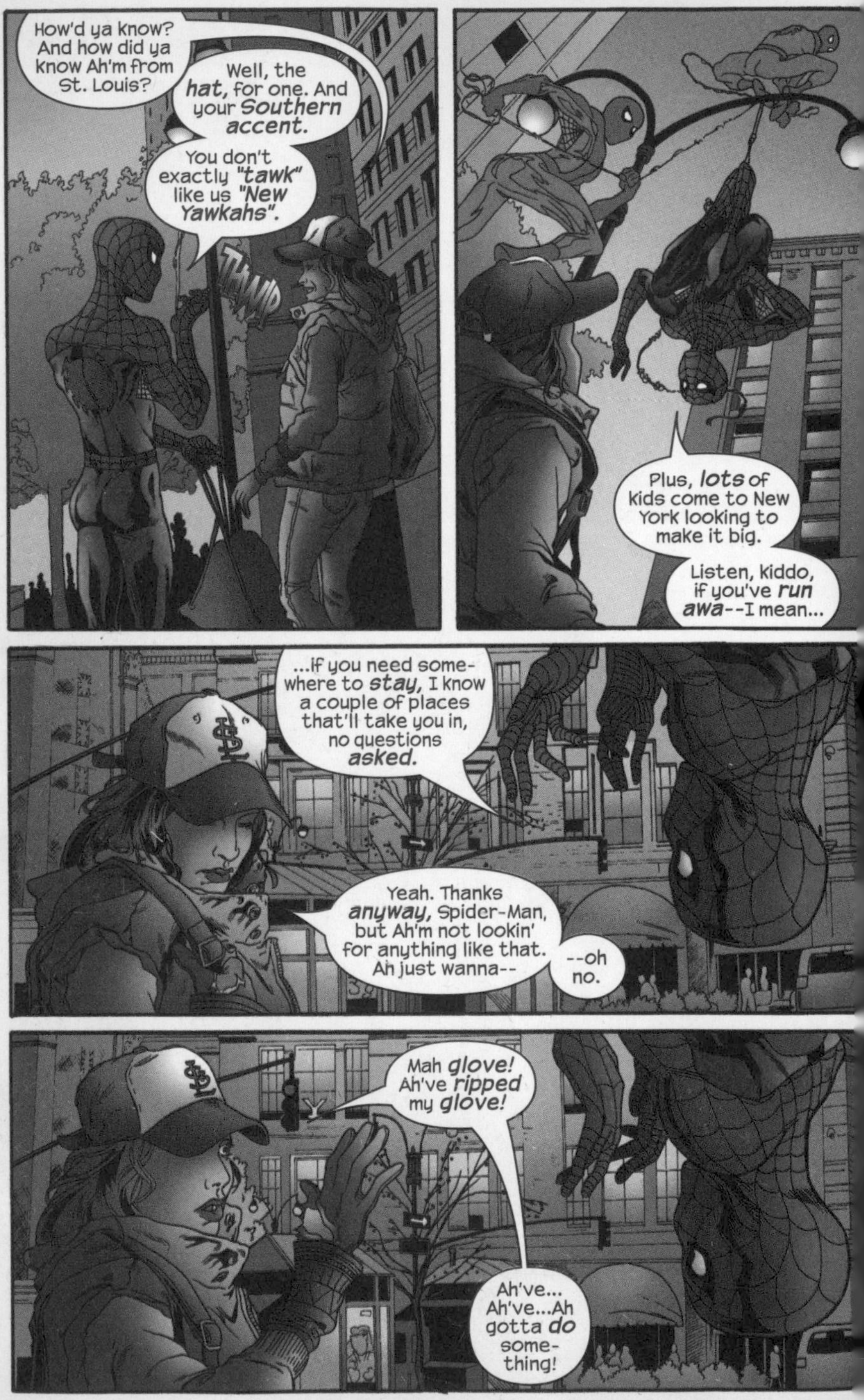
How'd ya know? And how did ya know Ah'm from St. Louis?
Well, the hat, for one. And your Southern accent.
You don't exactly "tawk" like us "New Yawkahs".
THAMP
Plus, lots of kids come to New York looking to make it big.
Listen, kiddo, if you've run awa--I mean...
...if you need somewhere to stay, I know a couple of places that'll take you in, no questions asked.
Yeah. Thanks anyway, Spider-Man, but Ah'm not lookin' for anything like that. Ah just wanna--
--oh no.
Mah glove! Ah've ripped my glove!
Ah've... Ah've...Ah gotta do something!

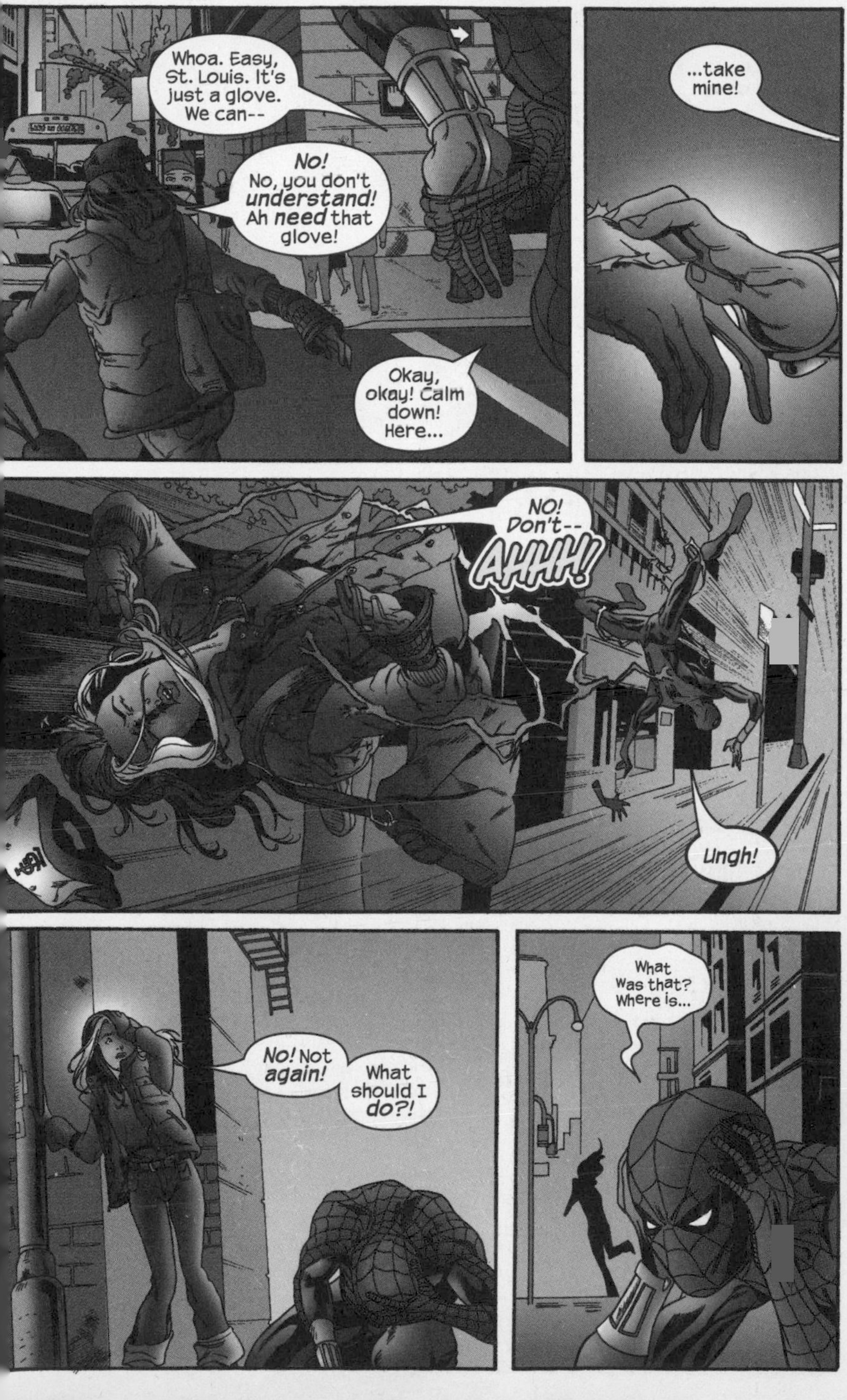
Whoa. Easy, St. Louis. It's just a glove. We can--
No! No, you don't understand! Ah need that glove!
Okay, okay! Calm down! Here...
...take mine!
NO! Don't--
AHHH!
Ungh!
No! Not again!
What should I do?!
What was that? Where is...

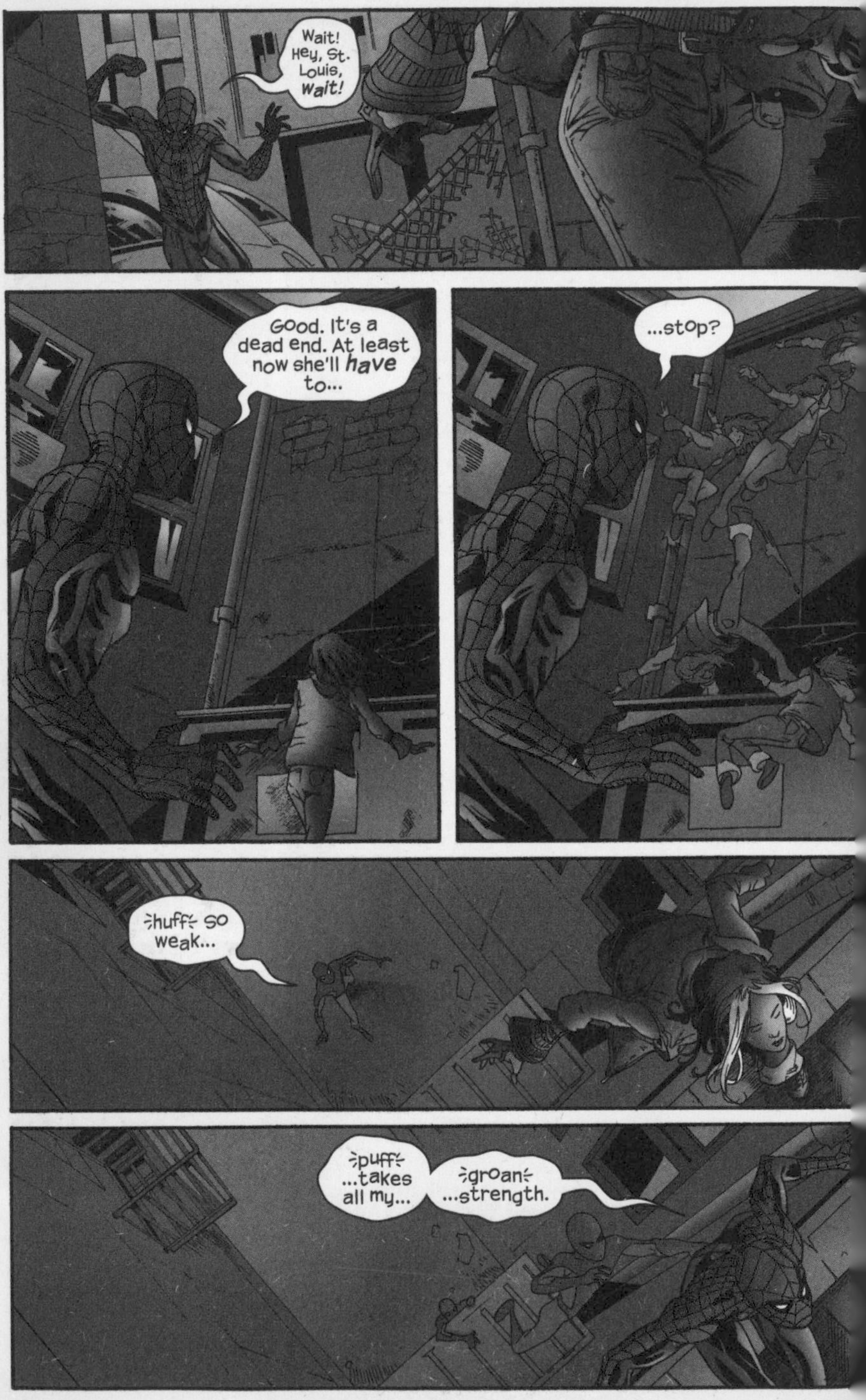
Wait! Hey, St. Louis, Wait!
Good. It's a dead end. At least now she'll have to...
...stop?
-huff- so weak...
-puff- ...takes all my...
-groan- ...strength.

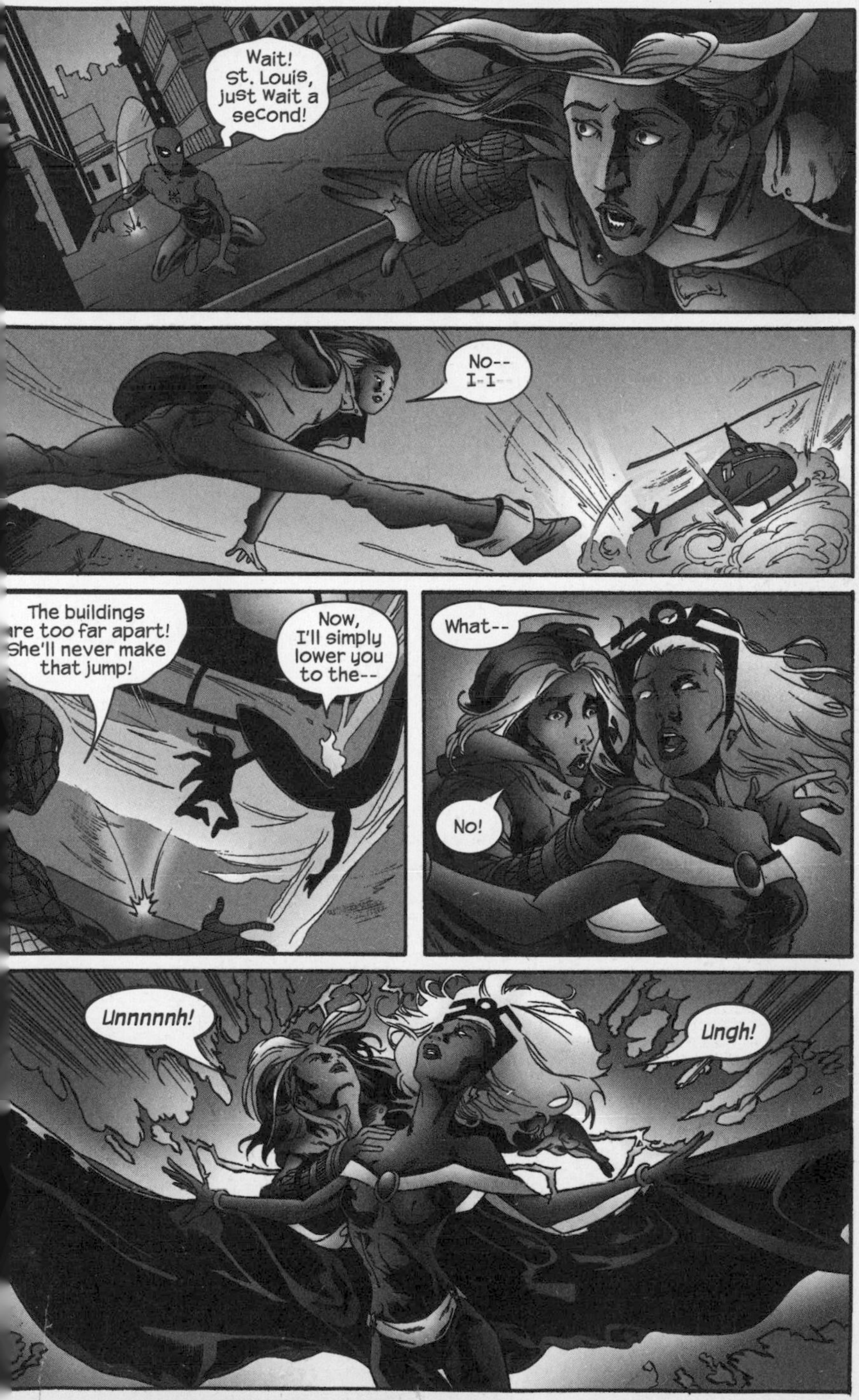
Wait!
St. Louis, just wait a second!
No-- I-I--
The buildings are too far apart! She'll never make that jump!
Now, I'll simply lower you to the--
What--
No!
Unnnnnh!
Ungh!

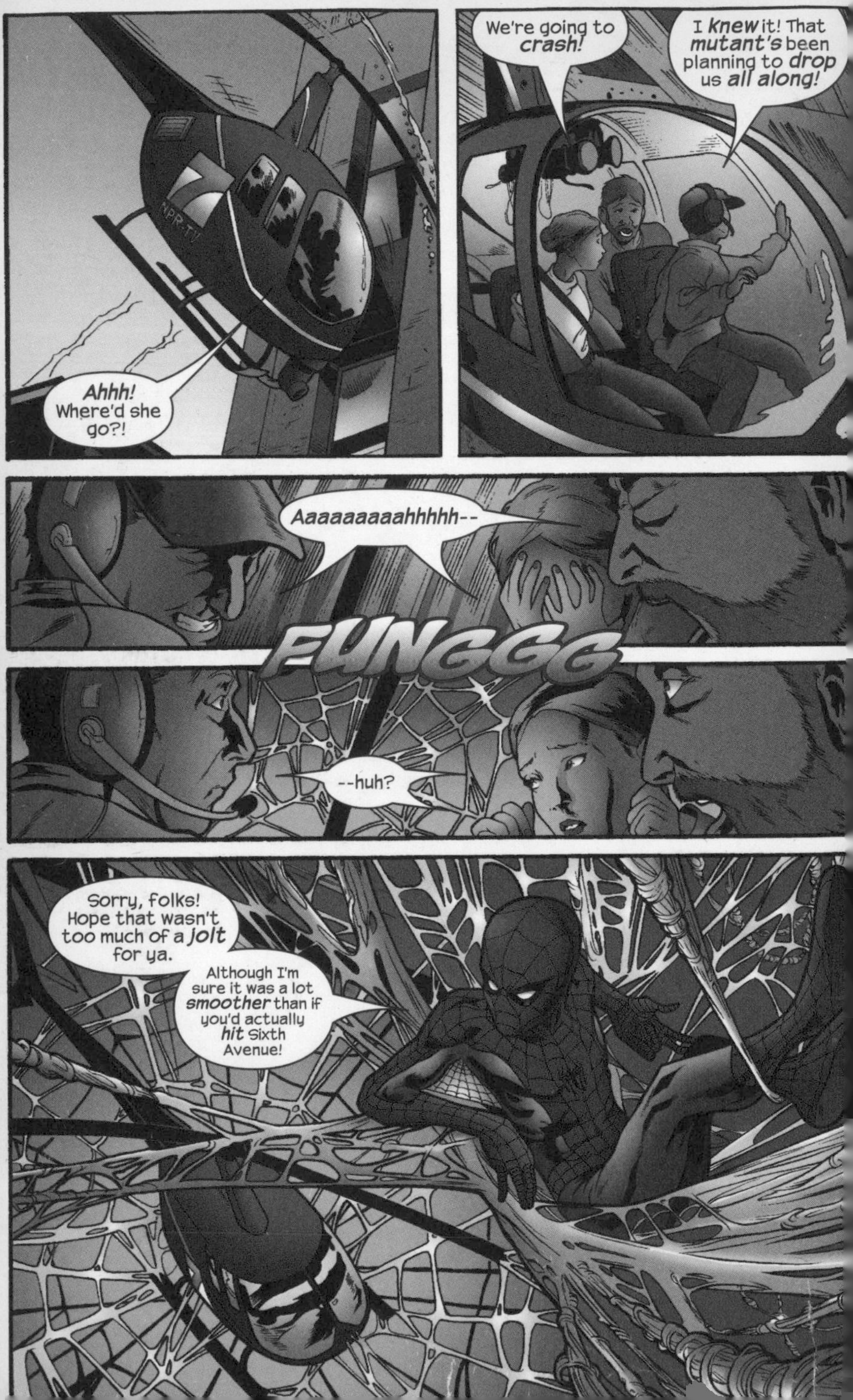
Ahhh! Where'd she go?!
We're going to crash!
I knew it! That mutant's been planning to drop us all along!
Aaaaaaaaahhhhh--
FLUNGGG
--huh?
Sorry, folks! Hope that wasn't too much of a jolt for ya.
Although I'm sure it was a lot smoother than if you'd actually hit Sixth Avenue!

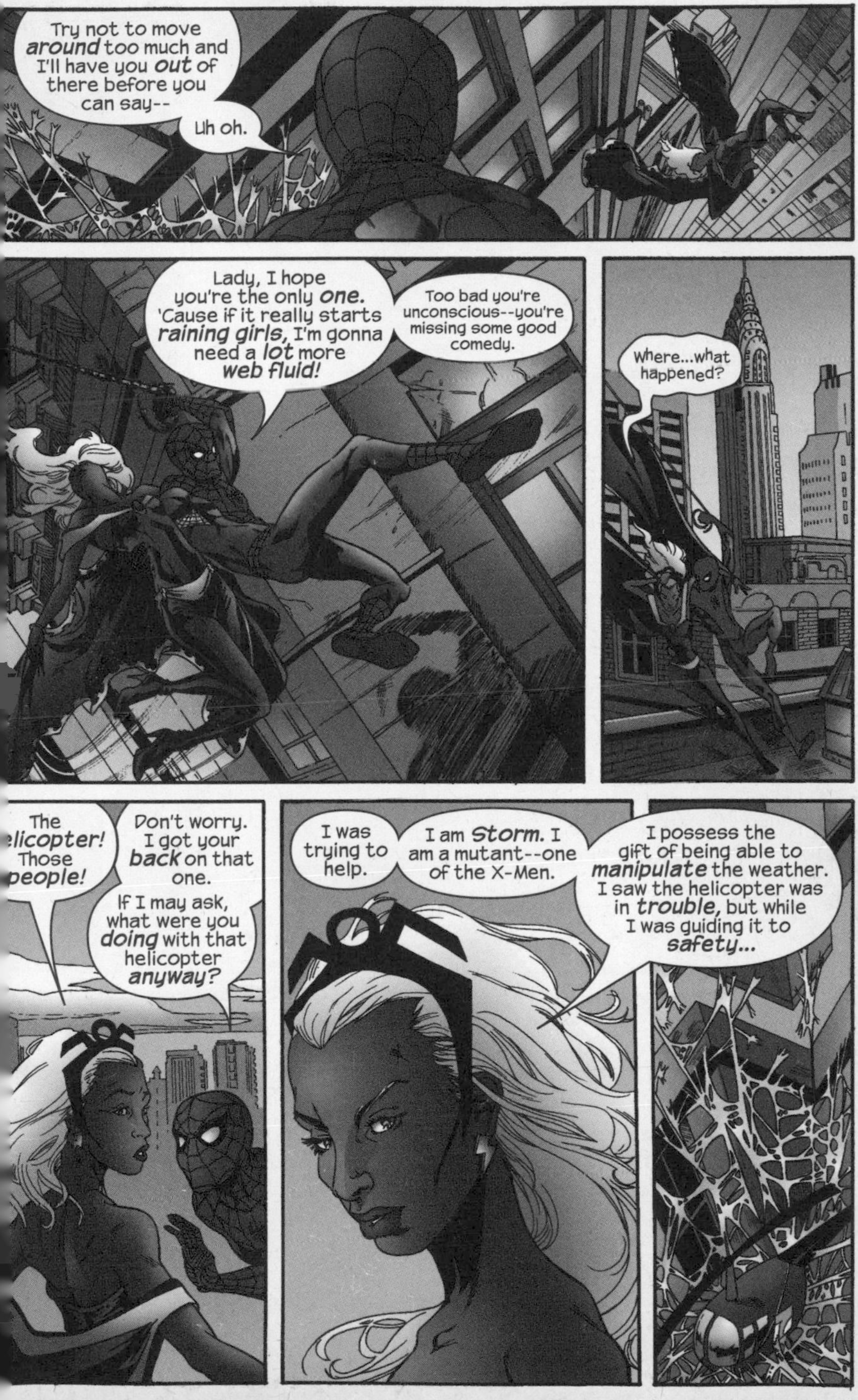

Try not to move around too much and I'll have you out of there before you can say--
Uh oh.
Lady, I hope you're the only one. 'Cause if it really starts raining girls, I'm gonna need a lot more web fluid!
Too bad you're unconscious--you're missing some good comedy.
Where...what happened?
The elicopter! Those people!
Don't worry. I got your back on that one.
If I may ask, what were you doing with that helicopter anyway?
I was trying to help.
I am Storm. I am a mutant--one of the X-Men.
I possess the gift of being able to manipulate the weather. I saw the helicopter was in trouble, but while I was guiding it to safety...

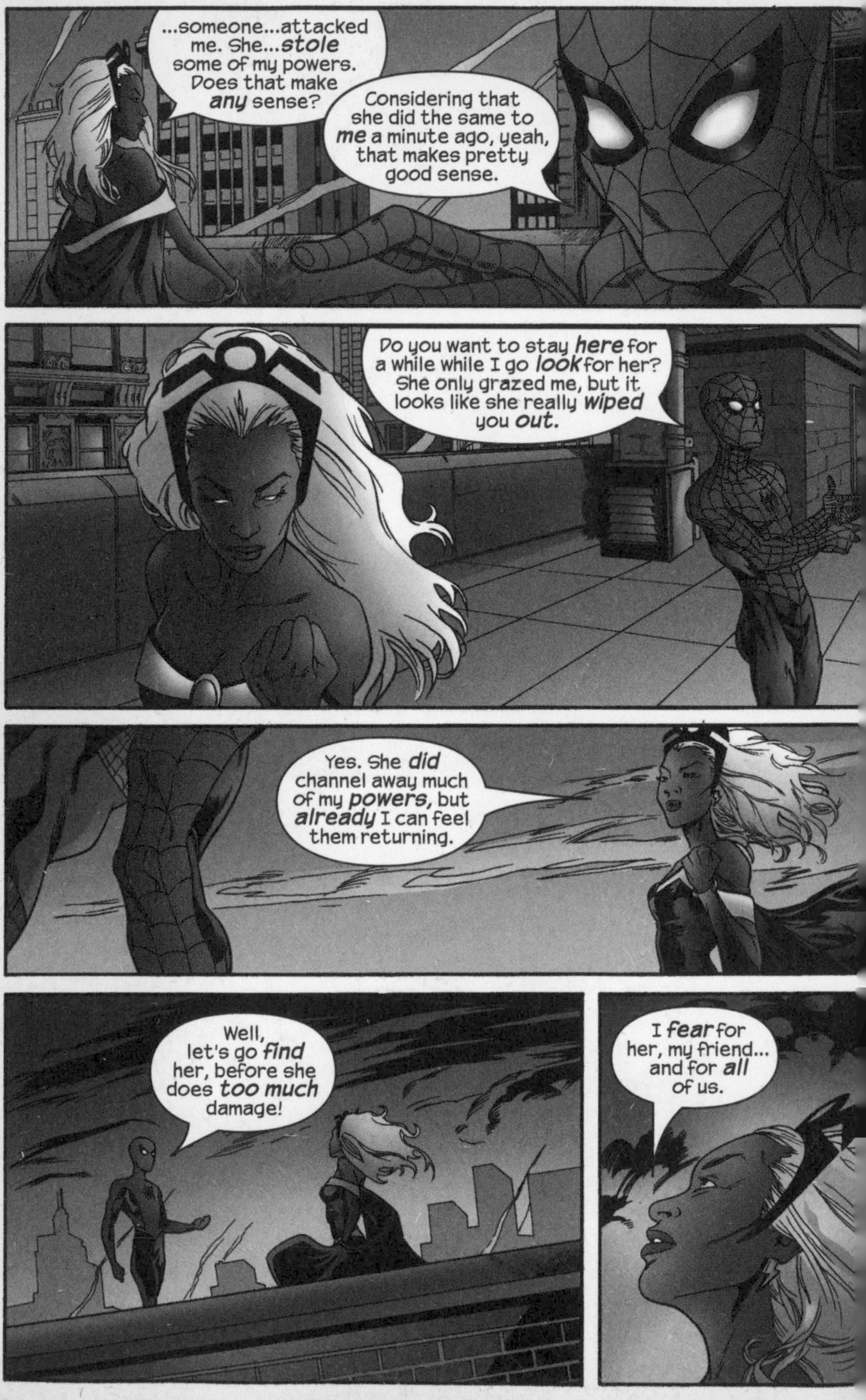

...someone...attacked me. She...stole some of my powers. Does that make any sense?
Considering that she did the same to me a minute ago, yeah, that makes pretty good sense.
Do you want to stay here for a while while I go look for her? She only grazed me, but it looks like she really wiped you out.
Yes. She did channel away much of my powers, but already I can feel them returning.
Well, let's go find her, before she does too much damage!
I fear for her, my friend... and for all of us.

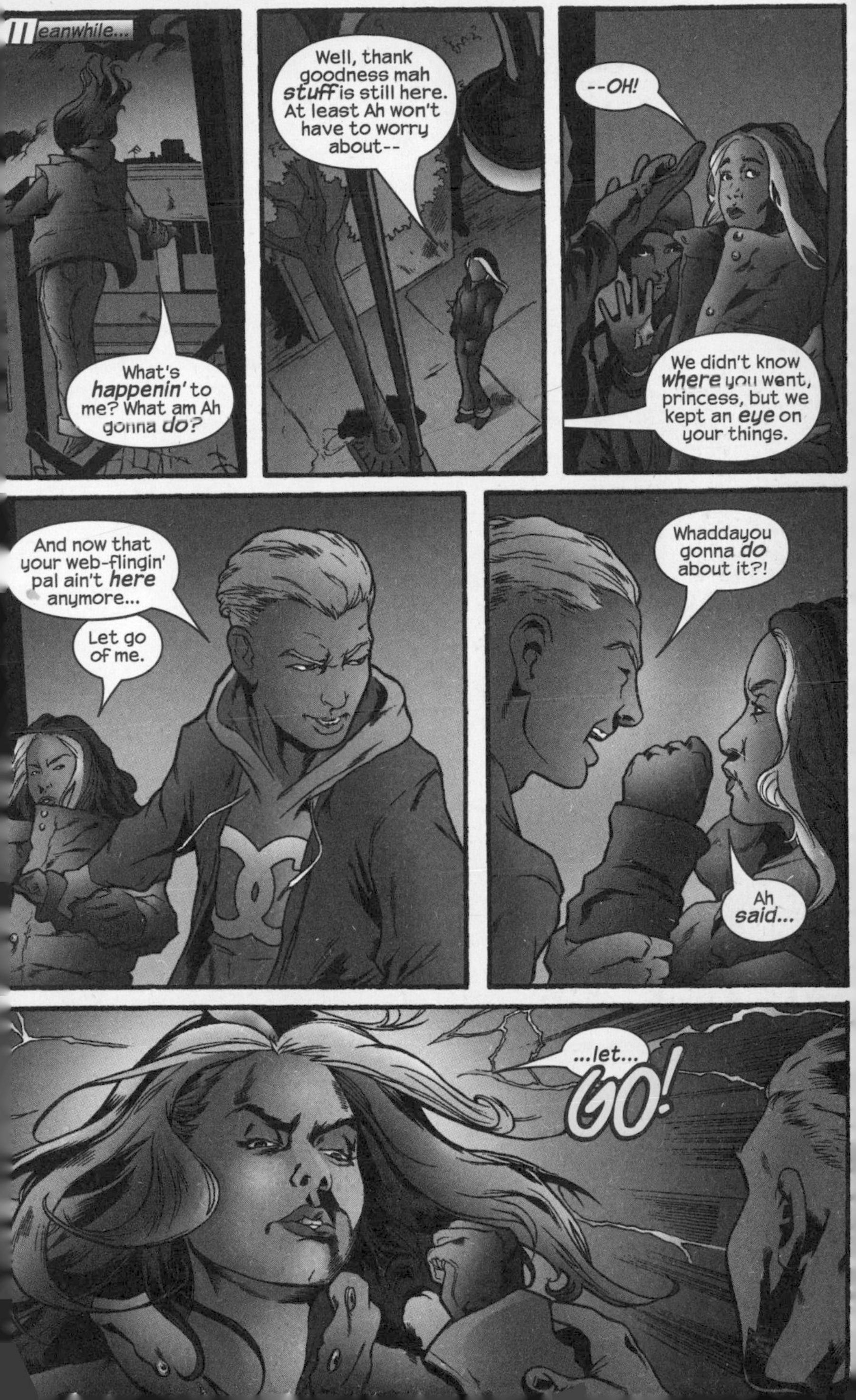
Meanwhile...
What's happenin' to me? What am Ah gonna do?
Well, thank goodness mah stuff is still here. At least Ah won't have to worry about--
--OH!
We didn't know where you went, princess, but we kept an eye on your things.
And now that your web-flingin' pal ain't here anymore...
Let go of me.
Whaddayou gonna do about it?!
Ah said...
...let...
GO!

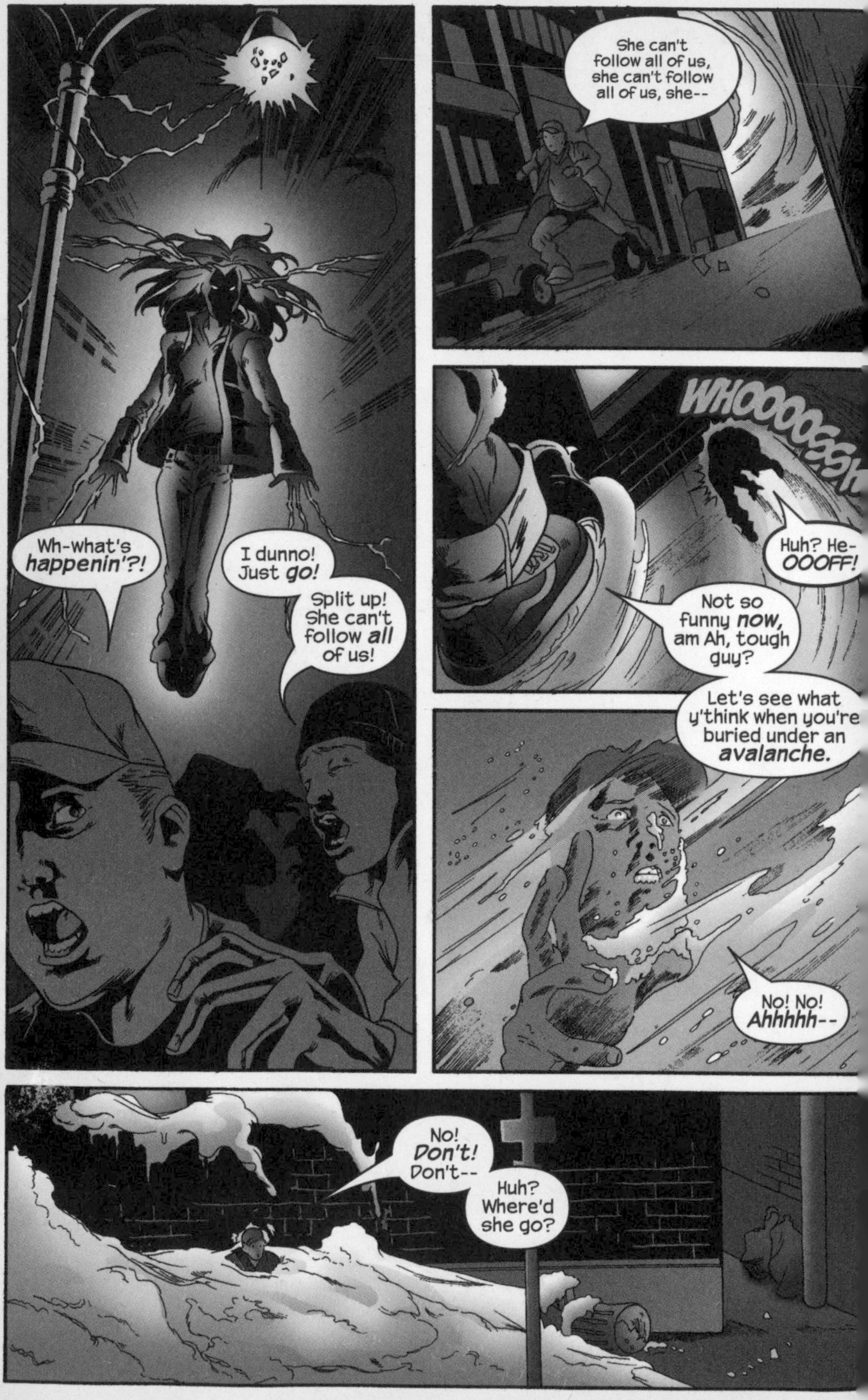
Wh-what's *happenin'*?!
I dunno! Just *go!*
Split up! She can't follow *all* of us!
She can't follow all of us, she can't follow all of us, she--
WHOOOOOSSSH
Huh? He- *OOOFF!*
Not so funny *now,* am Ah, tough guy?
Let's see what y'think when you're buried under an *avalanche.*
No! No! *Ahhhhh*--
No! *Don't!* Don't--
Huh? Where'd she go?

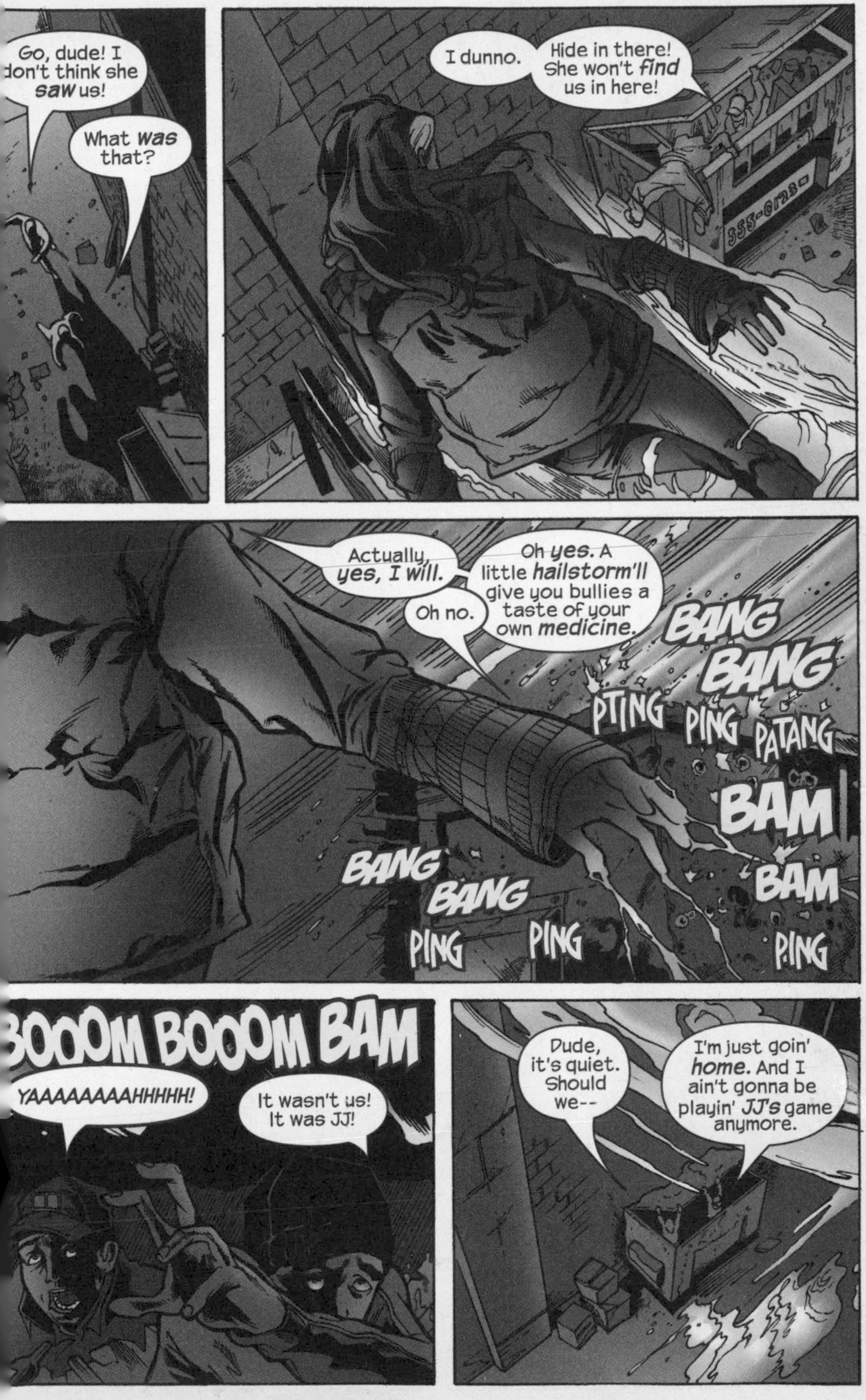

Go, dude! I don't think she saw us!
What was that?
I dunno.
Hide in there! She won't find us in here!
555-0728
Actually, yes, I will.
Oh no.
Oh yes. A little hailstorm'll give you bullies a taste of your own medicine.
BANG
BANG
PTING
PING
PATANG
BAM
BAM
BANG
BANG
PING
PING
PING
BOOOM BOOOM BAM
YAAAAAAAAHHHHH!
It wasn't us! It was JJ!
Dude, it's quiet. Should we--
I'm just goin' home. And I ain't gonna be playin' JJ's game anymore.

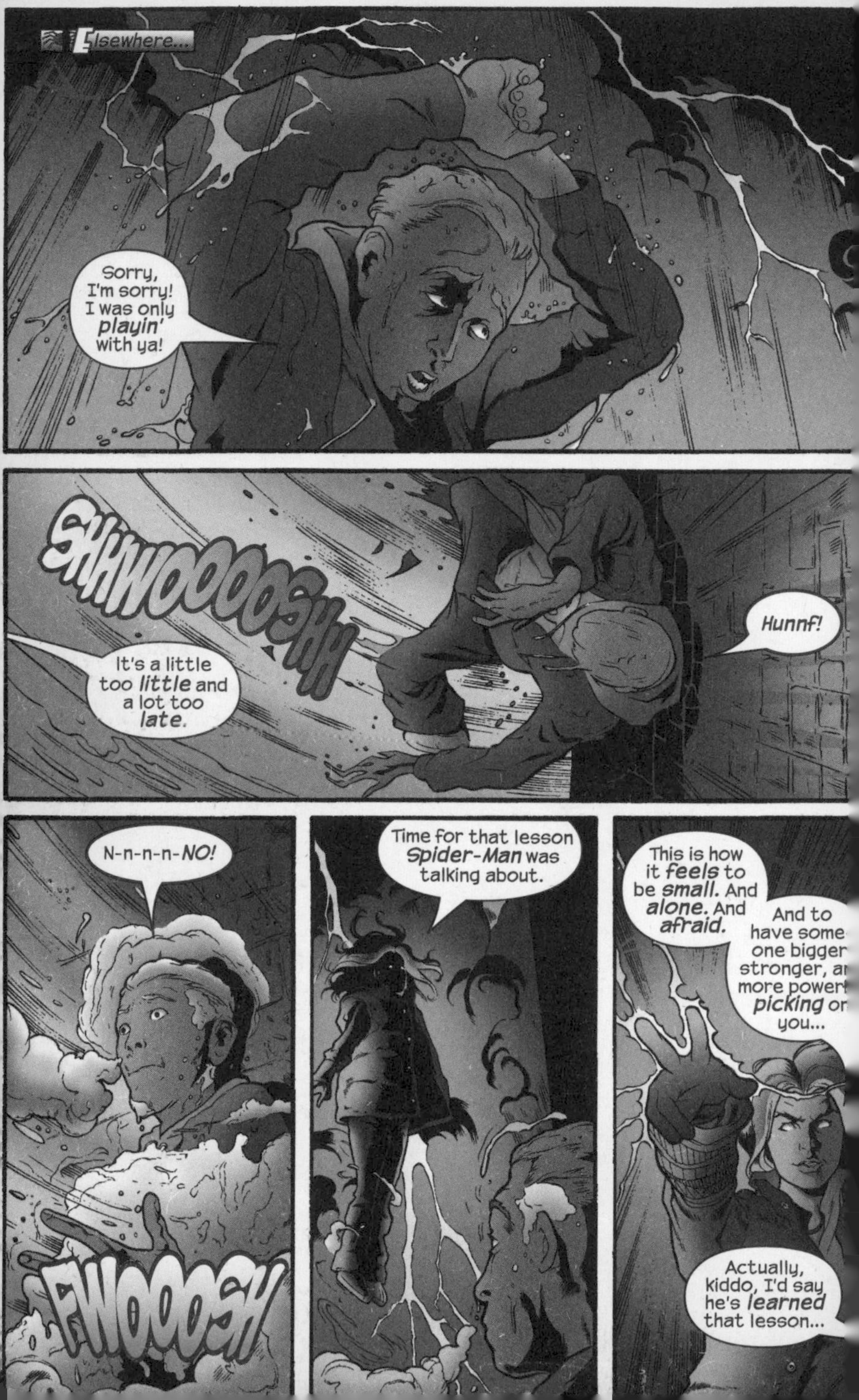
Elsewhere...
Sorry, I'm sorry! I was only playin' with ya!
SHHWOOOOSHH
It's a little too little and a lot too late.
Hunnf!
N-n-n-n-NO!
FWOOOSH
Time for that lesson Spider-Man was talking about.
This is how it feels to be small. And alone. And afraid.
Actually, kiddo, I'd say he's learned that lesson...

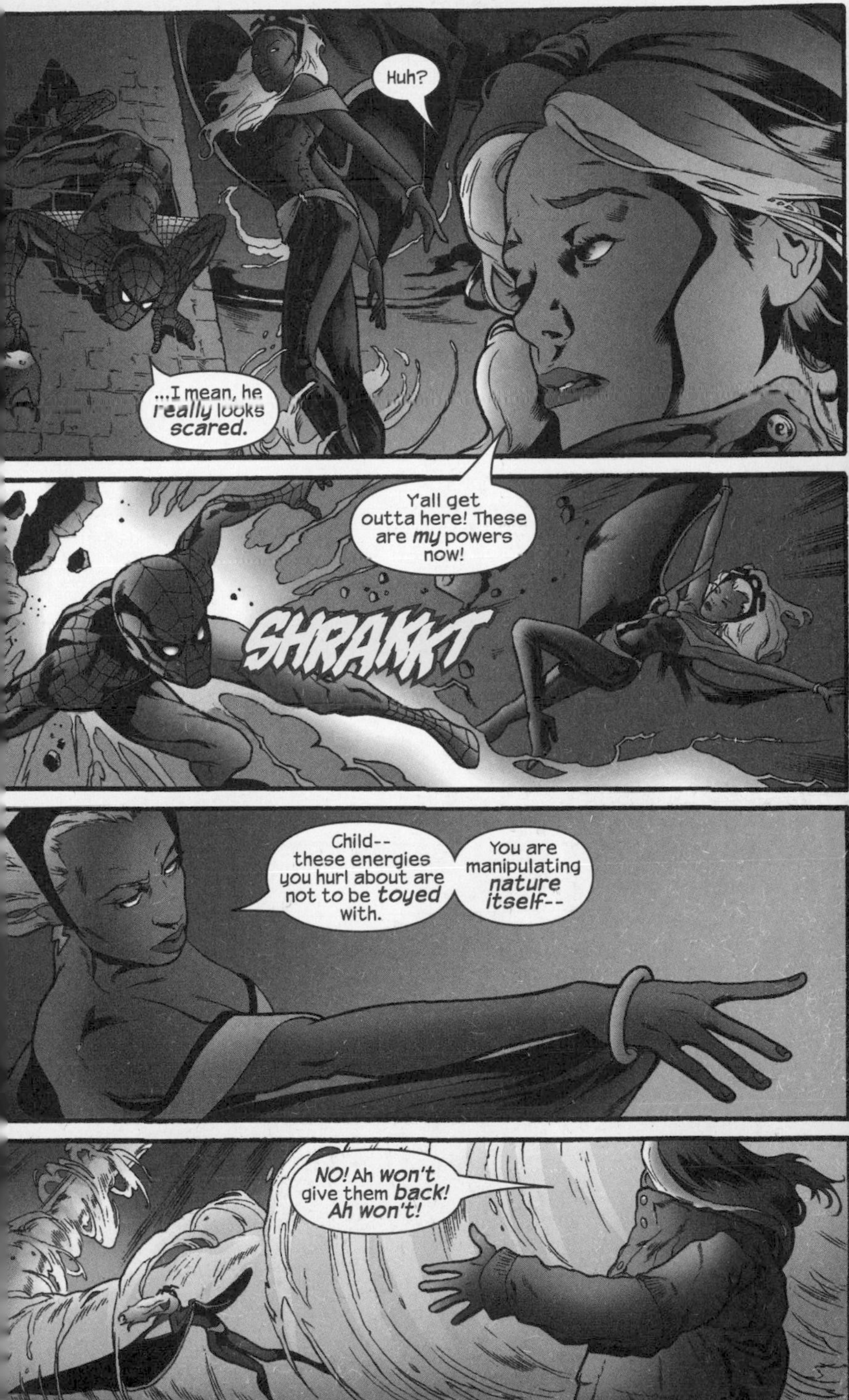

Huh?
...I mean, he really looks scared.
Y'all get outta here! These are my powers now!
SHRAKKT
Child-- these energies you hurl about are not to be toyed with.
You are manipulating nature itself--
NO! Ah won't give them back! Ah won't!

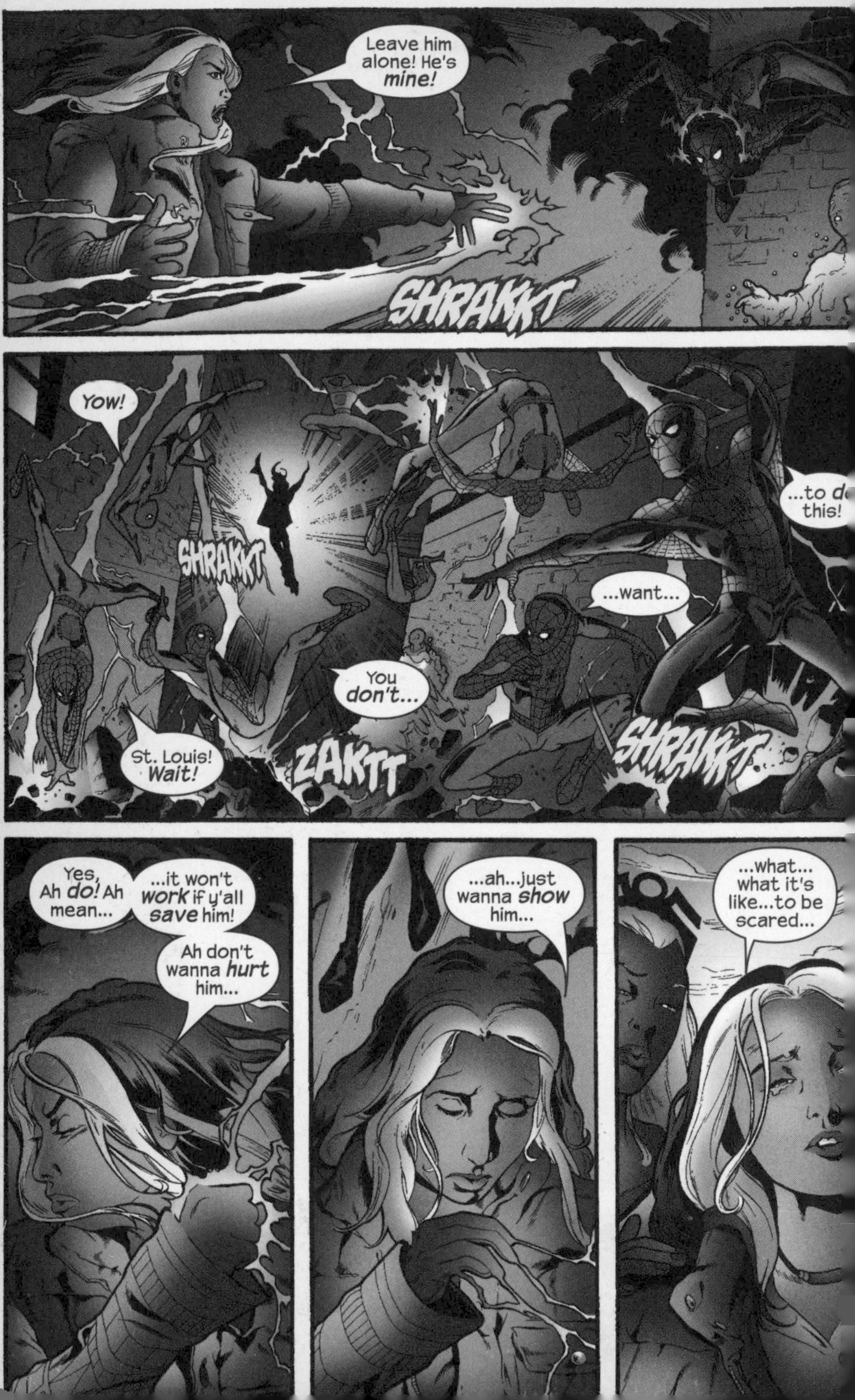
Leave him alone! He's mine!
SHRAKKT
YOW!
SHRAKKT
St. Louis! Wait!
ZAKTT
You don't...
...want...
SHRAKKT
...to d
this!
Yes, Ah do! Ah mean...
...it won't work if y'all save him!
Ah don't wanna hurt him...
...ah...just wanna show him...
...what... what it's like...to be scared...

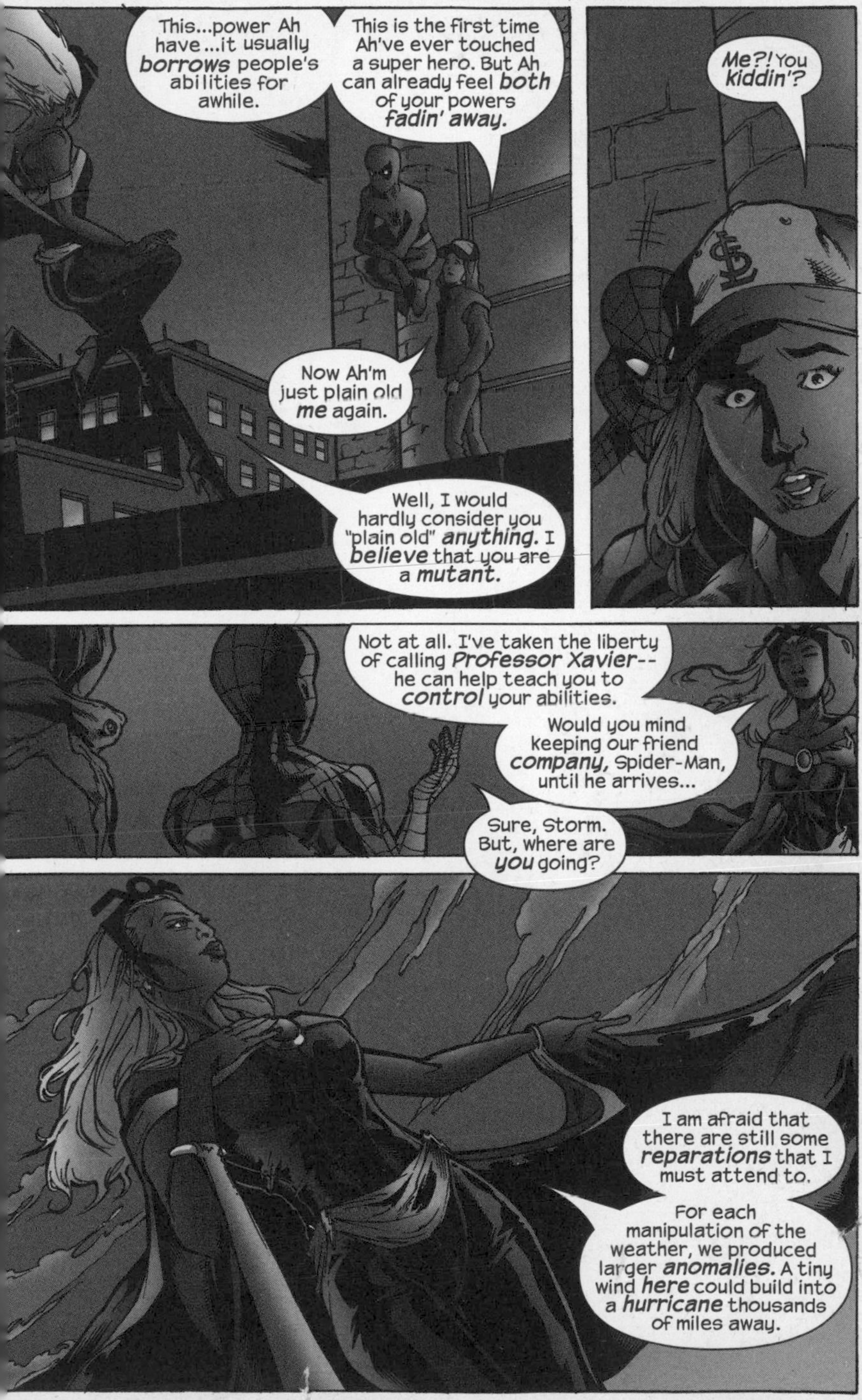

This...power Ah have...it usually borrows people's abilities for awhile.
This is the first time Ah've ever touched a super hero. But Ah can already feel both of your powers fadin' away.
Now Ah'm just plain old me again.
Well, I would hardly consider you "plain old" anything. I believe that you are a mutant.
Me?! You kiddin'?
Not at all. I've taken the liberty of calling Professor Xavier-- he can help teach you to control your abilities.
Would you mind keeping our friend company, Spider-Man, until he arrives...
Sure, Storm. But, where are you going?
I am afraid that there are still some reparations that I must attend to.
For each manipulation of the weather, we produced larger anomalies. A tiny wind here could build into a hurricane thousands of miles away.

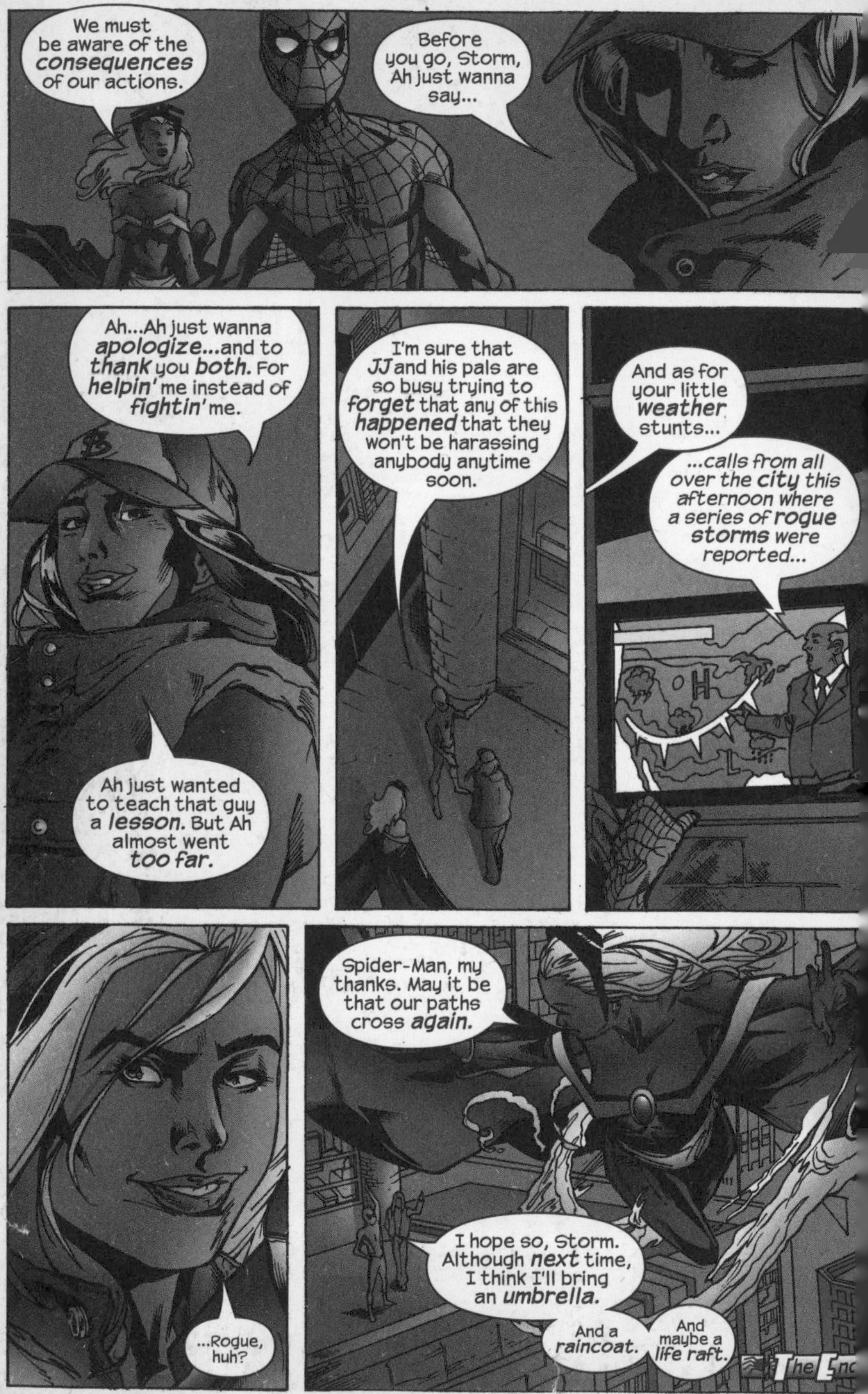

We must be aware of the consequences of our actions.
Before you go, Storm, Ah just wanna say...
Ah...Ah just wanna apologize...and to thank you both. For helpin' me instead of fightin' me.
Ah just wanted to teach that guy a lesson. But Ah almost went too far.
I'm sure that JJ and his pals are so busy trying to forget that any of this happened that they won't be harassing anybody anytime soon.
And as for your little weather stunts...
...calls from all over the city this afternoon where a series of rogue storms were reported...
...Rogue, huh?
Spider-Man, my thanks. May it be that our paths cross again.
I hope so, Storm. Although next time, I think I'll bring an umbrella.
And a raincoat.
And maybe a life raft.
The End

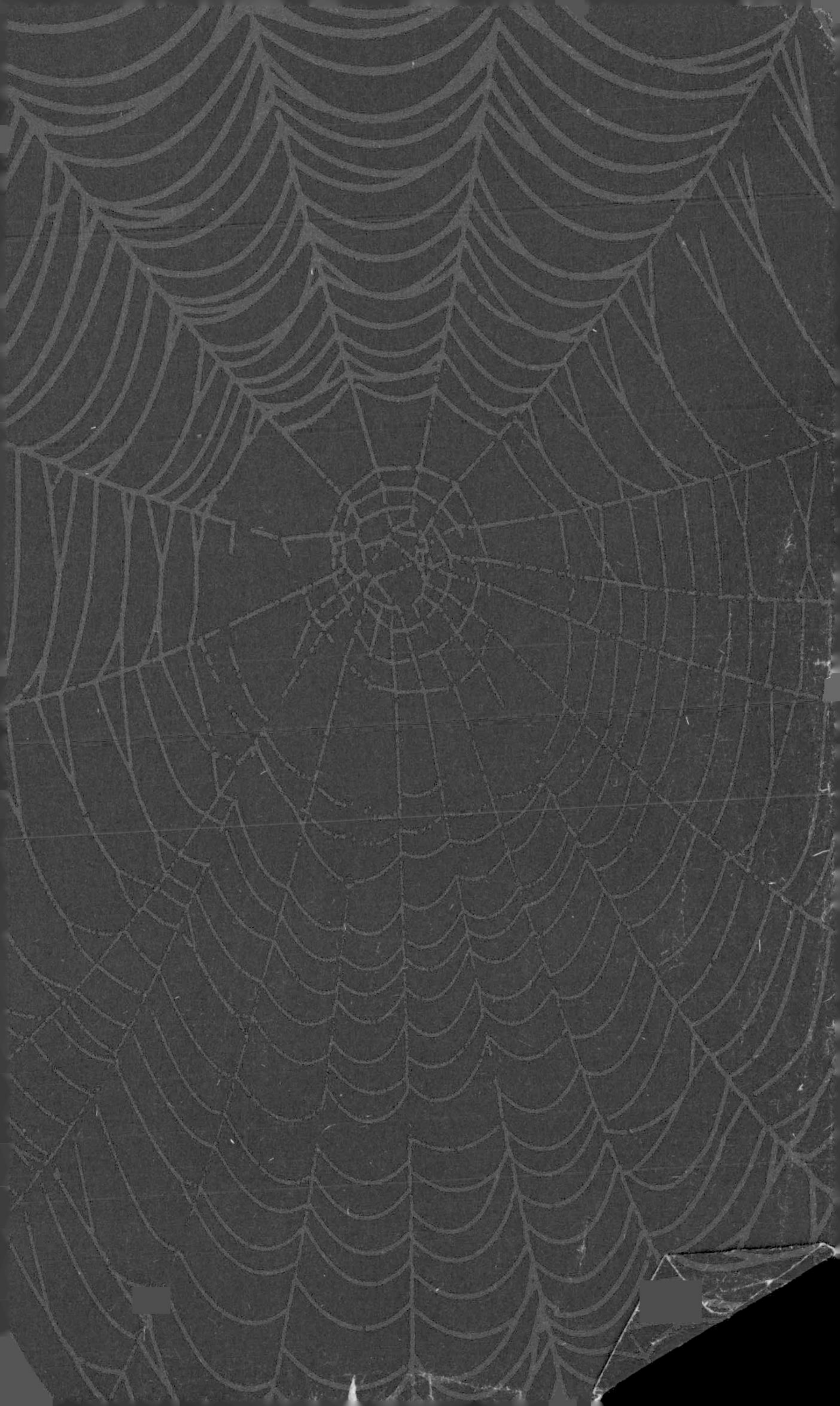

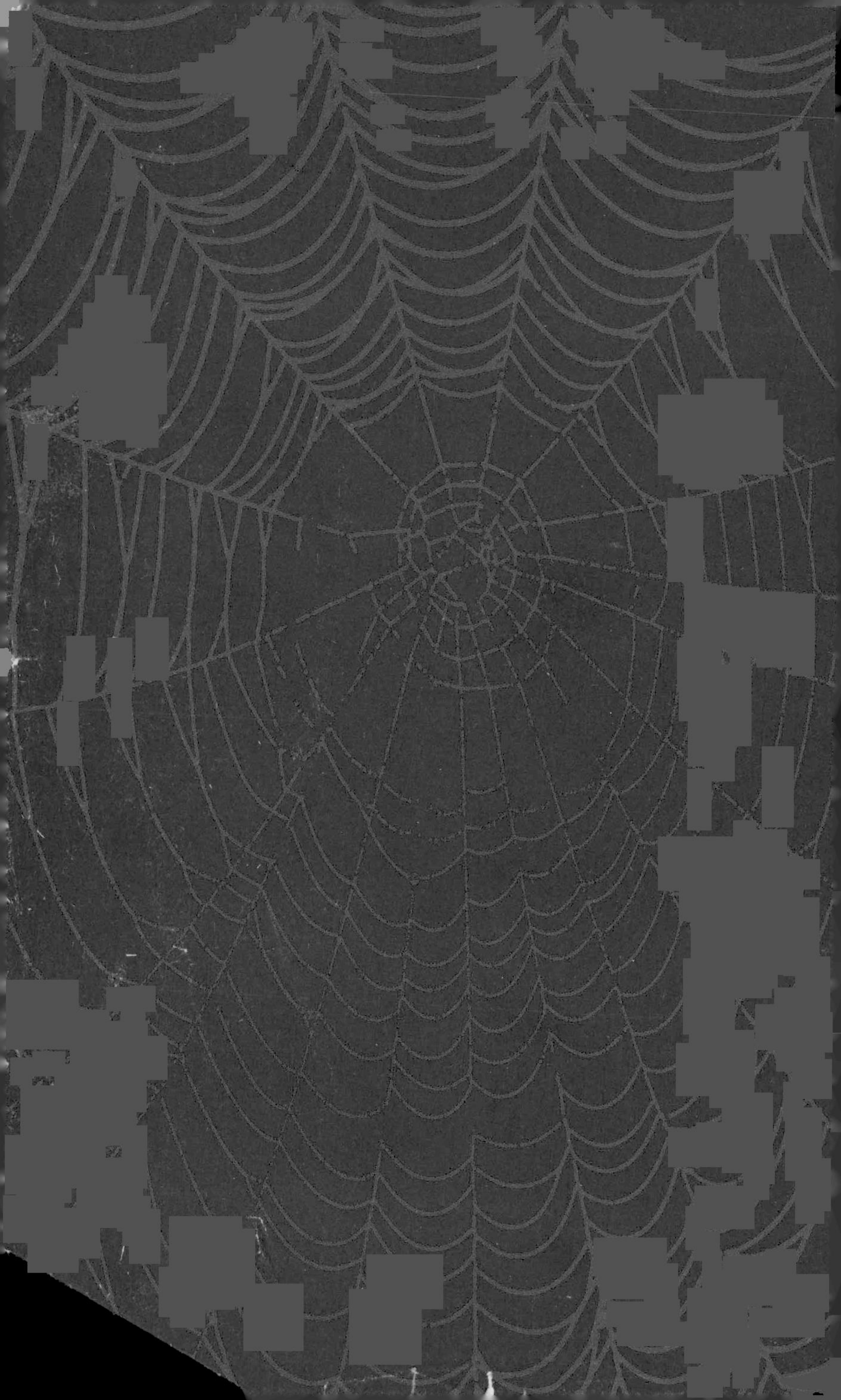